# Racializing Class, Classifying Race

## Labour and Difference in Britain, the USA and Africa

Edited by

Peter Alexander
*Senior Lecturer in Sociology*
*Rand Afrikaans University*
*Johannesburg*
*South Africa*

and

Rick Halpern
*Reader in the History of the United States*
*University College London*

in association with
ST ANTONY'S COLLEGE
OXFORD

First published in Great Britain 2000 by
**MACMILLAN PRESS LTD**
Houndmills, Basingstoke, Hampshire RG21 6XS and London
Companies and representatives throughout the world

A catalogue record for this book is available from the British Library.

ISBN 0–333–73092–5

 First published in the United States of America 2000 by
**ST. MARTIN'S PRESS, INC.,**
Scholarly and Reference Division,
175 Fifth Avenue, New York, N.Y. 10010

ISBN 0–312–22999–2

Library of Congress Cataloging-in-Publication Data

Racializing class, classifying race : labour and difference in Britain, the USA, and
Africa / edited by Peter Alexander and Rick Halpern.
    p.    cm.   — (St. Antony's series)
Includes bibliographical references and index.
ISBN 0–312–22999–2
1. Minorities—Employment—Case studies.   2. Group identity—Case studies.
3. Race relations—Case studies.   4. Working class—Case studies.   I. Alexander,
Peter, 1953–   II. Halpern, Rick.   III. Series

HD6304 .R33    1999
305.8—dc21                                                                99–052033

This book is printed on paper suitable for recycling and made from fully managed and sustained
forest sources.

10   9   8   7   6   5   4   3
09   08   07   06   05   04   03   02   01   00

Printed and bound in Great Britain by
Antony Rowe Ltd, Chippenham, Wiltshire

# Contents

*Notes on the Contributors*  vii

*Introduction*  ix

1. Empire, Race and Working-class Mobilizations  1
   *David Montgomery*

2. 'Mexican Labour' in a 'White Man's Town': Racialism,
   Imperialism and Industrialization in the Making of
   Arizona, 1840–1905
   *A. Yvette Huginnie*  32

3. The 'Lady' Telephone Operator: Gendering Whiteness
   in the Bell System, 1900–70
   *Venus Green*  57

4. The Elusive Irishman: Ethnicity and the Postwar World
   of New York City and London Dockers
   *Colin J. Davis*  87

5. A Racialized Hierarchy of Labour? Race, Immigration
   and the British Labour Movement, 1880–1950
   *Kenneth Lunn*  104

6. Racism and Resistance in British Trade Unions, 1948–79
   *Satnam Virdee*  122

7. Colonial Labour and Work Palaver: Labour Conflict in
   Britain and West Africa
   *Diane Frost*  150

8. Becoming 'Men', Becoming 'Workers': Race, Gender and
   Workplace Struggle in the Nigerian Coal Industry, 1937–49
   *Carolyn A. Brown*  168

9. 'Did Not Come to Work on Monday': the East London
   Waterfront in Comparative Perspective, *c.*1930–63
   *Gary Minkley*  193

10. Back to Work: Categories, Boundaries and Connections
    in the Study of Labour
    *Frederick Cooper*  213

*Index*  236

# Notes on the Contributors

**Peter Alexander** now Senior Lecturer in Sociology at the Rand Afrikaans University in Johannesburg, South Africa, was, until recently, a Research Fellow at St. Antony's College, Oxford. His latest book, *Workers, War and the Origins of Apartheid*, is forthcoming from James Currey. Currently he is working on a comparative study of Transvaal and Alabama colliers in the early twentieth century.

**Carolyn A. Brown** is an Associate Professor of History at Rutgers, the State University of New Jersey, and a specialist in West African labour history. Her book, *'We Weren't All Slaves': African Miners, Culture and Resistance at the Enugu Government Colliery, Nigeria, 1914–1950*, is part of Heinemann's Social History of Africa Series. Currently she is working on a social history of Enugu during the nationalist period.

**Frederick Cooper** is Professor of African History at the University of Michigan. His most recent book is *Decolonization and African Society: The Labor Question in French and British Africa*, and he has also edited (with Ann Stoler) *Tensions of Empire: Colonial Cultures in a Bourgeois World*. His research interests include the comparative study of colonial empires, conceptions of Africa within the social sciences, post-emancipation societies and labour history.

**Colin J. Davis** is Associate Professor of History, University of Alabama at Birmingham. His most recent publication is *Power at Odds: The 1922 National Railroad Shopmen's Strike*. Currently he is working on a comparative study of docker rank-and-file movements in New York City and London in the post-Second World War era.

**Diane Frost** is Lecturer in Race and Ethnic Studies at the University of Central Lancashire. She has published two books and numerous articles on West African migrant labour in Britain. Currently she is developing her research on Sierra Leonan migrants.

**Venus Green** is an Assistant Professor in the Department of History at the City College of the City University of New York where she teaches in Black Studies, Women's Studies and Labor Studies. Her book, *Technology, Women and Race: a Study of Women Telephone Workers, 1880–1980*, is forthcoming from Duke University Press.

**Rick Halpern** is Reader in the History of the United States at University College London. He is the author of *Down on the Killing Floor: Black and White Workers in Chicago's Packinghouses, 1904–1954* and currently is working on a study of race and labour in the sugar industries of Louisiana and Natal, South Africa.

**A. Yvette Huginnie** is an Assistant Professor in American Studies at the University of California at Santa Cruz. Currently she is working on a study of race, labour and politics in the US West from 1850 to 1920.

**Kenneth Lunn** is Reader in Social History at the University of Portsmouth. He has published on various aspects of race and immigration in modern British history and currently is working on a study of race and the British labour movement, 1870–1970.

**Gary Minkley** is Senior Lecturer in South African History at the University of the Western Cape, in Cape Town, South Africa. He has published on local South African labour histories and a manuscript, entitled 'Border Dialogues: Race, Class and Space in the Industrialisation of East London, South Africa', is in preparation. Currently he is working on the spatial and labour histories of Cape Town in comparative perspective.

**David Montgomery** is Farnam Professor of History Emeritus at Yale University. His most recent book is *Citizen Worker: The Experience of Workers in the United States with Democracy and the Free Market during the Nineteenth Century*. He is currently writing a history of the Left in the twentieth-century United States.

**Satnam Virdee** is Lecturer in Sociology in the Department of Government at the University of Strathclyde. His main research interests include racist and anti-racist collective action in trade unions; racist violence; and the political economy of racism. He is the author of *Racial Violence and Harassment* and co-author of the 1997 edition of *Ethnic Minorities in Britain*. Currently he is at work on a book on 'race' and organized labour in England.

# Introduction

The essays collected in this volume explore the interplay of race and class across three continents. Although the geographic sweep is wide – ranging from the copper belt of the American Southwest, to the docks of London's East End and the coal mines of Nigeria – the contributions all have a common concern with the construction of working-class identities. Similarly, although the various authors employ a range of methodologies and situate themselves in a number of academic disciplines, they share a materialist orientation to the study of the past. While sensitive to the roles of culture and ideology in shaping collective identities, they seek to ground group consciousness firmly within economic life and the labour process. In its empirical approach to recovering the past, this collection dissents from the notion that attention to language is the best – if not the only – way to analyse working people's motivations and thought. The international perspective afforded by this book emerges out of a conviction that the framework of the nation-state both confines and distorts labour history. Particularist and exceptionalist historiographic traditions limit historians' abilities to fully grasp processes of class formation, while the often unthinking adoption of the 'nation' as a unit of study cramps their understanding of the imperial – and, indeed, the global – dimension of working-class history.

If working-class identities are 'constructed', they are not assembled with complete freedom from a limitless range of possibilities. Workers' agency is a key feature in all the essays that follow, and many of these pieces probe the way in which working people imagine themselves as part of a collectivity larger than the workplace, the community and the nation. But at the same time the essays gathered here chart the limitations of this agency. They show how it is constrained, on the one hand, by the ability of employers to exacerbate pre-existing tensions and divisions within the working class and, on the other hand, by the cultural and ideological resources at the disposal of the state. Far from seeing identities as imposed from above – either by capital, culture brokers or political leaders – these essays regard them as the outcomes of processes of negotiation within which working people's power is limited and contingent.

This book originated with a conference on labour and difference held at St. Antony's College, Oxford, in the summer of 1997. This was a remarkable gathering of labour historians, certainly one of the largest ever convened in Britain, and it sparked a number of lively exchanges between Africanists, Americanists and British historians. David Montgomery provided the keynote address, and a revised version of his wide-ranging meditation on the international dimension of working-class mobilization opens this volume. It is followed by three pieces – by Yvette Huginnie, Venus Green and Colin Davis – which examine the way in which racial difference functions in three very different American settings: the Southwest, the workplace world of telephone operators in the twentieth century, and the heavily Irish New York (and London) docks. In each case, traditional assumptions about race are challenged. Huginnie shows how the fluid multiracial system of turn-of-the-century Arizona subverts the standard binary understanding of race as a black/white division. Examining employment practices within the Bell system, Green demonstrates the central importance of gender assumptions shared by both managers and workers in creating an ideology of 'whiteness'. And Davis, in a study of dock workers of Irish descent, contrasts New York, where there was an emphasis on Irishness, with London, where this was not the case, thereby pointing to the importance of broad societal influences in the construction of identities.

The next three essays focus upon Great Britain. Kenneth Lunn provides a critical reflection on the historiography of 'race' and labour, rejecting those accounts which either homogenize the history of immigrant workers – as in 'the black experience' – or oversimplify the impact of colonialism on working-class consciousness. Satnam Virdee's contribution analyses the relationship between Indian and Afro-Caribbean workers and the labour movement in the postwar period. He chronicles a shift from exclusionary to racially integrated practices, rooting his account in the increased prevalence of broadly-based, as distinct from sectional, trade union actions. Diane Frost employs an international framework to explore the role of race in structuring both class and intra-class relations in the ports of Liverpool and Freetown in West Africa. Focusing on the Kru – who were active in both seaports – she shows how their ethnic identity was wrapped up with a defence of occupational niches, recognizing that both these aspects of their lives were shaped by the requirements of empire.

These themes of domination, conflict and identity receive further elaboration in two other essays in African labour history. Looking at the Nigerian coal industry in the 1930s and 1940s, Carolyn Brown shows how miners rejected the racialized category of 'African worker' utilized by mine operators and colonial authorities. Drawing upon notions of British subjecthood and manliness, miners fashioned an identity for themselves that allowed a powerful challenge to employers and the state. Gary Minkley's essay also explores the interplay between colonial ideology and African labour. Placing the South African port of East London alongside the larger waterfront hubs of Durban, Lourenço Marques and Mombasa, he shows how the gradual shift from a casual to a permanent dock labour force changed the way in which colonial officials viewed the relation between race and class. He also makes clear how the distinctive pattern of working-class formation found in southern Africa – most notably its partial and incomplete nature – shaped workers' consciousness.

Frederick Cooper's essay on boundaries and connections in the study of labour rounds out this collection and serves as a conclusion. Elaborating upon themes that ran through the forty-odd papers presented at the Oxford conference, and amplifying the main arguments of the essays presented in this collection, Cooper suggests a number of different ways of understanding the relationship between race and class. Positioning his remarks in relation to recent scholarship in the United States, Africa and Britain, and linking the study of labour to ongoing political developments in these three locales, his essay both summarizes the contributions of this project to working-class history and serves as an agenda for future research.

***

This collection would not have been possible without the assistance of numerous individuals and institutions. For their financial support, special thanks are extended to St. Antony's College, Oxford's Rhodes Chair of Race Relations, the British Academy, the University College London Graduate School, and the Oxford-based Oppenheimer and Astor Travel funds. The editors are also grateful for generous assistance provided by Terence Ranger, Kenneth Lunn, David Holmes, Maniza Ntekim, Caroline O'Reilly, Leo Zelig and Rachel Cutler.

Peter Alexander, Johannesburg
Rick Halpern, London

# 1
# Empire, Race and Working-class Mobilizations

*David Montgomery*

Working-class mobilizations in England, South Africa and the United States have exhibited remarkable differences and remarkable similarities during the last 150 years. The purpose of this essay is to explore the relationship between the different trajectories of working-class movements in those three corners of the Atlantic world during the twentieth century and the changing patterns of imperial domination and rule, with the hope of formulating meaningful questions about the relationship of empire, race and class in modern life. Such an effort can build on decades of research into the diverse ways in which working women and men have burrowed their own enclaves of collective power into a global economy driven by the accumulation of wealth and shaped by market relations and military might. History remains a collective project, no matter how much pleasure and profit we may derive from controversies among ourselves.

To understand the lives and struggles of working people we must be prepared to think on three levels: local, national and global. The local setting is where workers have pursued their personal goals in familiar contexts, identified friend and foe through everyday encounters, and forged, or failed to forge, collective action. This is precisely why the best social history of the last generation has concentrated research on particular localities (often to the exasperation of its critics). Even when we research localities, however, we often encounter patterns of migration that link working people's behaviour and aspirations at their sites of employment to regions from which they have come, be they nearby native reserves or distant homelands. For black women and men who toiled in white households, the periodic journey between home and work, or even from kitchen to dining room within the employers' residence, was a trip from one racial context to

another. Moreover, for sailors, who were the first to engage in wage
labour on a large scale, the locus of their action included not only a
ship navigating the high seas, but also ports of call which might be in
several continents. In each of those ports local authorities might have
enforced a different type of racial hierarchy. We are obliged, in short,
to devote close attention to just what types of localities framed the
action of each group of workers.

The national synthesis has long provided the favourite domain of
historians of labour movements and of political action. It is at the
level of the nation-state that governmental power framed economic
activity in Britain, the United States and South Africa (although not in
important parts of the colonial world, such as the Dutch East Indies
and India), and it is at that level that the organized power and mere
presence of the working class have most obviously influenced state
policy. Much of our discussion will compare the political and social
consequences of class and racial confrontations in different nation-
states. But we must also concern ourselves with the role of class
struggles in informing workers' sense of their own nationality and in
creating new states. Conversely, state power has played a decisive role
in shaping the meaning of race, the character of labour movements
and the content attributed to the term 'working class' in popular
discourse. The global dimension has already surreptitiously slipped
into my argument through the reference to migration. Under modern
capitalism an ethnically homogeneous working class has been practically a contradiction in terms. On the eve of the Great War strike
initiators on the Witwatersrand, in Pennsylvania and in Arizona had
to address the miners in several different languages. Moreover, global
as well as national product markets and labour markets have been
forged, and continue to be forged, by governmental edicts and military force, as well as by economic pressures.

The hegemony created by the power of the United States during the
twentieth century has differed from the British Empire by involving
far less direct colonial administration. The heartland of the United
States' dominion lay in Latin America and the Caribbean.
Nevertheless, the crucial role of the conquest of northern Mexico and
of Native American peoples in shaping the ascendance of the United
States reminds us of three considerations, which are relevant to any
country we might study. The first is that race has seldom confronted
workers as a simple dichotomy of black and white. Mexicans who had
long inhabited the conquered region or who moved into it after it had
been annexed by the US, and European migrants, who varied from

Cornish to Greek and Finn, interacted with labourers and merchants from China's Taishan province, Japan's Hiroshima prefecture, the Philippines and Samoa.[1]

Second, people repeatedly reinvented races in the context of these encounters. This was *not* simply a question of European immigrants adopting 'whiteness'. For example, David Montejano has demonstrated that the racial self-definition of Mexicans changed over the course of a century and often varied from region to region. Moreover, for Mexicans in rural Texas, whether or not they were 'treated as white' reflected the dissimilar class structures of particular ranch and farm counties, in much the way that the social and legal implications of being called 'coloured' in Cardiff or Salford varied over time with British imperial maritime and immigration policies.[2]

The revolutionary epoch that spanned the years between 1775 and 1815 was of critical importance not only in the 'making of the English working class', but also in forging a new sense of the interplay of citizenship, slavery and complexion. Sylvia Frey has shown that the presence of slavery left an indelible imprint on the rhetoric, political alignments and military strategies of the American Revolution. Once the colonies had won their liberty, their political and intellectual leaders had to reconstruct the institutional and ideological underpinnings of chattel slavery, while they also imported thousands of new slaves from Africa. Subsequently, Haiti's struggles for independence and emancipation left their mark on the way the whole Atlantic world thought about citizenship and race. But let me just suggest a different example. When more than 1,000 American seamen were incarcerated in Britain's Dartmoor prison in 1814, during a war of little diplomatic significance but enormous ideological importance in the history of American democratic ideas, the republican white prisoners demanded that their monarchist jailers segregate them from the scores of black fellow seamen – and they got their way.[3]

Third, the experience of self-styled whites in the conquered territory suggests the importance of settler consciousness. Empire promised working people of the conquering nation the possibility of escape from the class oppression they suffered at home through the subordination or annihilation of previous inhabitants of the conquered territories. This promise was of decisive importance in the elaboration of 'the wages of whiteness' in antebellum America and Labouristic Australia, as well as in the readiness of British workers to enlist in the imperial cause.

The sailor Larry in Herman Melville's 1849 novel *Redburn* expressed the fantasy that saturated radical Democratic rhetoric in the United States of escaping one's own oppression by lording it over the imagined lawless domains of darker people:

> 'And what's the use of bein' *snivelized*?' he said to me one night during our watch on deck; 'snivelized chaps only learns the way to take on 'bout life, and snivel. You don't see any Methodist chaps feelin' dreadful about their souls; you don't see any darned beggars or pesky constables in *Madagasky*, I tell ye; and none o' them kings there gets their big tose pinched by the gout ... I might have been a great man in Madagasky; it's too darned bad! Blast Ameriky, I say.'[4]

Joseph Conrad explored the role of that delusion in the origins of modern imperialism. A basic theme of his writings was that Larry's fantasy could turn the poor man into a ruthless advanced guard of the very civilization he had sought to escape, free from the social obligations and scrutiny he had faced at home, and inflicting terrible suffering on the people he encountered, while leaving himself flirting with insanity. Carolyn Brown's research into the coal mines of Nigeria has produced a memorable image of this relationship: the 'hammock boys', who carried white supervisors back and forth each day between their residences and their places of work.[5]

Settler colonies assumed a complex role in the way the Second International regarded imperialism. Both Karl Kautsky and Bureau Secretary Emile Vandervelde distinguished between productive colonies (*Arbeitskolonien*), where European labour could advance socialist goals, and colonies of exploitation, which had been created by the lust of capital for accumulation, but were inhabited by 'backward' peoples. As the socialist movement came to grips after 1899 with news of immigrants' strikes and native resistance, it struggled to reconcile its faith in Europe's role as vanguard of civilization with the movement's hostility to wars of conquest and competition for empire. The socialist press in Europe denounced the 'Gold War' waged by the capitalists in South Africa, and advocated a 'return' of India and Egypt to self-rule. As for other colonies, Vandervelde wrote, the goal of the International should be:

> to expand the autonomy of the indigenous community step by step, to give them back possession of the soil, to suppress all forms of coerced labor, and, in general, to support all efforts and move-

ments that aim to free the natives from slavery and to make them independent.[6]

## Imperialism's reincarnation for the twentieth century

Formal and informal empires have defined the realm of possibility for working people in both imperialist countries and the portions of the world that those countries dominated. Vandervelde's programme of action both identified some basic features of the world order that emerged at the beginning of this century and evaded others. Only a few years earlier, W.E.B. Du Bois had suggested a quite different point of departure in his famous 1903 aphorism: 'The problem of the twentieth-century is the problem of the color-line, the relation of the darker to the lighter races of men in Asia and Africa, in America and the islands of the sea.'[7] But Thomas Holt recently has argued that the 'problem' cannot be *reduced* to 'race'. Said Holt: 'The development of racist thought was not a natural outgrowth of the legacy of slavery; it arose in part from the seemingly nonracist (or racially neutral) premises of liberal ideology.'[8]

Let us look more closely at the turn of the century, so that we might better understand the circumstances that transformed both 'racist thought' and 'liberal ideology'. At the end of the 1890s decades of protracted price decline, culminating in a world-wide depression, gave way to a spectacular leap in worker productivity and a wave of business consolidation in the highly industrialized countries. Mines, plantations and railways in the lands of the 'darker races' attracted investment capital and ambitious workers away from the North Atlantic areas that had been blighted by sluggish performance and fierce confrontations between capital and labour. While cities of the Northern Hemisphere hid grinding poverty behind their displays of unprecedented wealth, the colonies became, in another phrase from Du Bois, 'the slums of the world'.[9] In both domains, the gospel of separate development of the races enjoyed ardent acclaim in intellectual life and practical application in segregation laws, Native Land Acts and municipal zoning regulations.[10]

Political leadership in the industrial powers intervened vigorously in domestic economic and social life, while lavishing expenditures on military and naval strength. As Karl Polanyi summarized the transformation: 'society took measures to protect itself' from the 'self-regulating economy', which had grown to threaten the annihilation of its 'human and natural substance'. The new measures were summarized by an official British report on the coal mines of India in 1937 as the 'world-wide trend away from the competitive ideal towards formulas of public control'.[11]

The transformation Polanyi described was in its springtime when all of society's measures of self-protection converged in Britain's 'Liberal landslide' of 1906. Historians of the welfare state have hailed the old age pensions enacted by parliament during the ensuing half decade, along with unemployment insurance, eight-hour day for miners, health insurance through approved societies and expanded welfare services as the advent of citizen-entitlements in the Anglo-Saxon world. Students of labour movements have celebrated this same election for the improved legal framework for trade union action enacted on the eve of the voting and the subsequent emergence of the Labour Party as an organized parliamentary bloc.[12]

Henry Pelling raised challenging questions about the famous election of 1906. He noted that most working- class voters and most trade unions proved unenthusiastic about both the Liberal welfare proposals and expansion of the navy and the empire. His depiction of Gladstone, 'the most popular leader among the working class', as 'more hostile than almost anyone else to the extension of the power of the state', and favouring reconciliation with the Afrikaners, whom Britain had defeated in the recent war, bears a remarkable resemblance to the appeal of William Jennings Bryan for the American Federation of Labor in 1908. The walls and fences of urban Britain had been festooned during the election campaign with menacing depictions of Chinese, dramatizing the Liberals' protest against the recruitment of indentured workers from China for South Africa's mines.[13]

Pelling's view of the victorious Liberals as committed to 'the repudiation of the consequences of the South African war' has considerable merit, and it evokes comparison with the sometimes tacit, often explicit, endorsement by America's Bryan and Wilson Democrats of the spread of segregation laws in southern states. Ardent appeals to London by Africans to overturn the Act of Union and the Native Land Act were rebuffed by Britain's Liberal government.[14] Nevertheless, a view from South Africa reveals that far more was at work than simply British reconciliation with Afrikaner racism.

Shula Marks and Stanley Trapido, and more recently Saul Dubow, have pointed out that Sir Alfred Milner and his young colleagues of the so-called 'kindergarten', whose careful research and planning guided the formation of the new South African state and its labour policies in mining and agriculture, had been educated at Oxford in the neo-Hegelianism of T.H. Green. That doctrine, which was still an important part of the academic curriculum during the 1940s, inspired many progressives on both sides of the Atlantic to view the state as a creative force for the common good. The 'kindergarten's' way of thinking was cut from the same cloth as that of the authors of the pioneering Liberal welfare legislation. As Sidney Webb asked: 'What is the use of talking about Empire, if here, at its very centre, there is always to be found a mass of people, stunted in education, a prey to intemperance and congested beyond the possibility of realizing in any true sense either social or domestic life'?[15]

To be sure Milner often faced powerful opposition within South Africa from both British immigrant workers and Afrikaners, and he was censured by the Liberals in parliament on the eve of the 1906 election for authorizing the whipping of Chinese workers by mine supervisors. Nevertheless, his plan to introduce 60,000 Chinese workers under three-year contracts to work in Witwatersrand mines was designed to break the independence and reduce the wages of *black* miners. The effort to put an end to conditions that, mining companies complained, had produced a 'shortage' of African workers was a complete success. Even the electoral victory of the Afrikaner nationalist *Het Volk* (People's) Party in 1907 resulted not in the abrupt expulsion of the Chinese, but in government agreement to their phased withdrawal, in exchange for augmented recruitment of poor whites. When English-speaking miners subsequently struck against an increase in the tempo of work, the strikers were replaced by Afrikaner scabs, while Africans and Chinese continued to labour alongside whatever white men appeared at the mine face.[16]

The common intellectual origins of reform in the metropolis and in the colonies did not mean that the same formulas would apply to all locations. British authorities explained policy differences in the language of race. Thus as early as 1895 Colonial Secretary Joseph Chamberlain advocated both a constitutional style of union between England and those of her overseas domains where white settlers could govern themselves, and direct control of crown colonies where other races predominated. 'It would appear to me absurd', said Chamberlain, 'to apply to savage countries the same rules which we apply to civilized portions of the United Kingdom.'[17]

Milner had been every bit as explicit, when he explained the racial implications of his proposals:

The position of the whites among the vastly more numerous black population requires that even their lowest ranks should be able to maintain a standard of living far above that of the poorest section of the population in a purely white country.[18]

One cannot help being impressed ninety years later at the long-term success of this policy. Nevertheless, neither the history of South African public policy nor that of welfare state development in Britain and the United States can be understood as simply the fulfilment of the social vision shared by Milner and his contemporaries. The fierce class struggles that raged between 1909 and 1926 left their stamp on the statecraft of all three countries. In South Africa the strikes of white miners were treated very differently by the state from those of black miners, but both white and black strikes left their mark on the policies of the government and of mining corporations. The crushing of the 1922 Rand Revolt by the military and air power of Smuts' government broke the back of white working-class rebellion and culminated in bloody massacres of African residents of mining communities, but it also paved the way for the electoral victory of the Labour-Nationalist coalition scarcely two years later. It was that coalition, not the social engineering of Milner's kindergarten, that produced the economic and social legislation of interwar South Africa: the 'civilizing' of major sectors of the economy through reservation of specified jobs for whites, tariffs to encourage domestic manufacturing, and subsidies and marketing legislation designed to promote Afrikaner farming. South Africa's new Conciliation Act, which provided a legal frame-work for white trade unions, was the counterpart in timing and spirit to America's Railway Labor Act of 1926.[19]

The coalition's legislation also helped the mining companies accomplish the remarkable feat of preventing any increase in the earnings of African workers for almost half a century. The profitability – some would say the very survival – of South Africa's gold mining and the resuscitation of white agriculture depended not only on state assistance to whites, but also on an equally effective *suppression* of the wages of Africans. That effort too had global ramifications: it was part of the remarkable resurgence of labour coerced by penal sanctions *after* the abolition of slavery.

## Unfree wage labour

In both the United States and the West Indies former slaves struggled to secure economic independence from their former owners through obtaining land of their own, claiming possession of plantation homes and gardens whether or not all (or even any) family members were in the planter's employ, and enforcing their claims through both political associations and crowd action, in which men and women played visibly different roles. Their quest for peasant proprietorship has captured the attention of many historians, but not all have interpreted that quest in the same way. Eric Foner, writing about the West Indies, associated peasant proprietorship with isolation from markets and innovation, holding up Haiti as his prime example. Thomas Holt has argued that in Jamaica black peasants sought out areas where they could combine market gardening with wage labour, and that they moved quickly into the production of market goods, as well as subsistence crops. In a word, black men and women did insert themselves somewhat advantageously into the new framework of local and global capitalism. Similarly, Africans seized opportunities opened by early mine development on the Rand to grow commercial crops, before the 1913 Natives Land Act separated white-owned lands from isolated black reservations. African men, especially Zulu, also dominated household and laundry work, before pass laws herded them into the mines.[20]

These rural struggles are of great importance for our research for several reasons. First, they remind us that in the formation of African-American and colonial working classes the development of wage labour often did *not* entail radical separation from the land. We must look for ways in which men and women combined rural households and at least partial self-subsistence with wage labour, sometimes under conditions of people's own choosing, but increasingly under harsh options framed by the state. Planters often found that labour was most abundant at harvest time – when the work was the most arduous, we might note, but also when earnings were best. Conversely, in the American South, at least, the work of freed people that was most directly associated with their own aspirations for autonomy was women's work in and around the household, in stark contrast to the devaluation and 'pastoralization' of women's unpaid labour in Euro-American society, which Jean Boydston has analysed so tellingly.[21]

In many areas, however, women's work within the household also earned money. Look again at *All God's Dangers*, Theodore Rosengarten's narrative of a successful black farmer in Alabama, and consider the array of income-earning tasks undertaken by Hannah Shaw, who did *not* go to the cotton fields or to white women's kitchens: she sold honey, eggs, butter, vegetables and quilts, while also serving as her husband's legal adviser. Sugata Bose's conclusion regarding Bengal has validity far beyond the borders of India: capitalist development 'rested heavily on the forcing up of labour intensity within family units actually tilling the land'.[22]

Richard Roberts has demonstrated that in West Africa the increase of peasant cotton production brought with it a steady *expansion* of domestic weaving and spinning, rather than simply exports of raw cotton to the textile mills of England and France. A harsher aspect of the gendered link between peasant proprietorship and wage earning has been noted by John Higginson in the Belgian Congo. Men from the Lomami region often went to the copper mines in quest of wages, with their ultimate objective being to buy more wives, who could raise cotton for sale. Robert Shenton has observed that 'much of the writing of the last two decades on the changing position of African women under colonial rule has been focused on the battle between men and women over control of women's labor and productive assets such as land'.[23]

Second, as the discussion of African cotton production suggests, in many regions the great leap in commercial production of primary products, which called forth in turn state planning and coercion to produce a native wage labour force, occurred a long time *after* the abolition of slavery. Diamonds and gold in South Africa, tobacco in Sumatra and rubber in the Congo, not to mention the flourishing of settler agriculture in Kenya, all belonged to the new imperialism. Systematic employment of convict labour was an integral element in the development of coal mining, railway construction and turpentine extraction in America's New South, and the number of convicts employed grew rapidly in the 1880s and 1890s. The quest for a labour force that was both inexpensive and available at the behest of mining and agricultural capital also brought forth the new array of master-and-servant legislation in the colonies, in some cases more than half a century after the end of chattel slavery, and also after penal sanctions for refusal to work had been abolished in Britain by the famous Act of 1875, and in the United States by protracted popular struggle in the antebellum North and by Congressional overturning of the postwar Black Codes in the South. Although the Portuguese had abolished slavery in Angola in 1869, it was not until 1902 that their imperial legislation declared all Africans vagrants by nature and legally obliged to work.[24]

Moreover, both agricultural production for export and colonial coal, gold and diamond mining incorporated and transformed styles of employment that antedated wage labour. The 125,000 workers in

India's Jharia coalfields during the 1920s, for example, have been described by Dilip Simeon as '"low" caste, female and tribal'. They moved about incessantly, but were bound by obligations of debt and piece-rated family labour to contractors, in a complex network of subinfeudation that stretched from the coalfields to often distant homes. Intense controversies developed among administrators and nationalist intellectuals as to whether 'traditional' practices should be abolished or treasured. British managers of mines in India argued that *'the ethical standard of aborigines and semi-savages is hardly compatible with the principle of the minimum wage'*. Champions of 'native customs' within the British elite marshalled such arguments against what they denounced as the 'Westernizing' thrust of the India Congress Party and the African National Congress.[25]

Finally, we must probe the role of workers struggling within post-slavery regimes in the forming of nationalisms and of Pan-Africanism. Dealing with this question requires as much caution as is needed to study the relationship between industrial workers and socialism. Although trade unions in the colonial setting and struggles for national independence have been shaped by different social dynamics and often conflicting objectives, it has also often happened that each form of struggle opened political space for the other. For example, India's independence movement during the early years of the Second World War inspired British maritime authorities to grant important concessions to the wage demands of Indian seamen, who manned British vessels. More often it was the case that important strikes, like those of Jamaica's workers in 1938, pushed the question of independence for colonies into public discussion in the metropolitan country.[26] Conversely, Frantz Fanon has argued that the task of state-building after the achievement of independence invariably (or at least frequently) led to suppression and isolation of the new nations' trade union movements.[27]

I wish to draw attention at this point, however, to a rather different question: to the formulation of race, class and nation in working people's language of struggle. Consider the battle-cry of Paul Bogle during the rebellion of 1865 in Jamaica's Morant Bay: 'It is now time for us to help ourselves – skin for skin ... war is at us, my black skin. War is at hand.'[28] His appeal to 'black skin' was constructed, as Benedict Anderson would argue was the case with nationalism generally, 'in terms of historical destinies, while racism dreams of eternal contaminations, transmitted from the origins of time through an endless sequence of loathsome copulations: outside history'.[29] Bogle sought to create a sense of national unity based on the racial vocabulary white masters had created, to make someone else's language his own by populating it 'with his own intention, his own accent', to use the words of Mikhail Bakhtin.[30]

Evelyn Brooks Higginbotham, while endorsing Bakhtin's usage, also reminds us that race 'not only tends to subsume other sets of social relations, namely gender and class, but it ... suppresses ... its own complex interplay with the very social relations it envelopes'.[31] Bogle's call to the Maroons to join forces with Jamaica's former slaves, we might note, failed to overcome historic differences and suspicions, leaving the battle to peasant families and sugar workers. Even the most persuasive discourse can collide with the real world.[32]

But Higginbotham's warning about succumbing to the 'metalanguage of race' also brings to mind the provocative argument of Kevin Gaines about the class content of the uplift rhetoric, with which African- American leaders challenged racial oppression at the turn of the century. 'A rising race must be aristocratic', W.E.B. Du Bois wrote in 1901, 'the good cannot consort with the bad – not even the best with the less good'.[33] As Gaines observed: 'the middle-class character of the emphasis on positive representations of educated, assimilated blacks of sterling character was interdependent on the image of the so-called primitive, morally deficient lower classes', with its emphasis on dance halls, prostitution and gambling.[34]

Higginbotham's admonition draws our attention to what to my mind is the most valuable element of postmodernist analysis: its concern with the diverse and often conflicting narratives through which people who are differently situated in society construct their experience. This approach, rather than simply deconstructing the texts of dominant discourse, builds creatively upon labour historians' attention to the 'traditions, value-systems, ideas, and institutional forms'[35] through which working men and women handled their daily experience with capitalist relations of production. It is important for our purposes to recognize that popular cultures have been more than a residue of traditional norms, but are nurtured by both work experience and social relations outside the workplace, that they are often expressed in nonverbal forms, and they have been employed by working people in a creative interaction with the dominant discourse of their time and place. Within the vast domain of modern capitalism and empires, at least, we are never dealing with what Aileen Kraditor called 'autochthonous cultures', impervious to the teachings of bourgeois reformers and radicals alike.[36]

Robin Kelley and Tera Hunter in the United States and Charles van Onselen in South Africa have stressed the importance of such evidence as body language, cursing, loud talking, music and dance, all of which could provoke the revenge of the authorities. They have also noted the importance of 'dance halls and blues clubs' as places 'that enabled African Americans to take back their bodies, to recuperate, to be together'. Kelley adds that often 'the most intense skirmishes between such blacks and authority erupted during and after weekend gatherings'.[37] As Earl Lewis has put it: African Americans 'congregated' in a segregated society.[38] Such observations also remind us sharply that what mattered personally to working men and women was often quite different from what was couched in the programmes of labour or nationalist movements.[39]

Finally, let us note that creating a national identity involved not just an act of imagination, but also collective deeds. Julie Saville's path-breaking work on Reconstruction South Carolina has highlighted the role of self-organized paramilitary processions (even to and from cotton fields), platoons of new voters marching miles to the polls, and ritualized group confrontations with white authorities in the process through which men and women, who had lately been the property of different masters, became 'a people'. This transformation had been put into words by two handwritten documents found by a policeman on the streets of New Orleans in 1863, and signed simply 'A Colored Man'. The author proclaimed war aims of his people, which were not those of the United States. 'we care nothing about the union [.] we heave been in it Slaves over two hundred and fifty years', but he added, 'when we are free men and a people we will fight for our rights and liberty'. He concluded with a dazzling and defiant inversion of the political discourse then pronounced in Washington:

> we are the Blackest and bravest race the president Says there is a wide Difference Between the black Race and the white race But we Say that white corn and yellow will mix by the taussels but the black and white Race must mix by the root as we are so well mixed and has no tausels – freedom and liberty is the word with the Collered people.[40]

## Imperialism and internationalism

To ask what it meant for black and white (and other) races to 'mix by the roots' and what such mixing had to do with the mobilization of different groups of working people for 'freedom and liberty' is to pose the historical problem of human agency in the interaction of race and class. It is also a question that has evoked sharply opposing interpretations from different historians.

Much of the discussion recently has turned on the relationship between white racism and class consciousness. The best recent work has highlighted not only the frequent violent actions of whites against people of colour who were successful in business or who aspired to participate in political and social activity that whites considered their exclusive inheritance, but also the frequent shaping of class struggles around the militant demand of white workers for better treatment than employers accorded workers of other races. Consider the way white women hired for domestic labour in Johannesburg households insisted that their role was to supervise the black men, with whom they made beds and cleaned floors. Or the fact that it was a socialist preacher, Alexander Irvine, then investigating peonage in Alabama mines, who protested when the Italians with whom he was travelling were seated in a car marked 'coloured'. His ire rose when he asked a black porter, was there not a law on 'the separation of the races', and was met with the reply: 'Dere sho' is boss, but you ain't races. You is jes Dagoes, ain't you?'[41]

Persuasive analyses of the material and psychic advantages that white workers have gained, and continue to gain, by virtue of their complexions, of the saturation of workers' movement rhetoric with white supremacy doctrines in pre-Civil War America, and of the effective designation of Chinese as the class enemy in mobilizing trade union and labour party strength in many countries bordering the Pacific Ocean, have converged to change the tone of historical studies of working-class culture from one of celebration to one of denunciation. Herbert Hill's conclusion that trade unions are inherently racist has inspired both critiques of historical portraits of interracial collaboration as romantic myths and Bruce Nelson's ominous conclusion that democratic unionism does not lead to democratic social practice: to empower white rank-and-filers is to unleash racism.[42]

Such studies have served us well by drawing attention sharply to the racialized nature of class. It is important, however, not to allow that realization to close off examination of the specific circumstances that have encouraged or prevented various levels of collaboration and even solidarity among workers of different races. If we fail to probe the meaning of racialized encounters to the people directly involved and the ways in which workers' own conduct and programmes could, did and will in the future make a difference between reinforcing white supremacy and challenging it, we have thrown the whole burden of changing the world onto peoples of colour, with perhaps some noble white radicals as a cheering section.

When American soldiers marched into the Mexican city of Saltillo in 1847, they were greeted by a woman from New Jersey, who worked in a Mexican textile mill. 'Americans I am glad to see you,' she exclaimed. 'I have seen but one white man in eight months, a negro from New Orleans.'[43] Her greeting not only dramatized the contingency of race (which could be recounted through thousands of such tales), but also underscored the importance of local meanings. When Laura Tabili examined the 1930 protest in Salford's union hall against the employment of six Arabs, she found that the incident was resolved when a committee of two white and two black seamen satisfied itself that the Arabs were 'local men'. She also shows us that the same British port cities that saw whites assaulting racially mixed neighbourhoods in 1919 also produced frequent marriage between British women and colonial seamen and consequently kin networks that criss-crossed racial lines. Some of them also nurtured the inter-racial Seamen's Minority Movement.[44]

Tabili's work is especially important, however, for the ways it reminds us of the role of the state, business and union policies in shaping the racializing of class. Similarly, Thomas Sugrue has quite properly protested that 'in the current historiography on race relations and labor, employers are almost entirely missing'.[45]

The Great Depression reshaped state and empire in ways that were remarkably different in the United States, Britain and South Africa. Permit me to focus my remarks here on the experience of the United States. I do so both because the decisive economic power of the United States, as producer of more than 40 per cent of the world's value added by manufacture during the 1920s and as creditor to the other imperialist powers after 1914, meant that the collapse of New York securities markets brought the world economy down to ruin, but also because Depression era struggles in the United States can illuminate the relationship between working-class agency and race.

The American industrial unions of the 1930s were created during a period of such heavy unemployment that employers could be very choosy about the workers they hired. One consequence was an unprecedented homogenization of the industrial labour force, at the very time the new unions publicly repudiated racial and ethnic barriers to membership. Factory hirings averaged about 400,000 workers a month between 1933 and 1939. Those who were hired were over-whelmingly men (and increasingly women) with families to support, who were white, between the ages of 25 and 45, and graduates of more than eight years of schooling. Those who were specialists at the occupations to be filled and who had earned the highest wages on their previous jobs were the most favoured. Not only did the absolute number of black workers in manufacturing decline between 1930 and 1940, but a WPA survey of some 1,500 firms in Philadelphia's highly diversified industry found that only five – Atlantic Refinery, Franklin Sugar, Westinghouse, Diston Saw and Midvale Steel – had any black production workers.[46]

The United States had responded to the Depression with much the same turn toward autarchy that was evident elsewhere in the world. The New Deal's domestic reforms would have been impossible had the United States not broken with the world gold standard. Nevertheless, important features of American political life during the 1930s differed remarkably from those of most other industrial powers and of South Africa: party rivalries for office remained vigorous, Right-wing nationalism was confined to the role of opposition, and official policy encouraged workers of all races in manufacturing and mining to unionize.[47]

The revival of trade union strength is of special relevance to our investigation. American workers had gone through the 1920s with a union movement that was so widely committed to segregation as to make the unions that did not exclude or separate members of colour those in need of explanation.[48] The accommodations surviving unions had made by the end of the anti-union onslaught of 1919–22 resemble those Tabili found in the conservative British sailors' union. As Eric Arnesen has shown, the interwar legislative victories of railway unions empowered white workers often at the expense of black employees. Moreover, even in 1946, after union membership had exceeded 13 million workers, more than 7.5 million workers belonged to the American Federation of Labor. Most of its affiliates, including the electricians, machinists and teamsters who sparked the federation's growth, either barred non-whites from membership or consigned them to a subordinate status.[49]

Nevertheless, the new unions of the 1930s were involved in rather different racial dynamics from those that had shaped their precursors. All unions of the rival Congress of Industrial Organizations were publicly committed to enrolling everyone working in their industries, regardless of race or sex. On the West Coast fierce battles between the two federations were openly fought over race policy, especially in aircraft and shipbuilding. In the Southeast, African Americans provided most of the CIO's early recruits on riverfronts, in tobacco factories and in iron mines. The early defeat of unionism in the all-white textile industry magnified the importance of black workers in what union growth the region did experience.[50]

Within the automobile and steel industries, where large numbers of black and Chicano workers were employed, skilled white workers tended to hold aloof from the new unions, except in those auto and tool-making enterprises where whites constituted virtually the entire workforce. In one steel mill after another it was the black workers and those of recent immigrant stock who carried the day for the industrial unions, while the tonnage men, who had constituted most of the union members before 1919, clung to company-sponsored Employee Representation Plans, even at times after the CIO had been recognized.[51]

Looking specifically at Michigan automobile firms during the postwar decade, Thomas Sugrue observed that company policies created job categories and hiring pools that either excluded black workers almost entirely, as in the case of Chrysler and many General Motors affiliates, or reserved huge numbers of the most punishing job assignments for them, as in the case of Ford. All auto companies vehemently opposed proposals for a state fair employment practices law until lobbying by allied African-American and CIO organizations overcame their resistance in 1956. Most important of all, between 1947 and 1958 the Big Three transferred their operations wholesale out of Detroit to twenty-five new plants located in virtually all-white suburban areas.[52]

White workers exercised their own important initiatives in this process. The resistance of skilled tradesmen to the admission to their ranks of anyone who was not white was vigorous and successful, just as recurrent threats by those craftsmen to quit the United Auto Workers earned them special treatment by the union's leaders. Residents of the white suburbs in which new branch plants were built frequently resorted to violence against African Americans who attempted to move into the neighbourhoods. As John McGreevy has demonstrated, Catholic parishes formed community boundaries that were especially resistant to penetration, despite the postwar rise in appeals by Catholic clergy and lay intellectuals for inter-racial harmony.[53]

The story in the packinghouse industry played out somewhat differently. The crushing defeats of 1919–22 had left many workers wary of risking their jobs once again in the union cause. Those in better positions, like the older Polish women in Swift's sliced bacon department, openly feared that union victory would turn their jobs over to African Americans. It was black workers who spearheaded the new unionization in Chicago, despite the fact that their share of jobs in the city's packinghouses had fallen from 31.2 per cent to 19.6 per cent between 1930 and 1940. Consequently, the United Packinghouse Workers established a reputation for combating racism both on and off the job that no other national union could match – until the Chicago stockyards went out of business in the 1950s. It is important to add, however, that this achievement was accomplished by an alliance between black members and a left-wing minority of whites. It was supported, or at least tolerated, by the majority of white workers only when and to the extent that the union was successful in improving economic conditions. When union activists attacked residential segregation, however, they were openly, even violently, opposed by many white members.[54] Careful study of the packinghouse experience can tell us much about the impact and limits of workers' own activity in challenging the racialization of class.

A very influential book by Lisabeth Cohen has popularized the concept of the 'CIO's Culture of Unity', which enabled the goals of the new labour movement to be discussed in non-racial terms. Labour-oriented cultural expressions of the 1930s and 1940s depicted 'Americans' as 'working men and women of many races and nationalities'.[55] In stark contrast to South Africa's 1938 Great Trek commemoration, visions of history sponsored by the Roosevelt administration challenged Anglo-Saxon cultural supremacy in a way that framed in discourse an alliance between children of immigrants and African Americans. New Deal radio broadcasts such as 'Let Freedom Ring' (1937), 'Americans All, Immigrants All' (1938) and 'Freedom's People' (1941–2), slotted programmes about black Americans into the formula of 'a nation of nations'. Not only did that metaphor reflect the lines of support enjoyed by the CIO in heavy industry, but it had also been previewed by the 1926 Catholic Eucharist Congress in Chicago, when cardinals announced they had met 'thousands of Chicagoans of foreign birth or extraction', among them African Americans.[56]

Contradictions within the 'culture of unity' were made evident in the streets of America's cities by the Italian invasion of Ethiopia. Mussolini's escalating demands against Ethiopia and his invasion of that country in October 1935 had galvanized African American popular opinion like no previous foreign event since emancipation. Roi Ottley of the *Amsterdam News* observed that the teachings of black nationalists pervaded the conversation of black New Yorkers as never before. Moreover, the military assault in East Africa came hard on the heels of ardent 'Don't Buy Where You Can't Work' campaigns and the Harlem riot of 1935, in which the ubiquitous Italian store and bar keepers of Harlem were often singled out as targets.[57]

At the same time, Mussolini's invasion swelled the pride of Italian Americans. An editor of *Il Progresso Italo-Americano* explained that pride concisely:

> The Italians of America, who have known in the past the saddest bitterness, the Italians of America who have been so long in a world where Italians are looked down upon, today can raise their heads high and say to all the others: Hats off.[58]

Italian-American joy over the new international stature of their ancestral land turned into open enthusiasm for fascism after 6 May 1936, the day the Italian army entered Addis Ababa. Thousands of couples renewed their wedding vows at special Catholic masses using iron wedding bands, so that they could contribute their gold rings to the imperial cause. The mayors of Philadelphia and Paterson banned Italian victory parades, however, fearing bloody racial confrontation between two peoples, both of whom provided important constituencies of the new industrial unions.

The conflict in Harlem precipitated by the Ethiopian war not only dramatizes the tensions within the New Deal coalition, but also brings us back to the interaction of local, national and global history in shaping the classification of race and the racialization of class. The experience was not unique. Japan's invasion of China catapulted the left-leaning Chinese Hand Laundry Alliance into sharp confrontation with the established leadership of New York's Chinatown, while in San Francisco it precipitated the unionization of Chinese-American women at the National Dollar Stores – the first open participation of Asians in an AFL union. Protests against the Munich Pact cemented the alliance between Chicago's Slavic fraternal organizations and the CIO, just as subsequent Soviet conduct in Poland later disrupted it. Cardenas' reforms in Mexico, and especially the nationalization of American oil companies, strengthened the Left and the CIO among Chicanos in Texas and California.[59]

The links between local actions and the reshaping of world imperialism assumed both informal and institutional forms, which also deserve close attention. The inter-racial character and intercontinental role of maritime workers did not end with the nineteenth century. It persists in our own age of container ports, despite their isolation far out from urban centres, which has removed the ships and their crews from view. Out of sight, out of mind. We easily convince ourselves that the cargoes of a global economy somehow move about like our papers, in cyberspace.[60]

The Baku Congress of the Peoples of the East not only summoned European workers to 'form a close alliance with the working masses of the entire East, of the entire world', but also proclaimed the necessity 'to set up soviets even where there are no urban workers'. Revolution in the Russian empire had forged a physical link between insurgent industrial cities and insurgent Asia. Comintern chairman Zinoviev assured the delegates that 'only weeks will be needed before our Red Army stretches out its red hand once more toward Warsaw', advancing war 'against the imperialists around the world'.[61] Even though the revolutionary assault on the world order had been hurled back decisively on all fronts by 1927, the maritime world provided another geographic web for revolutionary activity. It was a seamen's journal, the *Negro Worker*, printed in Hamburg, Copenhagen, or wherever the police had not shut it down, through which the Comintern explicitly addressed people of African ancestry. Its first editor, George Padmore, quickly captures the attention of any historian who may be examining the Pan-African, world trade union or Communist movements.[62]

Those international links assumed a new importance during and after the Second World War. The war itself unleashed popular struggles and heightened workers' aspirations in both the metropolitan countries and their colonies in ways that proved difficult, if not impossible, for the governing authorities to contain. The defeat of the Axis powers, the achievements of the partisans and the electoral triumph of the Labour Party in Britain appeared to working people on both sides of the Atlantic to herald a new era, free from the destitution, repression, murderous racism and fear of impending war that had characterized the 1930s. In the United States a wave of postwar strikes matched the scale of those that had followed the First World War, but produced very different results. The new industrial unions turned back corporate efforts to reassert 'management's prerogatives' in the workplace and won major wage increases, which were of special benefit to lower-paid workers. Emboldened by its newfound strength, delegates to the CIO's 1946 convention adopted the most audacious programme in its history. They demanded statutory prohibition of racial discrimination and democratization of the American South as a 'Down Payment on the Four Freedoms': comprehensive economic planning, including price controls; governmental allocation of basic raw materials designed to direct production towards the needs of working people; exclusive government control of all uses of nuclear power; and United Nations control of atomic weapons. Although none of these proposals became law until the civil rights legislation of the 1960s, they articulated the working-class hopes that were soon to be snuffed out by the Cold War and channelled into the consumerism of the 1950s.[63]

Even more formidable was the rising tide of national independence struggles, which swept across the war-weakened empires of Britain, France and the Netherlands. General strikes in Nigeria and Sierra Leone, armed struggles in the Philippines and declarations of independence by Indonesia and Vietnam challenged Winston Churchill's reassurance that the principles of the Atlantic Charter applied only to Europe. Although the Cold War left its ugly and all-too often bloody imprint on the Third World's experience of independence, it could not halt the process of decolonization. The independence of India and Pakistan in 1947, the Bandung Conference of 1955 and the independence of Ghana two years later signalled the demise of the colonial empires which had appeared to be invincible half a century earlier.[64]

Faced with the revolt against colonialism, the political and intellectual leaders of the United States repudiated the ideology of white supremacy that had guided empire- and state-building at the turn of the century. Anti-colonial movements and the appeal of Soviet communism in nations which the United States sought to incorporate into its political and economic orbit, campaigns by African Americans in all parts of the country against both legal and *de facto* discrimination and the decisive role of urban political coalitions in presidential elections produced executive orders, court rulings and ultimately legislation, which prohibited racial discrimination and made verbal commitment to racial equality a crucial component of the 'liberal consensus'. By the end of the 1950s the hegemonic discourse castigated openly racist arguments as archaic and parochial.

In 1948, the very year the electoral triumph of Daniel Malan's Nationalists secured the future of apartheid in South Africa for more than four decades to come, the Democratic Party in the United States committed itself to a comprehensive programme of civil rights. Strom Thurmond's Dixiecrats, who left the party, protesting (quite accurately) that it had betrayed its historic commitment to white supremacy, initiated years of forceful but ultimately futile 'interposition' by Southern state governments against federal desegregation efforts. Neither that defensive effort nor the widespread popular support that bolstered the presidential campaigns of Alabama's George Wallace in 1964, 1968 and 1972, however, could restore the open celebration of white supremacy to the honoured status in national and international political discourse that it had enjoyed in the heyday of Woodrow Wilson and Jan Christian Smuts.[65]

The war and postwar years initiated a remarkable racial recomposition of the working class in both the United States and Britain. During the war the Depression's homogenizing effect on America's industrial labour force was reversed. Over the ensuing three decades a veritable depopulation of the Southern countryside made African Americans one of the most urbanized segments of the population. By the 1970s they constituted more than 20 per cent of the country's manufacturing and service workers. As their numbers in industry grew, so did their demands for access to more skilled jobs and to union leadership. Moreover, the doors to immigration had by then once again been partially opened. Immigrants from Asia and Latin America arrived in numbers that surpassed those of European newcomers in the late nineteenth century. The gradual shift of union leaders from support of the racial privileges of white members to endorsement of their newer members' demands and actions, which Satnam Virdee has found in England between the 1950s and 1970s, has a familiar ring to observers of the corresponding experience in the United States. By the elections of 1964 and 1968 major unions in the United States had come to identify George Wallace's appeal to their white members as a menace to the unions' own futures, which had to be combated vigorously, for the sake of the unions' political alliance with the Democratic Party and liberal organizations.[66]

Almost a century after the Liberal landslide of 1906, therefore, imperialism has assumed a very different shape from the one that was congealing at that time. One sphere of influence encompasses the globe, 'unleashing market forces' is its watchword, workers' movements have been humbled within the most highly industrialized countries, and the Soviet revolution is gone. Racism has simultaneously become the target of almost universal verbal condemnation and assumed an increasingly formidable presence in social and political practice. In former colonies state-building has become the pre-eminent concern, circumscribing both the space allowed workers' movements and economic policies. The most eminent intellectuals have repudiated their earlier faith in public control of economic life and staked their hopes for social improvement on profit-making enterprise. Even Jamaica's Michael Manley confessed before his death:

> I kept thinking that you could make the world economy submit to a system of political management to safeguard against injustice and inequity. I didn't realize the forces of production are too powerful, and their inherent logic too irresistible, to be made subservient to political barriers on a permanent basis.[67]

In short, at the end of the century of the colour bar the dialogue of race and class has not been resolved, but it is being subsumed into new forms of domination and conflict. But we mistake the nature of both past and future social struggle if we relegate the study of exploitation and class struggles to the historians' dustbin. To take that course is to write the past in the image of the shopping-mall present, to accept the new world order as natural and inevitable, and to close our eyes to the classification of race. It is also to ignore the boiling discontent of subordinated races and classes, which will make the new world empire's triumphal free marketism even more short lived than the political barriers that the Great Powers erected a century ago.[68]

## Notes

1  Howard Lamar, 'From Bondage to Contract: Ethnic Labor in the American West, 1600–1890', in Steven Hahn and Jonathan Prude, eds., *The Countryside in the Age of Capitalist Transformation: Essays in the Social History of Rural America* (Chapel Hill and London, 1985), 293–324.
2  David Montejano, *Anglos and Mexicans in the Making of Texas, 1836–1986* (Austin, 1987), 7; Laura Tabili, *'We Ask for British Justice': Workers and Racial Difference in Late Imperial Britain* (Ithaca and London, 1994).
3  Sylvia Frey, *Water from the Rock: Black Resistance in a Revolutionary Age* (Princeton, 1991); W. Jeffrey Bolster, *Black Jacks: African American Seamen in the Age of Sail* (Cambridge, MA and London, 1997), 105–6. See also C.L.R. James, *The Black Jacobins: Toussaint L'Ouverture and the San Domingo Revolution* (New York, 1963); David B. Davis, *The Problem of Slavery in the Age of Revolution, 1770–1823* (Ithaca and London, 1975).
4  Herman Melville, *Redburn, His First Voyage* (Anchor Books Edition, Garden City, New York, 1957), 96. The destructive potential of this fantasy for both races is explored carefully in John A. McClure, *Kipling and Conrad: The Colonial Fiction* (Cambridge, MA and London, 1981). Similarly, Japanese-Americans nationalists assured fellow inmates in the Manzanar concentration camp during the Second World War that after the war there

would 'be plenty of opportunity in Malaya, East Indies and Australia where you'll be able to live like kings'. Brian Masaru Hayashi, *'For the Sake of Our Japanese Brethren': Assimilation, Nationalism, and Protestantism among the Japanese of Los Angeles, 1895–1942* (Stanford, California, 1995), 144.

5  McClure, *Kipling and Conrad*, 90; Carolyn Brown, 'Becoming "Men", Becoming "Workers": Race, Gender and Workplace Struggle in the Nigerian Coal Industry, 1938–1948' (unpublished paper, presented at Racializing Class, Classifying Race – A Conference on Labour and Difference in Africa, USA and Britain, St. Anthony's College, University of Oxford, 11–13 July 1997. See also the brief but vivid description of colonists' pretensions in Benedict Anderson, *Imagined Communities: Reflections on the Origin and Spread of Nationalism* (London and New York, 1983), 137–9.

6  Emile Vandervelde, 'Die Sozialdemokratie und das Kolonialproblem', II: 'Die belgischen Sozialisten und die Congofrage', *Die Neue Zeit* 27 (1909), quoted in Preben Kaarsholm, 'The South African War and the Response of the International Socialist Community to Imperialism between 1896 and 1908', in Frits van Holthoon and Marcel van der Linden, eds., *Internationalism in the Labour Movement, 1830–1940* (2 vols., Leiden, 1988), I, 62. My translation from Vandervelde's German text.

7  W.E.B. Du Bois, *Souls of Black Folk: Essays and Sketches* (Premier Americana edition, Greenwich, Conn., 1961), 23.

8  Thomas C. Holt, *The Problem of Freedom: Race, Labor, and Politics in Jamaica and Britain, 1832–1938* (Baltimore, 1992), xix.

9  Eric J. Hobsbawm, *Industry and Empire: The Making of Modern English Society, 1750 to the Present Day* (New York, 1968), 171; Brinley Thomas, *Migration and Economic Growth, A Study of Great Britain and the Atlantic Economy* (Cambridge. Mass., 1954); Paul A. Baran and Paul M. Sweezy, *Monopoly Capital: An Essay on the American Economic and Social Order* (New York and London, 1966), 90–108; W.E.B. Du Bois, *Color and Democracy: Colonies and Peace* (New York, 1945), 17.

10  The political scientist Ernest W. Burgess worried that the industrial city nurtured 'areas of demoralization, or promiscuity, and of vice'. Like many of his peers, he proposed segregation as the remedy, because 'segregation offers the group, and thereby individuals who compose the group, a place and role in the total organization of city life. Segregation limits development in certain directions, but releases it in others'. Ernest W. Burgess, 'The Growth of the City: An Introduction to a Research Project', in Robert E. Park, Ernest W. Burgess and Roderick D. McKenzie, eds., *The City* (Chicago, 1967. First published 1926), 59.

11  Karl Polanyi , *The Great Transformation* (New York and Toronto, 1944), 3; the Burrows Report, quoted in Dilip Simeon, 'Coal and Colonialism: Production Relations in an Indian Coalfield, c. 1895–1947', *International Review of Social History* 41 Supplement 4 (1996), 106.

12  E.g. Maurice Bruce, *The Coming of the Welfare State* (London, 1961), 133–96; T.H. Marshall and Tom Bottomore, *Citizenship and Social Class* (London and Concord, Mass., 1992). It is fashionable among critical legal historians, if misleading, to depict this moment of one of fundamental divergence between the labour movements of Britain and the United

States. See, for example, William E. Forbath, *Law and the Shaping of the American Labor Movement* (Cambridge, Mass., 1991); Victoria C. Hattam, *Labor Visions and State Power: The Origins of Business Unionism in the United States* (Princeton, NJ, 1993).

13  Henry Pelling, 'The Working Class and the Origins of the Welfare State', in Pelling, *Popular Politics and Society in Late Victorian Britain* (London, 1968), 1–18, and 'British Labour and British Imperialism', in *ibid.*, 98. Pelling adds that efforts by Conservatives to counteract this sentiment by denouncing the immigration of Jews from Russia into England attracted few workers' votes outside London's East End. Joseph L. White discusses the weakness of the Liberal–Labour appeal to Lancashire cotton workers in *The Limits of Trade Union Militancy The Lancashire Textile Workers, 1910–1914* (Westport, Conn., and London, 1978), 146–61.

14  Pelling, *Popular Politics and Society*, 17; John W. Cell, *The Highest Stage of White Supremacy: The Origins of Segregation in South Africa and the American South* (Cambridge and New York, 1982), 266–7 ; C. Vann Woodward, *Tom Watson, Agrarian Rebel* (New York, 1938); Elliott Rudwick, *Race Riot at East St. Louis, July 2, 1917* (New York, 1972); Nell Irvin Painter, *Standing at Armageddon: The United States, 1877–1919* (New York and London, 1987), 278–9. Paul H. Buck hailed this epoch as the final healing of the wounds of Civil War. Buck, *The Road to Reunion, 1886–1900* (New York, 1937), 294–320.

15  Shula Marks and Stanley Trapido, 'Lord Milner and the South African State', *History Workshop* 8:3 (1979), 50–80. The quotation is on p. 55.

16  *Ibid.*, 58–65, 73; Saul Dubow, 'Colonial Nationalism, the Milner Kindergarten and the Rise of "South Africanism", 1902–1910', *History Workshop Journal* 43:2 (1997), 58. Dubow, *Segregation and the Origins of Apartheid in South Africa* (London, 1989).

17  Quoted in Holt, 332.

18  Quoted in Marks and Trapido, 66. This perspective informed the work of the Transvaal Indigency Commission. See Dubow, 'Colonial Nationalism', 65. It was shared by champions of the all-white textile industry in America's New South. See Alan Tullos, *Habits of Industry: White Culture and the Transformation of the Carolina Piedmont* (Chapel Hill, NC, 1989).

19  Cell, 64–81; Jeremy Kirkler, 'The Inner Mechanisms of a Racial Massacre'; Dunbar Moodie, 'Profitability, Respectability and Challenge: (Re)gaining Control and Restructuring the Labour Process While Maintaining Racial Order on the South African Gold Mines, 1913–1922'; Deborah Posel, 'The Office of van der Merwe: the Politics of Patronage and Labour Relations in the Apartheid Civil Service'; Eric Arnesen, 'The Death Knell of Jim Crow Unionism? Race, Law and Railroad Labor in Mid-Twentieth Century America' (all presented at the conference, Racializing Class, Classifying Race). In the United States government officials who had crushed the railway strike of 1922 were also repudiated at the polls, opening the way to the act of 1926. Colin J. Davis, *Power at Odds: The 1922 National Railroad Shopmen's Strike* (Urbana, Ill., 1997); David Montgomery, *The Fall of the House of Labor: The Workplace, the State, and American Labor Activism, 1865–1925* (Cambridge and New York, 1987), 435–7.

20  Eric Foner, *Nothing But Freedom: Emancipation and its Legacy* (Baton Rouge

and London, 1983), 29–38; Holt, 156 ; Cell, 215–19; Charles van Onselen, *Studies in the Social and Economic History of the Witwatersrand, 1886–1914* (2 vols., Harlow, 1982), I, 1–24, II, 1–110.

21  Holt, 156–63; Jeanne Boydston, *Home and Work: Housework, Wages, and the Ideology of Labor in the Early Republic* (New York and Oxford, 1990), 142–63.

22  Theodore Rosengarten, *All God's Dangers: The Life of Nate Shaw* (New York, 1974); Bose quoted in Samita Sen, 'Unsettling the Household: Act VI (of 1901) and the Regulation of Women Migrants in Colonial Bengal', *International Review of Social History* 41 Supplement 4 (1996), 135. See also Julie Saville, *The Work of Reconstruction: From Slave to Wage Labor in South Carolina, 1860–1870* (Cambridge and New York, 1994), 130.

23  Allen Isaacman and Richard Roberts, eds., *Cotton, Colonialism, and Social History in Sub-Saharan Africa* (Portsmouth, NH, 1995); John Higginson, *A Working Class in the Making: Belgian Colonial Labor Policy, Private Enterprise, and the African Mineworker, 1907–1951* (Madison, Wisc., 1989), 107–8; Robert Shenton, review of Isaacman and Roberts, *International Labor and Working-Class History* 51:1 (1997), 256.

24  W. Kloosterboer, *Involuntary Labour Since the Abolition of Slavery: A Survey of Compulsory Labour throughout the World* (Leiden, 1960), 194, 67; Frederick Cooper, *From Slaves to Squatters: Plantation Labor and Agriculture in Zanzibar and Coastal Kenya, 1890–1925* (New Haven and London, 1980); Alex Lichtenstein, *Twice the Work of Free Labor: The Political Economy of Convict Labor in the New South* (London and New York, 1996); Karin A. Shapiro, 'The Tennessee Coal Miners' Revolts of 1891–92: Industrialization, Politics, and Convict Labor in the Late Nineteenth-Century South' (PhD dissertation, Yale University, 1991); Daniel Letwin, *The Challenge of Interracial Unionism: Alabama Coal Miners, 1878–1921* (Chapel Hill, NC, 1997); Daphne Simon, 'Master and Servant', in John Saville, ed., *Democracy and the Labor Movement* (London, 1954), 160–200; David Montgomery, *Citizen Worker: The Experience of Workers in the United States with Democracy and the Free Market during the Nineteenth Century* (New York and Cambridge, 1993), 25–51. Charles van Onselen suggests that master–servant law was applied by Johannesburg magistrates primarily against whites, and with light sanctions, while pass laws provided the draconian sanctions against Africans. Van Onselen, II, 34–5.

25  Dilip Simeon, 'Coal and Colonialism: Production Relations in an Indian Coalfield, c. 1895–1947', *International Review of Social History* 41 Supplement 4 (1996), 83–108. The quotations are on pp. 89 and 103, with italics in the original. See McClure, 28–9 on the celebration of the 'true India' by Orientalists in the British elite. White American steam shovel and crane operators on the Panama Canal advised Samuel Gompers that black Jamaican labourers were unfit for an eight-hour day. T.J. Dolan to S. Gompers, 6 September 1906, quoted in Julia Greene, 'The Strike at the Ballot Box: Politics and Partisanship in the American Federation of Labor' (PhD dissertation, Yale University, 1990), 249.

26  Tabili, *'We Ask for British Justice'*, 162–6; Holt, 387–91.

27  Frantz Fanon, *The Wretched of the Earth*, translated by Constance Farrington (New York, 1968), 118–28.

28  Quoted in Holt, 262.

29 Anderson, *Imagined Communties*, 136.
30 Quoted in Evelyn Brooks Higginbotham, 'African-American Women's History and the Metalanguage of Race', *Signs* 17:1 (1992), 267.
31 *Ibid.*, 255.
32 Holt, 295–302.
33 Du Bois, 'The Black North', quoted in Kevin K. Gaines, *Uplifting the Race: Black Leadership, Politics, and Culture in the Twentieth Century* (Chapel Hill, NC, and London, 1996), 165. Cf. Du Bois's declaration of 1888: 'Bismark was my hero'. The Chancellor's mastery of the process that created a nation 'out of a mass of bickering peoples ... foreshadowed in my mind the kind of thing that American Negroes must do'. Quoted in Paul Gilroy, *The Black Atlantic: Modernity and Double Consciousness* (Cambridge, Mass., 1993), 35.
34 Gaines, 75, 158.
35 E.P. Thompson, *The Making of the English Working Class* (New York, 1966), 10. James E. Cronin argues that the methodological distance between Thompson's work and that of Gareth Stedman Jones, Joan Scott and other advocates of the linguistic turn has been exaggerated by the latter. Cronin, 'Neither Exceptional nor Peculiar: Towards the Comparative Study of Labor in Advanced Society', *International Review of Social History* 38 (1993), 59–75, note 10. A particularly perceptive scrutiny of 'narratives' can be found in James Gray Pope, 'Labor's Constitution of Freedom', *The Yale Law Journal* 106 (1997), 941–1031.
36 Aileen S. Kraditor, *The Radical Persuasion: Aspects of the Intellectual History and the Historiography of Three American Radical Organizations* (Baton Rouge and London, 1981), 297–321.
37 Robin D.G. Kelley, '"We Are Not What We Seem": Rethinking Black Working-Class Opposition in the Jim Crow South', *Journal of American History* 80:1 (1993), 84, 86 ; Tera W. Hunter, *To 'Joy My Freedom: Southern Black Women's Lives and Labors after the Civil War* (Cambridge, Mass., and London, 1997), 168–86. See also Gilroy, 75–85.
38 Earl Lewis, *In Their Own Interests: Race, Class, and Power in Twentieth-Century Norfolk, Virginia* (Berkeley, 1991), 91–2.
39 The *Alltagsgeschichte* current among historians of Germany has been constructed largely around this principle. See, for example, Alf Lüdtke, 'Polymorphous Synchrony: German Industrial Workers and the Politics of Everyday Life', *International Review of Social History* 38 (1993), 39–84. For an innovative study of the interaction of personal life and movement life, see Horst Groschopp, *Zwischen Bierabend und Bildungsverein: Zur Kulturarbeit in der deutschen Arbeiterbewegung vor 1914* (Berlin, 1985).
40 Ira Berlin, ed., *The Black Military Experience*, Series II of *Freedom: A Documentary History of Emancipation, 1861–1867* (Cambridge and New York, 1982), 155, 154.
41 'Van Onselen, II, 23–7; Alexander Irvine, *From the Bottom Up*, quoted in Kathryn J. Oberdeck, 'Popular Narrative and Working-Class Identity: Alexander Irvine's Early-Twentieth-Century Literary Adventures', in Eric Arnesen, Julie Greene and Bruce Laurie, eds., *Labor Histories: Class, Politics, and the Working-Class Experience* (Urbana, Ill., 1998).
42 Bruce Nelson, 'Class, Race and Democracy in the CIO: The "New" Labor

History Meets the "Wages of Whiteness"', *International Review of Social History* 41 (1996), 351–74. Among the pioneering works in this exploration are Alexander Saxton, *The Indispensible Enemy: Labor and the Anti-Chinese Movement in California* (Berkeley, 1971); Alexander Saxton, *The Rise and Fall of the White Republic: Class Politics and Mass Culture in Nineteenth Century America* (London and New York, 1990); Herbert Hill, 'Myth-Making as Labor History: Herbert Gutman and the United Mine Workers of America', *International Journal of Politic, Culture, and Society*, 2:1 (1988), 49–127; Hill, 'The Problem of Race in American Labor History', *Reviews in American History*, 24:2 (1996), 196–208; Herbert Hill and James E. Jones, Jr., eds., *Race in America: The Struggle for Equality* (Madison, Wisc., 1993); Theodore W. Allen, *The Invention of the White Race, vol, 1: Racial Oppression and Social Control* (London, 1994); Noel Ignatiev, *How the Irish Became White* (New York and London, 1995); David R. Roediger, *The Wages of Whiteness: Race and the Making of the American Working Class* (London and New York, 1991). Political implications of this development are explored by Staughton Lynd, 'History, Race, and the Steel Industry', *Radical Historians Newsletter* 76:1 (1997), 1, 13–16.

43  David B. Hill diary, 16 November 1846, quoted in Paul W. Foos, 'Mexican Wars: Soldiers and Society in an Age of Expansion, 1835–1855' (PhD dissertation, Yale University, 1997), 489.

44  Tabili, *'We Ask for British Justice'*, 1–2, 149–59. In Port Darwin, Australia dockside workers of Aborigine, Malay, Chinese, and Filipino backgrounds were supported by local unions and included in wage awards in the 1930s, provided they had been locally born.

45  Thomas J. Sugrue, 'Segmented Work, Race-Conscious Workers: Structure, Agency and Division in the CIO Era', *International Review of Social History* 41 (1996), 403.

46  Richard J. Jensen, 'The Causes and Cures of Unemployment in the Great Depression', *Journal of Interdisciplinary History* 19:3 (1989), 553–83; Walter Licht, *Getting Work: Philadelphia, 1840–1950* (Cambridge and London 1992), 30–1, 45–6, 51–3; E. Wright Bakke, *The Unemployed Worker: A Study of the Task of Making a Living Without a Job* (New Haven, Conn., 1940), 247–48.

47  Nancy J. Weiss, *Farewell to the Party of Lincoln: Black Politics in the Age of FDR* (Princeton, NJ, 1983); Earl Lewis, *In Their Own Interests: Race, Class, and Power in Twentieth-Century Norfolk, Virginia* (Berkeley, 1991), 110–98; Joe W. Trotter and Earl Lewis, *African Americans in the Industrial Age: A Documentary History, 1915–1945* (Boston, 1996); Raymond Wolters, *Negroes and the Great Depression: The Problem of Economic Recovery* (Westport, CT, 1970); Linda Gordon, *Pitied But Not Entitled: Single Mothers and the History of Welfare, 1890–1935* (New York, 1994); Gwendolyn Mink, *Wages of Motherhood: Inequality in the Welfare State, 1917–1942* (Ithaca, 1995); David Montgomery, 'Labor and the Political Leadership of New Deal America', *International Review of Social History* 39 (1994), 335–60; Eric J. Hobsbawm, *The Age of Extremes: A History of the World, 1914–1991* (New York, 1996), 85–141.

48  Sterling D. Spero and Abram L. Harris, *The Black Worker: The Negro and the Labor Movement* (New York, 1931); Dana Frank, *Purchasing Power: Consumer*

*Organization, Gender, and the Seattle Labor Movement, 1919–1929*
(Cambridge and New York, 1994); Charles H. Wesley, *Negro Labor in the
United States, 1850–1925; A Study in American Economic History* (New York,
1927).
49 Eric Arnesen, '"Like Banquo's Ghost, It Will Not Down": The Race
Question and the American Railroad Brotherhoods, 1880–1920', *American
Historical Review*, 99:4 (1994), 1601–33; U.S. Bureau of the Census,
*Historical Statistics of the United States: Colonial Times to 1970* (2 vols.,
Washington, D.C., 1975), I, 177. (The Bureau of Labor Statistics figures
showing a larger CIO membership are based on exaggerated claims.)
50 Christopher L. Tomlins, 'AFL Unions in the 1930s: Their Performance in
Historical Perspective', *Journal of American History* 65:4 (1979), 1021–42;
Robert H. Zieger, *The CIO, 1935–1955* (Chapel Hill and London, 1995);
Michael K. Honey, *Southern Labor and Black Civil Rights: Organizing Memphis
Workers* (Urbana, 1993); Steve Rosswurm, ed., *The CIO's Left-led Unions*
(New Brunswick, NJ, 1992); Jacquelyn Dowd Hall, et al., *Like a Family: The
Making of a Southern Cotton Mill World* (Chapel Hill and London, 1987).
51 James D. Rose, 'Shop Floor Representation without a Union: Skilled
Workers, US Steel, and the Employee Representation Plan during the
1930s' (unpublished paper, quoted by permission of the author); Nelson
Lichtenstein, *The Most Dangerous Man in Detroit: Walter Reuther and the Fate
of American Labor* (New York, 1995), 47–131; Prudence Cumberbatch, 'For
Liberty and Victory: Blacks, Unions, and the Bethlehem Company,
1937–1945' (unpublished seminar paper, Yale University, 1993); Peter
Gottlieb, *Making Their Own Way: Southern Blacks' Migration to Pittsburgh,
1916–30* (Urbana, 1987); Dennis C. Dickerson, *Out of the Crucible: Black
Steelworkers in Western Pennsylvania, 1875–1980* (Albany, 1986).
52 Thomas J. Sugrue, 'Segmented Work, Race-Conscious Workers: Structure,
Agency and Division in the CIO Era', *International Review of Social History*
41 (1996), 402; Sugrue, 'Crabgrass-Roots Politics: Race, Rights, and the
Reaction against Liberalism in the Urban North, 1940–1964', *Journal of
American History* 82:3 (1995), 551–78; Zaragosa Vargas, *Proletarians of the
North: A History of Mexican Industrial Workers in Detroit and the Midwest,
1917–1933* (Berkeley, 1993).
53 Sugrue, 'Segmented Work', 403; Sugrue, 'The Structures of Urban Poverty:
The Reorganization of Space and Work in Three Periods of American
History', in Michael B. Katz, ed., *The 'Underclass' Debate: Views from History*
(Princeton, 1993), 111–12; John T. McGreevy, *Parish Boundaries: The
Catholic Encounter with Race in the Twentieth Century Urban North* (Chicago
and London, 1996). McGreevy also reminds us: 'Simply invoking the talis-
man of "class" to explain racial tension ... is inadequate,' he argued. 'Even
the most working-class Catholic neighborhoods contained a core of physi-
cians, lawyers, city government officials, and police officers, and Catholics
were significantly more likely than white Protestants or Jews to structure
social networks along religious, and not simply occupational, lines'.
McGreevy, 107. The contrast between white workers' emphasis on class on
the job and on race in defining neighbourhoods is a central theme of
David Halle, *America's Working Man: Work, Home, and Politics among Blue-
Collar Property Owners* (Chicago and London, 1984).

54  Rick Halpern, *Down on the Killing Floor: Black and White Workers in Chicago's Packinghouses, 1904–1954* (Urbana, Ill., 1997); Roger Horowitz, *'Negro and White, Unite and Fight!' A Social History of Industrial Unionism in Meatpacking, 1930–90* (Urbana, Ill., 1997); Shelton Stromquist, *Solidarity and Survival: An Oral History of Iowa Labor in the Twentieth Century* (Iowa City, 1993). The figures on black packinghouse workers in Chicago are from Catherine Lewis, 'Trade Union Policies with Regard to the Negro in the Slaughtering and Meatpacking Industry in Chicago' (MA thesis, University of Chicago, 1946), 74–7.

55  Lizabeth Cohen, *Making a New Deal: Industrial Workers in Chicago, 1919–1939* (Cambridge and New York, 1990), 323–60; Michael Denning, *The Cultural Front: The Laboring of American Culture in the Twentieth Century* (London and New York, 1996), 126–36.

56  Barbara D. Savage, 'Broadcasting Freedom: Radio, War, and the Roots of Civil Rights Liberalism, 1938–1948' (PhD dissertation, Yale University, 1995); McGreevy, *Parish Boundaries*, 34. For all its limitations, this representation contrasted sharply with the Amos 'n' Andy image, and brought to the networks representations of black America advised and written by black intellectuals. Cf. the critique of Warren Sussman, *Culture as History: The Transformation of American Society in the Twentieth Century* (New York, 1984), 80, 205–12.

57  This discussion and what follows is based, unless otherwise indicated, on Nadia Venturini, *Neri e italiani ad Harlem: Gli anni Trenta e la guerra d'Etopia* (Rome, 1990). See also William R. Scott, *The Sons of Sheba's Race: African Americans and the Italo-Ethiopian War, 1935–1941* (Bloomington, Ind., 1993); Joseph E. Harris, *African-American Reactions to the War in Ethiopia, 1936–1941* (Baton Rouge, La., 1994). In 1895 black workers in São Paulo, who were being displaced by Italian immigrants, had clashed sharply with the newcomers over Italy's earlier invasion of Ethiopia. George Reid Andrews, 'Black Workers in the Export Years: Latin America, 1880–1930', *International Labor and Working-Class History* 51: 1 (1997), 13, 19.

58  Quoted in Venturini, 138. My free translation.

59  Renqiu Yu, *To Save China: To Save Ourselves: The Chinese Hand Laundry Alliance of New York* (Philadelphia, 1992); Judy Yung, *Unbound Feet: A Social History of Chinese Women in San Francisco* (Berkeley, 1995), 209–22; John J. Bukowczyk, *And My Children Did Not Know Me: A History of the Polish-Americans* (Bloomington, 1987), 80–9; Margaret Collingwood Nowak, *Two Who Were There: A Biography of Stanley Nowak* (Detroit, 1989); Mario T. Garcia, *Mexican Americans: Leadership, Ideology, and Identity, 1930–1960* (New Haven and London, 1989), 145–86; Mario T. Garcia, *Memories of Chicano History: The Life and Narrative of Bert Corona* (Berkeley, 1994), 59–66, 94–6.

60  See Allan Sekula, *Fish Story* (Dusseldorf, 1995).

61  John Riddell, ed., *To See the Dawn: Baku, 1920 – First Congress of the Peoples of the East* (New York and London, 1993), 68, 72, 49.

62  James R. Hooker, *Black Revolutionary: George Padmore's Path from Communism to Pan-Africanism* (New York, 1967), 18–28; Penny M. von Eschen, *Race against Empire: Black Americans and Anticolonialism, 1937–1957* (Ithaca and London, 1997), 48–52; Tabili, 'We Ask for British

*Justice'*, 158–9; Bruce Nelson, *Workers on the Waterfront: Seamen, Longshoremen, and Unionism in the 1930s* (Urbana, Ill., 1988), 1–38; Fernando Morais, *Olga: A Vida de Olga Bernario Prestes, Judia Communista Entregue a Hitler pelo Governo Vargas* (São Paulo, 1986), 202–32.

63 'What Are We Fighting For?' *Steelabor*, 28 May 1943, pp. 6–7; *Final Proceedings of the Eighth Constitutional Convention of the Congress of Industrial Organizations, November 18, 19, 20, 21, 22, 1946, Atlantic City, New Jersey* (n.p., n.d.), 36–43, 59–60, 73–87; Georges Gurvitch, *The Bill of Social Rights* (New York, 1946).

64 Von Eschen, *Race against Empire*, passim.

65 John Egerton, *Speak Now against the Day: The Generation before the Civil Rights Movement in the South* (New York, 1994), 471–512; Dan T. Carter, *The Politics of Rage: George Wallace, The Origins of the New Conservatism, and the Transformation of American Politics* (New York, 1995).

66 Satnam Virdee, 'Racism and Resistance in British Trade Unions, 1948–1979', in this volume.

67 Obituary for Michael Manley, *New York Times*, 8 March 1997.

68 See James Petras, 'Latin America: The Resurgence of the Left', *New Left Review* 223:1 (1997), 17–47; *NACLA Report on the Americas*, 30 (July/August, 1997).

# 2

# 'Mexican Labour' in a 'White Man's Town': Racialism, Imperialism and Industrialization in the Making of Arizona, 1840–1905

*A. Yvette Huginnie*

Early in the evening of 1 October 1904 a train climbed through Arizona's Peloncillo Mountains and made its regular stop at the Clifton depot just as the sun was starting to set. The neighbouring towns of Clifton, Morenci and Metcalf formed one of the United States' largest industrial copper mining districts and were a major population and commercial centre for eastern Arizona. That evening the train pulled a special car which carried several nuns, an orphanage agent and forty children from the New York Foundling Hospital. Sister Anna Michella peered outside; seeing a large crowd of people gathered on the platform she locked the door to protect her charges.[1] Father Constant Mandlin, the local priest in Clifton-Morenci, had arranged for some of his parishioners to adopt Catholic orphans. The Father had chosen the families who regularly attended church; to him, this seemed a good measure of character. His views, however, were not representative of the larger white community. The French priest, having recently arrived in the district, was apparently unfamiliar with southwestern race relations.[2]

White townspeople violently objected to Mandlin's arrangement that his Mexican parishioners should adopt what they saw as 'white' children. Middle-class white women repeatedly invaded the hotel rooms of the nuns and verbally harassed them about turning the children over to Mexicans, at times accusing the nuns of selling the children. The women also turned to white men in the district to help enforce the customary separation of the 'races'. The children had been with their Mexican adoptive parents less than two days when white men forcibly removed them. White townsfolk distributed twenty of the children to white families and allowed the nuns to leave with the rest. The legal battle which ensued between the New York Foundling

Hospital and the white families with the children eventually reached the Arizona Supreme Court; that body decided in favour of the white adoptive families.

The significance of the foundling controversy are multiple. Most obvious is that 'race' was one of the primary categories around which Arizona society was organized. As I shall demonstrate, white men and women came together across class lines to maintain what they saw as legitimate racial separations. Through their actions they affirmed and reinscribed their common understanding of both white and Mexican as distinct racial categories. Moreover, their effort to maintain this racialized line suggests a common notion of whiteness which bridged class, sex and ethnic differences among them. This combination of extra-legal and legal actions demonstrates that 'race' was itself an historical construct based on both ideological and structural factors.

Moreover, the foundling incident points to profound regional variations within US race relations. Most scholarship in US race relations focuses on black–white relations and presents bifurcated notions of race and of race relations. Couched as representative of the nation as a whole, this scholarship actually provides one regional slice of a larger mosaic of US race relations. While whites in Arizona did disenfranchise and segregate African Americans, their primary discursive and social struggles involved distinguishing between 'white' and 'Mexican'. As I shall demonstrate, both these categories were informed by multi-referent notions of other racialized groups, specifically Native Americans and African Americans; that is, definitions of 'Mexican' were based on perceptions of what was taken to be 'Indian' or 'Negro'. Race relations in the West were shaped by factors such as population characteristics, immigration and migration patterns, industrial development, agrarian policy and mythology, public policy and the region's relationship with other US regions. That is, the historical specificity of the West – like that of the Northeast and the South – gave its racial tapestry a unique pattern. Even in the West, distinct subregional patterns coexisted such as in the Pacific Coast states and in the US Southwest.[3] The specific working out of this identity – 'whiteness' – varied among US regions. My work looks at how it took shape in the Southwest.[4]

Racialization of the West grew out of the intersection of imperialistic expansionism, class formation and industrialization.[5] The terms 'Mexican Labour' and 'White Man's Town' suggest the contours of racialized, classed and industrial power structures and ideologies in Arizona. These social relations had their roots in the nineteenth century. I use the term 'racialism' to denote the type of thinking that increasingly framed American thought by the mid-nineteenth century. Racialist thinking understood peoples as divided among distinct racial groups, based on 'blood' and other supposedly immutable features, and positioned these 'races' in a hierarchy.

When the foundling case reached the courts, neither party called any ethnic Mexican[6] witnesses to testify. Both sides, the New York Foundling Hospital and the white families, apparently agreed that Mexicans were unsuitable to parent 'white' children even though the protests in the streets, hotels and eventually the legal case point to the ongoing process of solidifying those very definitions. Throughout the trial, the white community was portrayed as the aggrieved party, wounded by the Hospital's decision to allow Mexicans to adopt white children. Their exclusion from the trial is an indicator of the extent to which US settler colonialism marginalized ethnic Mexicans. The Mexican and Mexican American families who had sought to adopt the children were the subjects of US colonial rule, whereas the white men and women were its beneficiaries; therefore, the court records provide only whites' accounts of the event. This kind of treatment was commonplace in Arizona. White-run local newspapers, for example, rarely mentioned ethnic Mexicans even in towns where they were the majority. The court records none the less provide a window onto the particular southwestern development of racial categorization under US expansionism and industrialization.[7]

Mrs Laura Abrams had left the hotel which she and her husband owned and headed to the depot with her good friends Mrs Parks and Mrs Muriel Wright. Unwilling to wait until the children alighted from the car, Mrs Abrams peered in through the windows.[8] At the trial, Mrs Abrams recalled that what she saw when she peered in the window had shocked her:

> I heard that a car with about 40 little children was coming to Clifton to be given away to Mexicans ... I supposed that these little children being given to the Mexicans were Mexican children; of course out of idle curiosity I went over to the train to see them come in. ... When we went over to the train there was quite a crowd of Mexicans around the car, but of course naturally we wished to see the children; and we[,] Mrs. Wright and Mrs. Parks and myself, got in the vestibule of this private care and looked in; and I was greatly surprised to see perhaps 40 little American children.[9]

With 'but of course' suggesting the usual social divide between whites and Mexicans in the mining district, Mrs. Abrams' words provide important clues to identifying the characteristics upon which 'white' and 'Mexican' were defined in Arizona. Her and the other middle class white women's involvement had been prompted by curiosity about arrangements made in the socially distinct Mexican community, but once on the scene she asserted a presumed authority.

One of the distinguishing characteristics for Mrs Abrams and other whites in the district was skin colour. In the trial documents, she and many others repeatedly described the children as of 'fair complexion': '[The] [c]hildren [were] of fair complexion, all of them being of the Caucasian race, of unusual beauty and attractiveness.'[10] Throughout the trial, the lawyer for the white townsfolk referred to the children as 'white Caucasian child[ren] of the White-Saxon race'.[11] The redundancy of that description – 'white Caucasian children of the White-Saxon race' – points to both common assumptions that phenotype defines race and to the almost desperate need to fortify that belief system.

The rendering of the children, based merely upon sight, as 'American', 'white' and 'White-Saxon' – all terms used by White townspeople to describe the orphans – suggests a regional understanding of whiteness that differed from other areas of the United States. When the train left New York City, orphans Katherine Fitzpatrick, Joseph Ryan and Anna L. Doherty, among others, were probably considered to be 'Irish', but when they arrived in Arizona, they were 'American', 'white' and 'White-Saxon'. This regional notion of whiteness also eclipsed ethnic differences among the white men and women in Clifton-Morenci who would eventually adopt the children: John C. and Louisa Gatti, C. F. Pascoe, Samuel and Laura Abrams, and J. F. Kelley, among others. Their Italian, Cornish, Jewish, and Irish ancestries, respectively, did not exclude them from the category of 'white'.

The lack of ethnic tensions among Caucasian peoples in the Southwest, and in the West in general, and the ease with which they embraced a collective whiteness may be due to their joint participation in the US imperialist project that garnered the rewards of expansion for white people in a white republic.[12] Indeed, the terminology invoked, specifically 'American' and 'White Saxon', speaks to the historically specific regional race relations of the American Southwest. Hinting of the imperialism and conquest which lay at the heart of US acquisition of the Southwest, the term 'American' was used as a *racial* designator as opposed to indicating nationality. It fused nationality and whiteness, granting those of 'fair complexion' legitimacy within the region while delegitimizing those of darker complexion regardless of nationality. It associated, on the one hand, conquest with racial superiority, and, on the other hand, defeat with racial inferiority.[13]

In addition to overt characteristics such as skin colour, white towns-people particularly emphasized economic and class issues when they spoke of Mexicans. In doing so they indicated how class categories helped to constitute race. For example, T.J. Simpson, a machinist for the Arizona Copper Company, believed Mexicans to be unfit parents for white children. He told the court:

> I'll tell you. I don't pay much attention to them, you know, the Mexican class of people; but it [*sic*] just this way: you see them work around there, and all get very little salary ... the salary of the Mexican class of people is about two dollars a day, some of them two and a half, and very few of them gets three ... they all live in those little shacks about the size of 8 × 6 or 8 × 10, and most of them have no floor in them at all[,] no floor in the house at all.[14]

To Simpson, Mexicans' small homes and lower-class status were acceptable contexts for raising Mexican children – but not white children. Similarly, Charles E. Mills, manager of the Detroit Copper Company, emphasized Mexicans' class position: 'Mexicans when they went home, [they don't] really have a bed to sleep in; that is, one or two of them that was getting [only] two dollars a day[.]'[15] Mexicans', specifically Mexican men's, low-wage and low-class status made them unsuitable, according to Mills and Simpson, to raise these 'white' orphans. Their words suggest that being poorly paid and having a cramped small house was equivalent to being 'Mexican', that is, that class and cultural factors marked the racial boundaries between 'white' and 'Mexican'. The very essence of being lower class was conceived as antithetical to 'white' while functioning as a defining element of 'Mexican'.[16]

Simpson's and Mills' statements, along with others from the trial, indicate that 'class' involved a broad range of economic, social and cultural qualities: income, housing and language. Indeed, notions of 'class', like those of 'race', are historically contingent. As the manager of one of the largest companies in Arizona, Mills was well aware of the low wages of Mexican men. Clifton-Morenci was known for its employment of Mexican American and Mexican men at very minimal pay. The social relations of Arizona's copper industry directly helped to produce the class-based characteristics deemed so crucial in the construction of the racial category of 'Mexican'.

That both Mills and Simpson spoke with such assurance about the incomes of Mexican men suggests how important this issue was in constructing social relations in Arizona – between Whites and Mexicans, between white and Mexican working-class men, and among white men of different classes. Furthermore, the exclusive employment of men in the industry – whether as managers, tradesmen, miners or labourers – points to gendered aspects of these racial and class categories and relations.[17]

While class was explicitly connected to the definition of 'Mexican', it was a crucial though unmarked element in the configuration of 'white'. In that definition, there was a presumed level of income and material comfort which was taken to be standard. The underclass status of Mexicans differed from that supposed standard 'norm', thus enabling the construction of whiteness around an unmarked class position. Therefore Mills, the mill superintendent, and Simpson, the machinist, could accentuate their commonality of race and gender despite the differences in their own respective class positions. Throughout the court case, the lawyer for the white townspeople repeatedly emphasized that whites had the financial ability to care for these 'white Caucasian child[ren] of the White-Saxon race',[18] so calling further attention to the role class played in defining whiteness in Arizona.

Class relations within the copper industry were naturalized in racial categories. That 'Mexican' as a social position was overtly 'marked' by class while 'white' was less so, suggests the differing and complicated ways in which race and class intersected and constituted each other. Both 'Mexican' and 'white' were racialized and classed categories. The racial designations 'white' and 'Mexican' functioned as the language for the complex racialized and classed social structure.

In order to explore the social relations exemplified in the foundling incident, I shall focus on two critical historical periods that helped give rise to the racial and class categories underlying this controversy. The first, 1840–70, was particularly marked by the intersection of racialism and imperialism with an emerging class formation. During these decades, the United States extended its imperialistic arms around Arizona and much of what would become the US West. With this era I want to focus on two 'moments' in which racial understandings crystallized.

The first moment is the public discourse about Mexico during the mid-nineteenth century. The 1830s and 1840s were a period of US imperialistic territorial aggrandizement as the US incorporated one half of Mexico's territory. During this period, white Americans increasingly saw Mexicans as a weak race, backwards in their pastoral use of the land, religion and culture. Their weakness derived from being what white Americans termed a 'mongrel' race: One public figure said:

> Mexicans, like Indians, were unable to make proper use of the land. The Mexicans had failed because they were a mixed, inferior race with considerable Indian and some black blood.[19]

This concern about a 'mongrel' race was part of an overall cultural anxiety in the US about miscegenation, particularly black–white mixing, an act that was considered to degrade both races. This understanding of Mexicans helped to justify US imperialism and the seizure of Mexico's northern areas. Some anti-slavery politicians even rationalized that annexation of these territories would help solve the 'Negro' problem in the United States: 'both free blacks and slaves would migrate in their natural gravitation southward into a warmer climate. Among the 'mongrel' race of Mexicans, they would find more of their own'.[20] This quote illustrates what I refer to as a multi-referent system in racial thought. While race relations were and are often spoken of in binarisms, they often rest upon or utilize a larger system of references – references about other groups or about class or gender. Here 'Mexican' and 'Negro' are linked.

Concurrent with the racialization of Mexicans was a shift in how white Americans were thinking of themselves.[21] During this period, the notion of the United States as a nation of white people began to crystallize. According to the historian Reginald Horsman, in the process of seizing Mexico's northern territories, Americans increasingly moved towards thinking of themselves as a race of white peoples – white peoples of acknowledged English, German, Irish, French, Welsh and Scandinavian heritages. During the early and mid-nineteenth century, white Americans put less emphasis upon being a 'pure' White-Saxon race (which itself was without historical merit) and a more general embracing of whiteness. The superior American white race – so Romantic racialist thinkers postulated – was in a battle against inferior coloured races of the continent and the world.

The second moment that I want to examine takes us to Arizona in the 1860s. Although the US had acquired Arizona in the 1840s, there had been relatively little settlement or development of the region. Instead much of the United States' – and indeed the world's – attention was focused on California and the California Gold Rush. By 1859, however, gold placers in California had played out; this decline is significant for understanding the class tensions underlying the rush to exploit Arizona's gold placers. In the mid-nineteenth century, the social and economic differences among people had yet to solidify into our contemporary understanding of classes. Republican free labour ideology of the day understood citizenship as located among a 'producer' class of men. This group included a range of workers, journeymen and artisans who, it was thought, through their skills and hard work would rise above wage work into independent and honourable artisanal status. The advent of the industrial revolution at the end of the eighteenth century, however, increasingly undercut this social mobility.

When gold was discovered in California, many US Caucasian men flocked to the West in order to better their chances to attain that social mobility by literally digging up money. When California's gold placers dried up, so did that presumed social ladder. The likelihood of permanent wage work grew even greater.[22] And what happened across the West during the rest of the nineteenth century was that white American men – along with peoples from all parts of the globe – followed gold discoveries from one locale to another hoping to strike it rich and to better their chances in the changing social and economic world. When Arizona's goldfields were discovered in 1863, hundreds of men rushed in. Streaming into the region, white American men – many of whom saw themselves as rightful *victors* in the Mexican War – found themselves in competition with other men for the limited mining opportunities. White American men responded by limiting gold placer mining opportunities to white men.[23]

How could they do this? US mining laws authorized claimants in a mining district to establish regulations and laws for the local district. That is, those who staked claims could lay down the law.[24] This access to the mechanisms of the state enabled some men to restrict economic competition between themselves and Mexican men. Within weeks of establishing districts, White American men immediately limited who could have access to the placers. As the intended beneficiaries of US imperialism, White miners used their relationship to the state to promote racial exclusion and subordination. In June 1863, white miners in the Weaver district prohibited Mexican men from taking up claims. In a separate section entitled 'Mexicans' their law read: 'No citizens of Mexico shall hold or work claims in this District except the boy Lorenzo Para who is one of the original discoverers.'[25] White miners in other districts followed suit, writing laws to either exclude Mexican citizens or all men of Mexican heritage. Men in the Pioneer district excluded both Mexican men and Chinese men. Another district simply stated that only 'white' men could file claims.[26]

During the course of twelve months, the Pioneer district passed and reaffirmed their restrictions against Chinese and Mexican men four times. The frequency suggests that there was tension around such exclusionary laws: that is, it was necessary to fortify the laws against challenges from Mexican and Chinese men and perhaps some white men. As the following resolution indicates, the very terms and categories these local lawmakers were using were themselves a matter of some contention:

> Resolved, that the law already passed with regard to Mexicans remains unchanged[.] Resolved that Asiatics and Senorians [*sic*] be excluded from working in the Dis't[.] Resolved That a committee of three be appointed who *shall decide who are & who are not Mexicans* subject to the law of exclusion from taking up and holding claims in the Dist[.][27]

These categories – both the 'marked' 'Mexican' and the unmarked 'white' categories – were being constructed and delimited even as they were being used to limit economic competition. The fact that a committee had to determine who was a 'Mexican' illustrates two points: first, that these categories were not 'natural' as Romantic thinking postulated; and second, that slippage between them occurred.

The exclusion of Chinese and Mexicans takes on more significance when one learns that there were a few African American men in Arizona's goldfields: an escaped slave and another man of 'mulatto' and English heritage mined in the Weaver district. The presence of these men is suggestive of the complex contours and boundaries of race relations in Arizona. None of the districts formally prohibited African Americans from claiming mining sites.[28] This lack of prohibition, however, did not mean that these African American men were welcomed – one has been inscribed into Arizona local history as 'Nigger Ben'. One reason for the lack of restrictions placed on African Americans may have been their small numbers in the territory during the mid-nineteenth century. Census figures cite only 26 blacks in 1870.[29] Yet the same census lists only 21 Chinese in the territory – so numbers alone do little to explain why African Americans were not excluded while Chinese were. Certainly, anti-Chinese sentiments originating in Gold Rush California and Chinese immigrants' limited political rights in the United States help to account for this treatment of Chinese in Arizona.[30]

While population figures alone cannot account for the character of racial tensions, they do suggest one reason for the principal binarism being between whites and Mexicans. The small number of African Americans and Chinese is in sharp contrast with the large number of people of Mexican descent in Arizona. In 1862, of the estimated population of 6,500, 5,900 were of Mexican descent – over 90 per cent.[31] By 1870, even with increased migration of white Americans from New York, Pennsylvania, Ohio and Missouri, and European immigrants from Ireland, Germany, Canada and England, ethnic Mexicans – whether born in Arizona, California or Mexico – still comprised 60 per cent of the population. The sheer numbers alone – as well as the preceding shift in thinking about race and the United States' imperialistic war against Mexico – suggest why, in the early 1860s, the few hundred native and foreign-born white men might see Mexican men as their principal competitors in the newly discovered goldfields.[32] Because their political and economic rights were circumscribed, Mexican men's economic opportunities were more limited. The effect of these laws was to confine Mexican men to wage work.

The competition between White and Mexican men did not end with the prohibitive laws. In the both the Pioneer and Weaver districts, White men sought not only to exclude Mexican men from claims – thereby confining them to wage work – but to limit Mexican men's agency as free wage labourers. The Weaver district law required that:

> should the miners employ any of the said citizens of Mexico, they will be held responsible for their good behavior, and should the said employer fail to comply with this article he or they shall forfeit all interest in the mines and leave the District.[33]

Mining districts in the Globe, Prescott and Wickenburg areas passed similar laws. In the Pioneer district, White men who employed Mexican men had to inform the local authorities. That law read:

> That all persons bringing in Mexicans or have them in their

employ, record the names of said Mexicans at the office of the Dis't Recorder[.] That persons employing Mexicans in *any* capacity be held responsible for all depredations upon property proved to have been committed by them[.] That upon the discharge of each or any such Mexican from employ notice be given the Recorder by the employer[.] That the fee for Recording each individual name be fixed at four bits[.][34]

Under this law, Mexican men were not free to come and go and to barter their labour as they pleased. Unregistered Mexican men could be forced to leave the district. Moreover, these laws heightened white surveillance and encouraged white control of Mexican men. The laws also suggested that 'Mexican labour' was prone to violence or somehow destructive.[35]

Such restrictive laws also helped to establish the unmarked 'white' category as a distinct social status. This position was created in opposition to what was considered 'Mexican' or, more specifically, 'Mexican labour'. This is what the laws said about white men: they were either self-employed or the employers of Mexican men. They were responsible and constructive. They were entitled to the riches of the goldfields. In addition to positioning 'white' and 'Mexican' as dichotomized opposites, the laws fortified these constructed positions with the threat of economic punishment – to lose one's own claim – for those white men who disregarded this division. Such legislation forced whites to accept this artificial separation between white and Mexican, inscribing and reinscribing both as distinct racialized and classed categories.

The white American men in Arizona who actively and passively supported such practices and laws were establishing a *herrenvolk* democracy – a democracy for white men only. The type of exclusion practised in Arizona's goldfields was rather commonplace, not only in the West – and here I am referencing the 1850 and 1852 Foreign Miners' Tax in California – but also in the South. These Arizona laws are akin to the 'Black Codes' passed by Southern legislators in 1865 and 1866. Those laws established rigid codes for regulating the labour of newly freed blacks – limiting them to agricultural or domestic work, making unemployment a crime and in other ways restricting their economic behaviour. My point here is that there was a larger pattern in the US of attempting to restrain the economic opportunities of 'marked' racialized groups for the benefit of 'unmarked' groups; what I document in Arizona is a regional variation on this larger theme.[36]

A critical piece of this regional variation is the fact that in the Southwest, the often unmarked 'white' category included a wide range of Caucasian ethnic groups. Men with Irish surnames were especially prominent in Arizona's gold district. This is of particular interest given the level of anti-Irish antagonisms in the northeastern and southeastern regions of the United States during the mid-nineteenth century. In those regions, Irish people were commonly deemed 'non-white', whereas in Arizona they were assimilated into the category of White. In claiming land, that is, participating in US imperialism, a variety of European ethnic groups at odds in other parts of the country were consolidated under the common identity of 'white'.[37]

The Irish are a particularly interesting example. Most studies of Irish immigrants and Irish nationals depict Irish Americans as part of an ethnically distinct immigrant community vis-à-vis the dominant white Protestant community.[38] In the West, however, Irish Americans and Irish immigrants could and did assume a higher place in the regional racial hierarchy. Carlotta Silvas Martin's recollections of her childhood in the copper town of Superior, Arizona, show the interplay between ethnicity and whiteness as a racial position. Because she grew up on the white side of town – her grandmother was the only Mexican person who owned land on the white side of town – Martin recalls that, 'I grew up playing with white children and speaking English. Most of my friends were the Mahoneys, a big Irish family from Utah.' Yet when she entered high school, she had to go to the Mexican school which was located outside the town, while the Mahoney children went to the white school which was near her house.[39] Martin recognized both the particular ethnicity of the Mahoneys and the degree to which it did not undermine or preclude their racial status as white.

This Southwestern regional understanding of whiteness is an important point to look at, both in terms of mapping out the complex terrain of regional US race relations and engaging in the historiographies of race and ethnicity in United States. I am not disregarding or discarding the significance of ethnicity among Caucasian peoples in the United States. What I am asking for is greater understanding of the difference between ethnicity and race. Too often these two categories are used synonymously – often divided by a slash – when in fact they are two separate categories and historical phenomena. US immigration historians study the experiences of European immigrant groups. While usually this scholarship examines issues of assimilation or acculturation into the larger American society, it does *not* tend to explore the character or extent to which becoming 'Americanized' meant taking on the racial consciousness of being 'white'.

The second critical time period, 1870–1905, is marked by the spread of oligarchic copper operations across Arizona and the accompanying stratification of Arizona's social structure. In 1870 Arizona was in a semi-peripheral relationship to the northeastern core of the US; by 1905 it was integrated into the capitalist economy as a hinterland from which essential commodities were acquired using various kinds of free and unfree labour. Copper was king; by 1905, there were six major centres for copper production in Arizona, several across the border in Sonora, and scores of small mines. That year, Arizona had become the nation's largest producer of copper, easily exceeding centres in Michigan and Montana. The industry directly employed tens of thousands of men and indirectly even more in the support industries of construction, fuel, and transportation. The rise of copper spurred massive migration into the territory, particularly from Mexico, southern and eastern Europe, and the rest of the United States. The rapid rise of corporate capitalism within Arizona's mining industry helped to structure class relations and solidify the formation of a distinct working class. It is on this historical moment that I wish to concentrate.

The extension of corporate industrial capitalism into Arizona was directly responsible for generating the notion of a 'White Man's Town'. US capitalists and their promoters had been eyeing Arizona since the 1860s; for them it was a prime area for development and one which only they could truly bring to fruition. J. Ross Browne, an adventurer and government agent, surveyed Arizona's mineral and agricultural potential for both the US Department of Interior and his capitalist associates. Throughout his account, he stated that 'Americans' will be the ones to develop this potential. He continually invested 'Americans' with 'productivity', 'civilization' and 'industriousness'. For example, Browne rejoiced upon entering a white American-owned mining town:

[H]ere, at least, a living nucleus of American civilization – ... A mill, with smelting furnaces and a small engine, had just been erected for reducing the ores, and would be put in operation as soon as the necessary facilities for working the mine could be obtained.[40]

The specific references to the mill and engine, as well as the larger discourse that they referenced, were gendered, classed and raced. Like the white American men in the goldmining districts, Browne was speaking of men's 'public' world of work. Note that his focus is on the capital acquisitions – the mill and the engine – that will enable mass production of copper. He envisaged 'ingenuity' and 'drive' – terms he used frequently – as the characteristics of white elite men with the financial resources to construct such facilities. Labouring men, he rarely mentioned.

Like many other capitalists of the era, Browne tended to see the characteristics of productivity and industriousness in racial terms, that is, as rooted in innate racial qualities. Since industriousness was Browne's central discursive concern, that was the criterion upon which Browne measured men, and thereby races. Throughout his report and other writings, 'American' was constructed in opposition to the notion of 'Mexican'. While white American elite men were industrious, Browne saw Mexican men as lazy and unmotivated, and even destructive; he blamed this condition on their 'mongrel' heritage. In fact, he judged the Mexican race as inferior to Pimas Indians, whom Browne saw as more productive in their activities because of their racial purity. His judgement of the Mexican race extended even to Mexican elite males. At one point, he went so far as to denigrate a successful Mexican-owned mine, which previously he had admired for producing a profit within its first two years. Now he said that Americans could run it better.[41]

The idea of an 'American' or 'white Man's town' therefore was associated with white American capitalistic economic dominance. Browne and others assumed that their dominance would 'naturally' transcend political boundaries. For example, a 1905 newspaper description of the Greene Consolidated Copper Company of Cananea, Sonora, depicted that northern Mexican town as an 'American' town:

> Cananea, the mining town of Greene Consolidated company in Sonora, has grown to be quite a little city. Fully 5,000 are on the payrolls of the camp. Three big smelters with combined capacity of 900 tons a day are in operation, while a fourth smelter of 400 tons capacity is nearly completed. The railroad is now within nine miles of the camp. It is in every sense an American town, although located forty-five miles below the international line in Sonora.[42]

Again, note the emphasis on equipment, rate of production and infrastructure. Because it was part of a productive, enterprising, capitalist venture, it could only be an 'American' town – even if it is in Mexico.

Hidden beneath such descriptions was the unseen and ignored work of Mexican and white working-class men. In positioning themselves as the vanguard of American male industry, white American capitalists by necessity tried to displace or deny the significance of others' waged work on which their own productivity and profits were based. Therefore, it is not surprising that these capitalists rarely acknowledged the labour of working-class men. In the Southwest, this contest had particular racial contours. The availability of Mexican men to work in white-owned enterprises was one of the major attractions of Southwestern economic development. In a mutually reinforcing opposition, depictions of Mexican working-class men invested white American male capitalists with the aura of industry. Their conceptions of 'Mexican labour' established their own roles as leaders of industry and as 'handlers' of labour. In mining industry journals, government reports and travel accounts, white American capitalists and their agents discussed and defined 'Mexican labour'. Central to these discussions was the notion that Mexican working-class men were both 'cheap labor' and infinitely malleable labour. An October, 1904 issue of *Leslie's Weekly*, for example, described the predominance of Mexican workers in Clifton-Morenci: 'Mexican laborers are largely employed because they work much [more] cheaply than the white generations to conditions not far removed from actual servitude laborer and are easier to handle.'[43] Another article characterized Mexicans as 'a simple-minded people, accustomed for generations to conditions not far removed from actual servitude and who have not yet learned to act on their own initiative'.[44] Such depictions were also gendered. Essayists in the industry journals imbued Mexican working-class men with less than manly qualities. They were depicted as childlike, emotional and in need of governance. One article states: '[Mexican men] have no initiative – they can do nothing alone.' Thus the accomplishments within the industry were credited to white capitalists who provided governance or leadership, as well as capital.[45] Again, the hierarchical relationship between these two groups was naturalized: the control of Mexican labourers by white owners and managers was frequently said to be rooted in shortcomings within the Mexican 'race' and strengths within the (usually unmarked) white 'race'.

While articles in industry journals uniformly agreed that Mexican working-class men needed to be 'handled' and were 'cheap labour', they offered varying assessments of Mexican working-class men's intellectual abilities and skills. Some white managers wrote that

Mexican men lacked both intelligence and skill, often attributing this deficiency to their race. Others recognized a range of skills and the ability to learn new ones. This suggests that depicting Mexican working-class men as unskilled and lacking in intelligence was less crucial to managers than positioning them as malleable and 'cheap'.

White working-class men developed a different notion of 'Mexican labour'. As noted earlier, the rise of the corporate capitalist copper industry had reduced most men, including most white men, to the status of wage earner. In their struggle to come to terms with this new social location, white working-class men drew distinctions among kinds of work. Their developing understanding of 'Mexican labour' had roots in the 1870s and 1880s with the rise of the copper industry. White capitalists had used Mexican working-class men to build much of the infrastructure of the industry. At the completion of this work, some white owners hired these Mexican men to work on in the mines and mills while others turned to white workers. From that period on, a social division of labour developed that categorized certain types of manual work as most appropriately performed by Mexicans. For example, working above ground (as opposed to below, in mines) was considered 'Mexican work', as was providing fuel for smelters. White working men relied on such distinctions – often very fine distinctions – among work tasks to differentiate themselves from Mexican working men. For example, Mexican underground workers who did the initial excavation for new mines were considered below white men who performed day-to-day underground excavation. White working class men defined 'Mexican labour' as unskilled and degraded. In opposition, they themselves were skilled and honourable.

According to one source, if a white man performed 'Mexican labour', 'he would soon be hooted out of the camp by his fellow countrymen and his Mexican competitors'.[46] This description implies that this social and work division was well known, commonly practised and agreed on even by 'Mexican inferiors'. Historically, differing kinds of work have been denigrated – whether as 'coolie work', 'stoop labour', 'nigger work' or, in this case, 'Mexican labour' – in white working-class men's complicated discursive and social struggles to maintain a perceived difference between themselves and other working men.

White men in Arizona used a variety of tactics during this period to exclude Mexican working-class men from copper work or to limit their participation in certain kinds of work. These tactics included passing laws, taking part in extra-legal actions or violence, as well as develop-

ing a union movement which appealed directly to white men to organize against Mexican men. In these assorted actions, they struggled
not only against white capitalists but also against Mexican working-
class men. While never successful in totally excluding Mexican men,
white working-class men were able to establish a racialized job hierarchy in many of Arizona's copper towns. Two patterns developed. One
was that, in copper towns where white men predominated, the best
paid and most highly skilled jobs were reserved for them. The term
'White Man's Town' therefore had an alternative meaning among
white working-class men, one that spoke to the presence of a racialized job hierarchy that privileged white over Mexican men. Ironically,
the fact that white men had designated some jobs as degraded
'Mexican labour' opened the employment door to Mexicans even in
those copper towns where white workers predominated. The second
pattern existed in copper towns where Mexican men were the majority of workers. There, white men held supervisory positions while
Mexican men occupied a full range of highly skilled to unskilled positions. These early laws and practices created structural inequalities
between Mexican and white working-class men; later with the advent
of corporate mining and the development of a white man's regional
labour movement, the Western Federation of Miners, these inequalities were further solidified. These actions constructed a racially
stratified division of labour with the industry.[47]

Just as white capitalists and white working-class men held different
though coinciding understandings of the 'White Man's Town', their
respective understandings of 'Mexican labour' shared a basic
commonality. Both understandings of the term 'Mexican labour' – as
'cheap' and malleable labour of varying skill levels according to white
capitalists, or as unskilled and degraded labour according to white
workers – rested on the practice of the 'dual wage system'. Until the
mid-twentieth century a dual wage system, sometimes known as a
Mexican wage system, operated throughout the Southwest, and also
in northern Mexico.[48] Under this system, workers of Mexican
heritage, regardless of their nationality, received lower wages for the
same work performed by white American workers. On average,
Mexicans, skilled and unskilled, received 50–70 per cent of the wages
of their white counterparts. In 1880 the daily wages were $1.50 for
Mexicans versus $2.50 for whites. In 1900, the average wages were
$2.15 and $3.40, respectively.[49] White American capitalists who
employed Mexican workers clearly benefited from this system; the low
wages paid to Mexican workers underwrote the rapid expansion of

white corporate capitalism in Arizona, the Southwest and northern Mexico. Mexican workers were a regional pool of 'cheap labour' in much the same way that African Americans were to southern capitalist enterprises of the same period. For white workers, the dual wage system fortified their belief in the distinctiveness of their work and capabilities as 'white men'.

Ironically, the dual wage system also served to destabilize white working-class men's actual, if not ideological, position in the industry. White capitalists turned increasingly to Mexican men in their continued expansion of the mining enterprises. Indeed, this was the paradox for white American copper workers: their racial identity and notions of white American superiority bound them to the copper owners, but divisive class interests made white workers and white bosses, at best, superficial allies. White working class and elite men held different understandings of the meanings of racial difference; these meanings were mediated by class, skill, and gender. Race – specifically 'Mexican' and 'white' – was relational, stemming from struggles over class, gender, colonization, skill and authority.

To return to the foundling case which began this essay, the protest and then removal of orphans from Mexican people's homes was part of a larger self-conscious enforcement of racial and class domination, premised on interactions that consolidated a white settler regime in Arizona. Therefore when the mine manager Mills and machinist Simpson spoke of the 'Mexican class of people' as being unfit to rear the orphans, both men spoke from common and distinct investments in Mexican men's low wages. Both spoke and acted to reify the constructed material and ideological lines that defined 'Mexican' and 'white'.

The materials I have set out here engage a number of different fields: western American history, Chicano Studies, US labour history and US race relations. In many ways, my work challenges all of them to encompass the historical complexity of US society. For western American history and Chicano Studies, my work presses for class and class distinctions to be more seriously integrated into the analysis of both the emerging western social structure and the structural pattern of race relations that pressed peoples of Mexican heritage into a regional labour pool of 'cheap labour'. Similarly, US labour history needs to utilize better 'race' as an historically contingent factor affecting class relations. Furthermore, US labour history needs to give weight to the historical specificity of the West – for example, to the role of mid-nineteenth century US imperialism, proximity to Mexico and rapidity of corporate capitalist development. Finally, I call on scholars of US race relations – including the recently emerged field on the historical construction of whiteness – to move beyond the black–white dichotomy. My work shows the centrality of 'white' and 'Mexican' as the crucial dichotomy within the Southwestern social structure. And while the principal ideological and material struggle in Arizona was between white and Mexican, these categories were themselves constituted within a multi-referent matrix of racial categories. My research on the category of 'Mexican' demonstrates that it was constructed in dialogue with the categories of 'Chinese', 'Indian' and 'Negro', as well as those of class and gender. My examination of the category of 'white' – which included native-born whites, northern and western Europeans, and usually (but not always) southern and eastern Europeans – brings to the fore a regional variant in the historical construction of 'whiteness'.

## Notes

1  My account of this incident relies heavily on the work by A. Blake Brophy, *Foundlings on the Frontier: Racial and Religious Conflict in Arizona Territory, 1904–1905* (Tucson, 1972), 27–41, 52, 60–1. I have also examined the court testimony from the resulting law suit. Brophy's work is largely based on this testimony. I rely on Brophy because he apparently had access to the full testimony; the portions of the testimony which have been microfilmed are less comprehensive than those Brophy used during his research. Brophy understands this incident as a religious conflict. My reading, however, shows that religion was, at best, only a minor issue in the conflict. In fact, not until the very end of the ensuing legal case between the New York Foundling Hospital and the white men and women who kept orphans did the lawyer for the hospital even bring up the question of religion and whether the children would be raised as Protestant or Catholic. Instead, both sides argued their position based on issues of race and class. For both parties, raising the children as 'white' children – a term which, as I demonstrate, encoded both race and class issues – transcended religion. Arizona Supreme Court, Microfilm 36.2.9, Case #209 (Arizona State Library and Archives, Phoenix, Arizona) (hereafter Foundling Case #209) Sister Anna Michella, 32–3.

2  Father Mandlin, however, was not completely outside any understanding of racialism. According to Sister Anna Michella, he specifically asked that among the orphans 'there should be no negroes, or any indians sent, or Chinese'.

   While Southwestern scholars often use the term 'Anglo', there was a multitude of terms used to describe non-Mexican Caucasians during the time period of my study. 'White', 'Caucasian', 'White Folks' and 'Anglo-Saxon' were all used, though predominantly the former. 'Anglo' apparently became more common in the 1940s among Mexicans Americans as they sought to carve a space at the white table for themselves by focusing on ethnicity and not race, in response to the kinds of racialization that I am discussing. For discussion of self-identification and terminology by whites in the US Southwest, see Orick Jackson, *The White Conquest of Arizona: History of the Pioneer,* published by the West Coast Magazine (Los Angeles, 1908); David Montejano, *Anglos and Mexican in the Making of Texas, 1836–1986* (Austin, 1987); Reginald Horsman, *Race and Manifest Destiny: The Origins of American Racial Anglo-Saxonism* (Cambridge, 1981).

3  Even within the Southwest there are significant differences in the character of race relations among Texas, New Mexico, Arizona and southern California. See Sarah Deutsch, *No Separate Refuge: Culture, Class, and Gender on an Anglo-Hispanic Frontier in the American Southwest, 1880–1940* (New York, 1987); David Montejano, *Anglos and Mexicans in the Making of Texas, 1836–1986* (Austin, 1987); Albert Camarillo, *Chicanos in a Changing Society: From Mexican Pueblos to American Barrios in Santa Barbara and Southern California, 1848–1930* (Cambridge, 1979).

4  By using the term 'racialism' I do not mean to deny the then current practice and effects of racism. Rather, I seek to understand the development of racial and racist thought within the historical context of the nineteenth-century US and to show the movement within the US towards organizing society along perceived race-based differences.

As Horsman says, white Americans, particularly those in slave-owning or frontier areas, readily accepted this notion of thinking, in part to justify their own aggressions, slavery and colonialism. Horsman disputes the argument that white Saxonism had any cultural or biological merit. The English were themselves a mix of different peoples, and Americans were no less heterogeneous. Racialist ideology distinguished white peoples in the US from blacks, Mexicans, Spaniards, Asians, and Indians, and yet it could be inclusive enough to include Irish immigrants or at least their children. See Horsman, *Race and Manifest Destiny*, especially chapters 6, 8, 9 and 10. Mine manager Mills berated orphanage agent Swayne, arguing that his New York sensibilities had no place in Arizona, which further points to the regional aspect of this particular set of race relations. Foundling Case #209, Statement of Facts, p. 4 provides a list of the children, their Mexican adoptive parents and their white adoptive parents.

5  My concern is with the racialization that occurred with US settler colonialism in the nineteenth century. The US Southwest, of course, has been shaped by conquests other than that of the US. The first European intruders were the Spanish, who arrived in Texas in 1519 and New Mexico in 1540; they created distinct understandings of culture, civilization and race. George M. Fredrickson, *White Supremacy: A Comparative Study in American and South African History* (Oxford, 1981) identifies the founding of Jamestown, Virginia as the 'beginnings of' the first 'White settler' society 'emanating from northern Europe' (4). In this case, he focuses on colonialism from northern Europe and isolates Spanish colonialism as limited to Central and South America. Later in his discussion of settler colonialization, he distinguishes between the English version that desired land for its growing population and that of the Dutch that sought riches through trade. In the end, he brings together Spanish and English colonization:

dentdentdentdentuginnieuginnieuginnieuginnie

'Spain and later England were the most successful practitioners of the kind of direct subjugation and colonization that enlarged the system itself' (20–1). Settler colonialism is an unusual form of colonialism. The process of claiming land or nativity is fundamental in shaping the national character of settler societies, e.g. in the US and South Africa. (One might argue that Chicanos' claim to nativity in the Southwest is part of their own settler colonialist ideology.)

6  'Ethnic Mexicans' means peoples of Mexican descent regardless of their nationality; it is appropriate since many of Arizona's discriminatory practices operated along that line as opposed to nationality. I borrow the term 'ethnic Mexican' from historian David G. Gutierrez, 'Sin Fronteras?: Chicanos, Mexican Americans, and the Emergence of the Contemporary Mexican Immigration Debate, 1968–1978,' *Journal of American Ethnic History* 10 (1991), 5–37.

7  In my book manuscript I examine Mexican and Mexican American resistance patterns to this racialization.

8  Foundling Case #209, Mrs Laura Abrams (Respondent Witness), 148–9.

9  *Ibid.*

10  Foundling Case #209, Statement of the Facts, p. 2.

11  See Statement by Respondent, Foundling Case #209, 2–11, and examination of Respondent witnesses.

12  For a comprehensive examination of racism's origins as a justification of expansionism and creation of a *herrenvolk* republic, see Alexander Saxton, *The Rise and Fall of the White Republic: Class Politics and Mass Culture in Nineteenth Century America* (London, 1990).

13  I have found Pamela Scully's discussion of whiteness, blackness and gender in South Africa to be helpful in my thinking; Pamela Scully, 'Rape, Race, and Colonial Culture: The Sexual Politics of Identity in the Nineteenth Century Cape Colony, South Africa', unpublished paper presented at the Berkshire Conference on Women, 1993.

14  Foundling Case #209, T. J. Simpson (Respondent Witness), 191–2.

15  Even though Mills was a pivotal character in the resolution of the conflict and held a very important social position in the district, he did not testify at the ensuing trial. Simpson and Clifton's Deputy Sheriff L. J. Dunagan both recounted the exchange between Mr Mills and Mr Swayne. Foundling Case #209, pp. 74, 194–5; Brophy, *Foundlings on the Frontier*, 28–41.

16  Elite Mexican Americans often used or were referred to as 'Spanish' in an effort to distinguish them from being *mestizo* or 'Mexican'.

17  The low wages of ethnic Mexican men also affected the women and children in their lives. My work shows that a much higher percentage of ethnic Mexican women worked for wages than native born white, northern and western European, or southern and eastern European women. This surely was directly related to low incomes of their male family members.

18  See Statement by Respondent, Foundling Case #209, 2–II and examination of Respondent witnesses.

19  Horsman, *Race and Manifest Destiny*, 210.

20  Horsman, *Race and Manifest Destiny*, 214–17.

21  Both Fredrickson and Saxton look at Native Americans but neither give attention to Mexicans.

22 Placer deposits are gold particles, eroded and carried away by water from mountain deposits, which have settled in the bottom of streams. To retrieve the gold, men scooped up dirt from the river bed into pans, rockers or long toms, and used water to separate gold from the dirt. Placer mining was highly lucrative. In the mid-1850s, gold miners on average made 5 dollars a day. In fact, employers in the West complained of the difficulty of finding and keeping skilled wage labourers because goldmining offered such an attractive alternative. Richard H. Peterson, *The Bonanza Kings – The Social Origins and Business Behavior of Western Mining Entrepreneurs, 1870–1900* (Lincoln, Nebr., 1977), chapters 1 and 8; Joseph F. Park, 'The History of Mexican Labor in Arizona During the Territorial Period' (MA thesis, University of Arizona,1961) [American], 171–3; Rodman Wilson Paul, *The Far West and the Great Plains in Transition in the Far West, 1859–1900* (New York, 1988), 2. The appeals of placer mining, however, went beyond potential earnings. Western placer miners were self-employed. The work was arduous and labour-intensive, but did not require a large capital investment. Men could work alone, in cooperative partnerships or hire men to work for them. Most of the placer deposit sites were in central Arizona near present-day Prescott. Arizona's mineral resources were at the centre of nineteenth-century development of the territory. In the 1850s and 1860s, that effort took two paths: individual conducting gold placer mining in central Arizona and small- and medium-sized companies mining and producing silver in the southern part of the territory. James Monroe Patton, 'The History of Clifton' (MA thesis, University of Arizona, 1945), 147. Charles H. Dunning, with Edward H. Peplow Jr., *Rocks to Riches: The Story of American Mining, Past, Present and Future...as Reflected in the Colorful History of Mining in Arizona, the Nation's Greatest Bonanza* (Phoenix, 1959), 68, 78; Park, 'The History of Mexican Labor', 2–3.

23 Through restrictive legislation, white American men in Arizona, and elsewhere, sought to preserve the fortunes and benefits of gold placer mining for themselves. In her book on British racialism, Laura Tabili identifies employers and other elites as creating the initial racialized stratification that would shape the meanings and experiences of Black peoples in England. My work differs in that it locates this initial impulse among working-class men and not their employers. Ultimately we need to think about definitions of the state and working-class and other peoples' (particularly men's) relationship to the state under colonial situations and later; see Laura Tabili, *'We Ask for British Justice': Workers and Racial Difference in Late Imperial Britain* (Ithaca, NY, 1994).

24 US government statutes for mining districts required that miners lay claims to specific pieces of land, mark the boundaries of a local mining district and call a meeting of local miners to establish laws for that district. Each mining district enacted its own laws. White men were able to use these mining codes to restrict other men's access to placers.

25 According to Bryd H. Granger, one or more Mexicans were part of this party of men and they were the ones who found the gold. 'Weaver, Yavapai County', in *Arizona Place Names*, (Tucson, 1985), 362. The next month they extended the time period of exclusion for another six months.

Clarence King, compiler, *The United States Mining Laws and Regulations thereunder, and State and Territorial Mining Laws to which are appended Local Mining Rules and Regulations* (Washington, DC, 1885), 254, 256.

26  King, *The United States Mining Laws,* 254, 256. Miners at Walnut Grove Mining district required claimants to be US citizens. I have no information about how this law was applied and whether it applied to European immigrants; see King, p. 253. Only some of the placer mining districts in Arizona enacted these restrictive laws, pp. 256–66. Some districts restricted 'Asiatics and Senoranians' from making claims for a specific duration, such as the first year of the district, and others did so indefinitely. Harwood Hinton, 'Frontier Speculation: A Study of the Walker Mining Districts', *Pacific Historical Review* 29: 3 (August 1960), 246, 248–9, 251; *Jerome Chronicle*, 6 April 1895, 2; *1880 Mine Census*, Reel 1880.1, 247–71; Park, 'The History of Mexican Labor', 111; Robert L. Spude, 'The Walker-Weaver Diggings and the Mexican Placero, 1863–1864', *Journal of the West* 14 (October 1975), 64–74.

27  Emphasis added. King, *The United States Mining Laws,* 254. Mexican and Mexican American men did stake claims in these gold districts despite these laws and practices, and thus resisted efforts to marginalize them economically and politically.

28  Wagoner says that segregation was proposed first in the state constitution in 1912; Harris, however, cites a 1909 decision to segregate high school-aged black children. Richard E. Harris, *The First Hundred Years: A History of Arizona Blacks* (Apache Junction, Arizona, 1983), 59–61; Jay J. Wagoner, *Arizona Territory, 1863–1912: A Political History* (Tucson,1970), 472.

29  Harris, *The First Hundred Years*, pp. ii, 30, 100. Of the few African Americans in the region, most were in the army and thus posed little economic competition to white men whereas large numbers of Mexican men, many with experience of mining in Arizona and Sonora, did pose such a threat.

30  In this White Republic, Chinese men presumably challenged white folks' decent living standard. Campaigns against Chinese laundries were justified as a way to protect white women's paid economic niche in mining towns. In 1850, white miners in California had imposed a Foreign Miners' Tax on foreigners in the goldfields. This excessive tax, at times in combination with mob actions by white miners, drove Asian and Mexican and some European men from the fields. Similarly, white men blocked Chinese men from the Oregon and Idaho goldfields until the fields were nearly played out. US naturalization laws also forbade any Asian from become a US citizen. Suscheng Chan, in *Bittersweet Soil: The Chinese in California Agriculture, 1860–1910* (Berkeley, 1986), argues that Chinese men went into railway construction work, in part, because white Americans prevented them from engaging in more lucrative gold mining work; see Chan, pp. 37–40, 51–8.

The exclusion of so few Chinese men suggests some of the rational and irrational competition that white men might have felt. It also hints at the multi-referential nature of race relations. Even though the vast body of the discourse and social and economic competition was between white and Mexican men, white men none the less consciously situated themselves within a matrix of racial groups and associations about these groups.

31  This census figure is based on the non-Indian population in the Arizona territory.

32  Wagoner, *Arizona Territory*, 27; *Ninth Census of the United States: Statistics of Population*, Tables II, III, IV, VII.

33  King, *The United States Mining Laws*, 251.

34  *Ibid.*, pp. 254, 256.

35  Park, 'The History of Mexican Labor', 2–3. Because their political and economic rights were circumscribed, Mexican and Chinese men's economic opportunities were more limited, and they were more likely to engage in waged work because of the legal and extra-legal actions by white American men.

36  American Social History Project, *Who Built America?*, volume 1 (New York, 1989), 483–5.

37  Whiteness or Americanness was bestowed on Caucasian ethnic groups, who otherwise were suspect in other regions of the US. Horsman notes the tendency in the Far West for ethnic differences among Caucasian peoples to be less important than in other regions of the country.

38  Examples include James R. Barrett, *Work and Community in the Jungle: Chicago's Packinghouse Workers, 1894–1922* (Urbana, Ill., 1987) and David M. Emmons, *The Butte Irish: Class and Ethnicity in an American Mining Town, 1875–1925* (Urbana, Ill., 1990). For an examination of the racialization of Irish immigrants as 'white', see Noel Ignatiev, *How the Irish Became White* (New York, 1995).

39  Interview with Carlotta Silvas Martin in Patricia Preciado Martin, *Songs My Mother Sang to Me: An Oral History of Mexican American Women* (Tucson, 1992), 206.

40  J. Ross Browne, *Adventures in the Apache Country: A Tour through Arizona and Sonora, with Notes on the Silver Regions of Nevada* (New York, 1869), 195.

41  Browne, *Adventures in the Apache Country*, 228–9, 265, 269, 282–4. Browne seems to express a notion of 'Americanness' and 'whiteness' which is primarily based on American men and notions of industriousness. This quote is reminiscent of some of the distinctions made in the foundling case. The passage locates productivity and industriousness, as well as certain standards or comforts of living, as 'American'. Yet the same industriousness and sense of business when used to Browne's disadvantage are seen by him as being lacking. Throughout their journey, Browne and his companions had to purchase scarce firewood from Mexican and Indian peoples they encountered. The high prices they were forced to pay infuriated Browne, who frequently talked about the economic promise of the region, but that was a promise only for 'Americans'.

42  *Copper Era*, 26 December 1901, 1.

43  Quoted in Brophy, *Foundlings on the Frontier*, 16.

44  Quoted in James D. McBride, 'The Development of Labor Unions in Arizona Mining, 1884 to 1919' (MA thesis, Arizona State University, 1974), 66–7.

45  Alonzo Crittendon, 'Management of Mexican Labor', *Mining and Scientific Press* 123 (20 August 1921), 267.

46  Park, 'The History of Mexican Labor', 180.

47  Ethnic Mexican miners resisted the racialized labour structure through the

formation of *mutualistas* (fraternal associations) and by striking. The Clifton-Morenci district was known as a stronghold of Mexican activism; one of the first large-scale copper strikes in Arizona was by Mexican and Italian men in the 1903 Clifton-Morenci strike in which the Mexican men asserted the right to work an eight-hour day and to end the dual wage system. Termed a 'riot' by local white citizens, the Arizona Rangers and National Guard broke up the strike and imprisoned the strike leaders. See discussion in Thomas E. Sheridan, *Los Tucsonenses: The Mexican Community in Tucson, 1854–1941* (Tucson, 1986, 1992), 176–8.

48  P. Manuel, ed., *An Awakened Minority: The Mexican-Americans* (Beverly Hills, 1974), 28–9.

49  Park, 'The History of Mexican Labor', 245.

# 3
# The 'Lady' Telephone Operator: Gendering Whiteness in the Bell System, 1900–70

*Venus Green*

Dear Mr. Morgan
The question of a female's qualification to be a Commercial Representative has arisen due to a vacancy in Charlotte. I strongly urge that we not consider a female for this job.

   One of the Commercial Representative's main functions is to make visits to customers' premises to solve difficult problems. Most of these visits are under unfavorable, defensive, or argumentative circumstances and usually to areas such as slums and negro ghettos. To send a woman to such localities would be an open invitation to assault, rape, or death, in addition to profanity and other verbal abuse.[1]

Written some eighty years after the Bell System began constructing its image of the ideal telephone woman, this letter illustrates how greater societal notions of white womanhood are absorbed and transformed to 'gender' whiteness in the workplace. The 'woman' referred to is vulnerable and needs protection. Her genteel feminine nature would be insulted by 'profanity' given her high moral character. This woman's identity is shaped by defining African Americans as 'others'. By this definition white women possess innate qualities that black women do not and cannot obtain.

   Even with its explicit sex discrimination, few would argue that the letter includes African American women among the women in need of protection. Implicitly, black women live in 'slums and negro ghettos' where they are accustomed to and may in fact participate in crime and profanity. The nineteenth-century creation of the virtuous and pious 'white lady' in need of seclusion from the public and the 'negro' threat of 'assault, rape, or death' to her physical body as well as her virtue is well established in historical literature.[2] What this twentieth-century letter shows is the necessity to continuously recreate this racialized image, not just in the larger society but in the workplace as well. These images help to justify a white identity that is connected to a system of privileges and advantages based on a socially constructed concept of race – whiteness.

Over time, political, social and economic conditions may shape or transform this system, but a belief in racial practices and policies that disadvantage African Americans remains constant and is its ideological foundation.[3] For example, limited opportunities for women in the telephone industry contributed to the exclusion of African American women as telephone operators in the 1910s, whereas expanded opportunities for white women opened telephone operating to black women, but segregated and restricted them mostly to that job during the early 1970s. Each generation reproduces whiteness in a variety of forms, and each form is distinctively inaccessible to African Americans.

Some theorists suggest that the creation and dissemination of racial ideology is from the top down – from capitalists to workers.[4] This essay will explore a more dynamic process in which whiteness is constructed in the workplace by both the capitalists and the workers. Employers are usually the more powerful in this equation and therefore can implement their own racial policies and practices as they either accept or reject those demanded by workers. Despite this disparity in power and difference in motivation, the goal of maintaining white privileges frequently crosses class lines.[5] The desire for control over the workplace and the work process in the pursuit of higher profits motivates employers to contribute to the concept of whiteness by establishing a racially segmented workforce.[6]

White workers, who believe that it is in their interests to reduce black competition for jobs, partly accept and sometimes even demand the capitalists' imposition of a racial hierarchy in occupational structure.[7] From their contribution to the construction of whiteness, they gain not only economic rewards (higher wages and the cleaner, lighter and/or less dangerous jobs), but also a 'psychological' wage (a 'deference' manifested in racial privileges and a social status that is always higher than African Americans).[8] The 'psychological' wage affirms a meritorious white identity composed of inherent cultural characteristics (not just white skin) which make special privileges appear natural rather than socially determined and allocated. Unfortunately, this 'wage' blurs common interracial working-class interests.

The production and distribution of these 'wages of whiteness' is a gendered process.[9] How white women workers accepted racist ideology and participated in the construction of whiteness has been neglected in an historical literature that concentrates on working-class formation among nineteenth-century white male workers. Studies that examine whiteness among women or the construction of white womanhood focus on a middle-class paradigm to which perhaps many working-class women aspire, but fail to achieve.[10] While they both receive 'the wages of whiteness', men and women employers and employees experience this process differently because whiteness is structured hierarchically. All white women receive the advantages of whiteness through the prism of white male domination. Consequently, twentieth-century white women workers, concentrated in low-level, low-paying, sex-segregated jobs, have received more 'psychological' wages than economic when *compared* to white men.

This essay shows how Bell System management and white women telephone operators interacted in the construction and perpetuation of whiteness during the twentieth century. It argues that telephone managers used the 'psychological' wages of white exclusivity to compensate women for their low pay, poor working conditions and lack of access to male-dominated work. Ironically, telephone operators achieved higher status on the job than in the general society. Outside of work, they may have enjoyed segregated housing, schools and recreational facilities, but in most cases these environments were clearly distinguishable from those of the upper classes. On the job, however, racial segregation ensured their position above domestic and factory workers.

Indeed, the image of the 'white lady' operator obscured the 'factory-like' working conditions of the job and to some extent diluted resistance.[11] This model encouraged operators to ignore the reality that required them to defer like servants and, more significantly, it helped operators forget that they actually could never become the 'ladies' upon whom their mystique was based. Despite their working-class status, white women telephone operators consciously embraced the 'white lady' identity by participating in company activities that demeaned black people and by insisting upon the exclusion of black women in the workplace. As members of the white Bell System family, women telephone operators invested in the concept of whiteness and enjoyed the rewards of that investment.

## The Bell System constructs its model operator

When the Bell System began replacing boy operators with young women during the late 1870s, managers initiated what was to become a long history of reproducing 'whiteness'. Infamous for swearing, beer drinking and fist fighting, boy operators had been rude and unruly with customers. Male and later even female managers accepted the idea that it was *natural* for boys to behave in this way. According to John J. Carty, a boy operator who rose to Chief Engineer of AT&T, these boy operators 'were not old enough to be talked to like men ... not young enough to be spanked like children' and were 'but a little lower than the wild Indian'![12] Katherine M. Schmitt, also a pioneer operator, concurred: 'As I listened to them I used to think that all the Indians had not yet left Manhattan. In short, nothing could be done with those boys, until, by common consent, they were abolished.'[13] The feminization of telephone operating entailed the substitution of a near-savage non-white male image with a civilized, white female ideal.

In an effort to counter the unruly boys' negative effect on business, management created the 'white lady' image as a method of seducing customers away from the telegraph, soothing customers frustrated by the still unreliable equipment, and keeping customers away from their competitors.[14] B.E. Sunny, General Superintendent at Chicago Telephone Company, thought it especially important 'to get girls of the right character' and 'to keep the standard of intelligence and morality high'.[15] N.W. Lillie, manager of the Boston exchange in 1879, hired the first woman operator, Emma M. Nutt (a nice girl who lived across the street from him) 'to reduce the shouting' and confusion in the switch room.[16] One New York manager found girls 'generally polite and obliging, while boys are inclined to be impudent and boyish'.[17] This idealization of white women presented a demure and 'ladylike' image that commanded the highest reverence.

White women regardless of class accepted this idealization and sought to behave in conformity with it as Miss Schmitt's racist characterization of Indians demonstrates. Women of all racial and ethnic groups in this era aspired to some version of this identity, but all women were not acceptable to the economically and racially dominant classes. The men of these classes were socialized to 'respect' and 'protect' young white women, regardless of what they considered to be the primacy of their own position. For example, Frank Rozzelle remembered 'cussing' out boy operators when he became angry over 'busy' lines, but with the girls 'we simply hang up the receiver and picked on our office partners or whoever happened to be handy ... because we could not swear at a girl'.[18] Management instituted rules to ensure that telephone operators would not be subjected to profanity. In 1890, The Delaware and Atlantic Telephone and Telegraph Company warned: 'Improper talk by subscribers or their employees, or others over the Exchange wires, must be promptly traced and stopped. In an extreme case the subscriber's instrument must be removed, the wires must be protected in the interest of all concerned.'[19]

Over the years, the telephone industry perfected and perpetuated this gendered model of whiteness by utilizing several strategies. First and most important, the companies established a racially segregated workplace by rigid hiring, selection and training policies during the early years of telephony. Immediately prior to the First World War, the Bell System developed a comprehensive plan of paternalism designed to re-enforce attributes the company deemed important to success. And finally, Bell literature openly projected demeaning images of black women and management explicitly articulated its rationale for the rejection of black women as operators.

## Hiring and selection process

In 1915, F.H. Bethell bragged that the New York Telephone company accepted only 10 per cent of those who applied.[20] Managers usually hired young, single, native-born white women who lived with their parents.[21] Friends and relatives of employees recommended the majority of applicants. All Bell companies requested references, particularly if the applicant had left another job. Some companies solicited churches or schools, and in emergencies personnel officers tried 'newspaper advertising, notices posted in women's clubs, lunch rooms and charitable organizations'.[22] Recruitment through personal and social channels (white networks) ensured the employment of workers with the desired 'cultural attributes'.

Operating companies, except in extremely rare individual cases, had an explicit policy against hiring blacks and most immigrants as operators.[23] Managers frequently rejected immigrants on the grounds of their strong accents.[24] The New England Telephone & Telegraph Company did not hire Jews because of an objection to the observance of Jewish holidays, fear that they were labour agitators and general anti-Semitism.[25] When their Jewishness could not be immediately discerned, a few Jews did slip through the discriminatory bars. Some companies found women from English-speaking countries such as

Canada, Ireland and England acceptable. In the Mid-West where there were pockets of foreigners, it would not be unlikely to hear a Norwegian or Scandinavian accent on local lines.[26] However, African Americans were excluded from telephone operating on the basis of skin colour.[27]

Since the Bell System trained all its newly hired employees, neither special training nor prior work experience weighed more heavily than race as a prerequisite to employment. A 1910 Investigation of the Telephone Companies showed that one company rejected 2,229 of 6,152 applicants. Among those rejected were eleven Jews who refused to work on Jewish holidays, 90 women with accents, and seven 'colored' women.[28] This highly selective personnel policy reinforced the Bell System's carefully cultivated image of the telephone operator and insured the selection of white women as operators until the Second World War era.

After personnel managers hired potential operators, special training in voice, the physical manipulation of the switchboard and Bell System ideology became necessary. Katherine M. Schmitt, manager of the first modern operating school, described the fully trained operator as someone 'docile enough to deny herself the sweet privilege of the last word' and who could 'assume that the subscriber is always right, and even when she knows he is not her only comeback must be: "Excuse it please", in the same smiling voice'.[29]

Operators who completed the telephone training programme were expected to behave in a 'ladylike' manner in the workplace and at home. Employment officers frequently visited the potential operator's home to ensure that she met a specific moral standard. According to F.H. Bethell, 'Every girl who is passed into a central office must satisfy competent and experienced chiefs that she is in every way qualified to become one of this great army. Once in, the girls are protected in every way that can be devised ...'[30] This protection applied especially to the 'white lady' image.

Bell System advertisements and other literature continuously reinforced this image by depicting African Americans, particularly women, in historically familiar stereotypes. The New York *Telephone Review* published two covers in one year (1911) portraying African American females in subservient roles.[31] Black women cast as domestic servants reassured telephone women that they were ladies, not servants, despite their rigorous training in how to provide 'service with a smile'. The April cover showed a black girl who has delivered the wrong hat to a white woman. It is unclear whether the girl misunderstood the written instructions or simply could not read them. The October–November issue portrayed the stereotypical 'Aunt Jemima' serving dinner to a white family. She, of course, is amazed by both the telephone and a young white boy's ability to use it. These portrayals of African American women as subordinate, stupid and unattractive contributed to the continuous reproduction of whiteness during the pre-First World War era. The appeal to white female gentility in these images was directed at the middle-class white public who were the primary users of the telephone at that time and to white women workers. Like sales clerks and to some extent waitresses, telephone operators sought to identify with the people they served.

For example, operators endeavoured to live up to an elite self-perception by wearing expensive clothes. When New England Telephone and Telegraph Company in 1913 imported over 1,200 strikebreakers, the strikebreakers 'looked more like chorus girls from some high-class theatrical show than they did telephone operators'.[32] The strikers themselves wore 'Furs, hats of chic design, and smart-looking shoes'.[33]

Class-conscious Chicago operators refused to pass through an alley to get to work 'owing to the low character of the saloons in this alley way and to its dark and dirty condition ... When an effort was made to compel them ... they struck and were successful after much notoriety for the telephone company in the newspapers.'[34] Ladies did not walk through alleys of ill repute. The progressive reformer Elizabeth Beardley Butler explained that women in Pittsburgh accepted lower wages and desired work in the telephone industry because of the short training period and most importantly, because 'a telephone girl ranks higher socially than a factory operative.'[35] Part of this social rank was derived from nativism and racism since many factories employed large numbers of immigrants and, in some places, African Americans. Telephone operators in 1920 were still isolated from these groups of people.

## Bell System welfare capitalism: employee benefit plans

Bell System welfare and benefit plans contributed to the construction of a gendered whiteness in the workplace as they sought to secure employee loyalty against the appeal of unionism.[36] In addition to sickness, disability, pension and stock ownership plans, AT&T and other companies provided well-lit and ventilated 'retiring' rooms supervised by matrons, free tea and coffee and, in some places, lunches free or at cost. Special rest rooms, where women could see a nurse who would administer first aid in emergencies or give medications for 'simple indispositions', became commonplace in big cities like New York.[37] To show its concern for the employees, the company established vacation camps, employee magazines, employee societies, company awards and prizes for good work and attendance, after-work educational programmes, libraries, sports and other activities. At a time when public facilities were segregated, the company guaranteed a continuation of white privilege and indeed enhanced white working women's illusion that they could participate in all the privileges of their race.

Like other corporate programmes established during the early twentieth century, the Bell System welfare programme encouraged employees to see themselves as a family. Of course, the Bell family was white. Indeed, F.H. Bethell declared that 'Since the creation of the Employees' Benefit Fund we have felt more than ever that we are just one big family with every employee having a seat at the family table'.[38] Compared to male telephone workers, and male workers in general, the plate in front of the majority of women telephone workers contained a meagre meal.[39]

Nevertheless, compared to female factory and domestic workers, operators who remained in the Bell System feasted relatively well. Two-week paid vacations became institutionalized by 1929 and, in many areas of the country, operators went to vacation camps or resorts provided by the company. Operators with two or more years of service received prorated sickness and disability benefits, while pension, stock, savings, insurance and other thrift plans were enhanced for those eligible to participate in them. Many operators found opportunities for advancement as clerical workers in the accounting, commercial and plant departments that were growing as a result of business expansion and the various policies set in motion to gain public favour. The pages of internal Bell System magazines are filled with dozens of examples of telephone operators with over 25 years' service who were able to accumulate stock, receive pensions, and benefit from mortgage plans that allowed them to buy homes, even though many of them were single. Clearly, management projected the idea that being a member of the white Bell family had certain economic advantages for those who remained loyal to it. And, above all, white women continued to enjoy their racist homogeneity created and fostered by Bell System hiring practices.

## Company associations: the Bell System concept of family

F.H. Bethell's meticulous choice of the family metaphor in 1915 became a key strategy of company paternalism in the decades following the First World War. The Bell System faced a complete breakdown in service, employee demoralization and low productivity in the postwar period. In its effort to improve and restore the system to normal during the 1920s, the Bell System established employee associations (company unions). The advent of these associations among telephone workers marked not only the decline of independent trade unions but the replacement of unions by the Bell System concept of 'family'.[40] Using AT&T guidelines, operators in the Long Lines Department organized one of the first associations. In December 1919, they adopted a constitution that limited its membership to 'any white employee ... after active service of three or more consecutive months in the employing Company.'[41] The operators had accepted the executives' proposal to keep the Bell family white.[42]

Managers developed a variety of methods for persuading employees to accept their roles in the family enterprise. Executives designed activities to enhance public relations and to keep operators occupied in unthreatening activities under Bell System surveillance. In the associations meetings, officials familiarized employees with First Aid training, Rest Homes, the Pink Ticket Plan, 'What I Did Today', company courses, picnics and other entertainment in which participation was expected.[43] 'What I Did Today' suggested that employees 'write a brief story ... on any act which would help the public to a better appreciation of telephone service, policy and practices'. Managers emphasized that 'we let ourselves be known as employees of the telephone company when performing any service'.[44] Company magazines and posters publicized these stories. The Pink Ticket Plan elicited operators' suggestions (on pink slips) for improvements in methods or solutions to any problems. Any ideas particularly appealing to management's goals would be published with the operator's name and picture.

Even the most reluctant groups of operators eventually participated in these activities.[45] Initially, a certain amount of compulsion would account for their behaviour but their stories show that many of them had absorbed Bell System indoctrination. One enthusiastic operator reported:

I fell in company a few days ago with an elderly gentleman and, after having learned where I was employed, he seemed very much interested about our line of work.

He said, 'I wish you would tell me how the Company in general treats its employees where the majority of them are girls.' I explained to him all about our rest room, silence room and matron, and the care we received when ill. He said, 'Do you mean that you have a rest room and beds and cafeteria furnished like that all at the expense of the Company?' I told him that was what I meant. He then asked if I was an operator, and I said I was a Maple operator. He said, 'Well, don't you have chief operators and supervisors?' I said 'Yes, sir.' He asked how they treated us and I told him about how they took things up with us and how we could go to them with anything we could not solve ourselves. Then I told him about our Association and the entertainments it furnished.

I invited this gentleman up to our next open house and he said he certainly was coming and would bring his wife, and when I started to get out of the car he said, 'Well, your Company has a wonderful system.'[46]

This operator believed that she was a part of the Bell System family from which she received protection and comfort. Her remarks assured the 'gentleman' (i.e. the respectable white public) that her work environment was appropriate for 'girls' and even his wife. Whether they genuinely believed in the family concept or not, many operators conformed their behaviour to it.

## The Bell System enlists the workers in the creation of whiteness

Throughout the 1920s, 1930s and 1940s, Bell managers continued to deploy the racist pre-First World War imagery to cast the company and its customers as white. But the companies advanced beyond simple cartoons and drawings and enlisted the employees in the production of denigrating images of African Americans. Telephone company men and women blackened their faces and staged shows for company functions to which the white public was invited. Obviously, the white public and the performers shared a familiarity and agreement about the content of these shows. Company publications, including pictures, advertised and reported these events. Most common were pictures of 'blackfaced' white women dressed in male and female costumes acting out skits that ridiculed African American people's intelligence, speech and other behaviour.[47] For example, in 1939, *The Telephone Review* reported that 'the old south,' complete with plantation, 'Aunt Jemima' and 'Lazybones', was a 'principal feature' of the annual Christmas party held for operators in Buffalo, NY.[48] As late as September 1955, the 'Sodus Minstrels' staged 'minstrel shows for Pioneer parties, the Business and Professional Women's Club and the Grange'.[49] As their names show, many of these women were the native-born children of immigrants. Their participation in these performances demonstrated their desire to identify with the 'white lady' image and it also indicates a continuity in the process of perpetuating that image.[50]

## The rationale for rejecting African American applicants

Print and dramatic caricatures of African American people were merely a graphic representation of an ideology Bell System managers frequently expressed in other more subtle but effective ways. Managers used language to obfuscate their own opinions and behaviour and to shift responsibility away from themselves for the exclusion of African American women from the operating forces. Before the Second World War, Bell managers' explanations ranged from vague references to tradition and custom to statements which blamed either white women telephone workers or black women applicants. In 1920, when the telephone industry suffered a tremendous labour shortage and advertised for 1,000 operators, New York Telephone Company refused an offer to supply it with 'neat and intelligent ... colored girls', free of charge, made by Eugene McIntosh, proprietor of the Harlem Employment Agency.[51] To this offer of '100 per cent American' girls who would 'prove competent and loyal', E.J. Anderson, the employment manager, blandly replied that while the company had 'given consideration to employing colored girls as telephone operators', it was 'not in a position to do so at the present time'.[52] Anderson gave no further explanation, but a Mr Schultz, assistant to the vice-president, responded to a similar offer made by the League for Democracy by disclaiming any personal objection to black workers, asserting that the white operators would quit if they had to work next to black women and also claiming that white women would not train black women.[53]

By the late 1920s, New York Telephone Company managers seemed impervious to appeals for justice and they no longer offered these meagre apologies for their policies of racial exclusion. In 1927, when

George S. Schuyler of *The Messenger* inquired about the number of blacks employed by the company, vice-president T.P. Sylvan, replied that there were some blacks on the payroll 'assisting ... in the conduct of ... restaurant and lounge facilities'.[54] To Schuyler's follow-up letter asking why there were no black operators, Sylvan answered that he had already discussed this matter with other 'distinguished' blacks and that he believed that he had 'satisfied them that the position which we have taken with reference to their employment has been a proper and necessary one'.[55] According to a New York City Mayor's Commission Study in 1935, 'Mr. R.H. Boggs, Vice-president in charge of personnel of the New York Telephone Company did not regard the exclusion of Negroes ... as discrimination but only as a customary practice'.[56]

Even after New York State passed a law in 1933 which forbade public utilities to 'refuse to employ any person in any capacity, in the operation or maintenance of a public service on account of the race, color or religion of such person', the exclusion of black women from the operating forces continued.[57] Indeed, during the 1930s, in testimony given before government investigators, New York managers insisted that the absence of African American women from operating and clerical work was an indication of black women's incompetence.[58] Consider the testimony of Walter D. Williams, New York Telephone General Traffic Manager in New York City, before the New York State Temporary Commission on the Condition of the Urban Colored Population in 1937.

> Q. What explanation have you for the failure of any Negro telephone operator to be employed out of those 4500? A. That in the opinion of the interviewers, they are not qualified to fill the position of telephone operator. ...
> Q. Have you ever had a Negro Telephone Operator who has been qualified, in your experience? A. Not in my experience.
> Q. What prevents them from being qualified, in your opinion? A. Our job, of course, in the Central Offices, is to give telephone service; that is done by a group of girls and we work together. They are white girls, and in our judgment it would not be possible to give a proper grade of telephone service if we put the Negro girls in with the white girls.
> ...
> Q. I understood the tenor of your remarks to be, Mr. Williams, that even if an applicant should possess all other qualifications, the fact

that such applicant was colored – a colored applicant – would in your judgment be a proper reason for refusing employment because of what you feel – of seating that colored employee next to a white person in the switchboard exchange. A. That is correct.

Q. In other words, having perfectly competent colored applicants, you would feel it your duty to refuse to accept those applicants, and you would feel it your duty to give those jobs to white applicants, of no better or equal qualifications, merely because of that fact? A. That is correct, yes, I would say.[59]

Throughout his testimony, Williams asserted the company's right to exclude black women and that the company was not in violation of the law to do so.[60] He acknowledged the justice of hiring African Americans, but concluded that 'unfortunately all the things in this world are not decided on straight questions of justice'.[61] The 'white lady' image of the telephone operator prevailed.

Even during the severe labour shortages of the Second World War, New York Telephone Company and the Traffic Employees Association (representing 98 per cent of the operators) continued to reproduce 'whiteness' among operators.[62] In 1944, the Fair Employment Practices Committee (FEPC) conducted an investigation into the personnel practices at New York Telephone company which found that the company had begun to employ African Americans as clerks, typists, messengers, kitchen men, lounge attendants, stenographers, tellers, coin collectors and business representatives and matrons, 'but not as operators'.[63] Even though the company had reported 'difficulty filling labor needs for operators due to relatively low wages', managers claimed in November 1943 that they could not 'hire Negroes because of speech and diction limitations'.[64] By 20 July 1944, company managers explained to FEPC investigators that they were willing to hire black operators 'if given just a little time'. D. McClure, Assistant to the First vice-president, stated 'that the company for the present felt it better to place non-white workers on individual jobs and not on "team play" jobs. ... a great deal of cooperation was necessary in the operation of a switchboard where a large group of operators is employed and ... Negro and white workers would not get along well on such a board.'[66]

## Telephone unions contribute to the production of whiteness

On 24 July 1944 when pressed by the FEPC investigators, McClure said that the company had already agreed to a programme 'for a slow, gradual process whereby Negroes would be hired in other divisions of the company and gradually moved into operators jobs'.[67] Despite this agreement, he said that he 'would be willing to hire Negroes as operators now except for the very determined attitude of the telephone operators' union that Negroes not be put on such jobs'.[68] When the FEPC investigators discussed these allegations with representatives from the Traffic Employees Association:

> it was discovered that a very large percentage of the operators now employed by the company are Catholics and that many of them had been originally recruited through various Catholic churches. It was also learned that a very large proportion of them had at various times expressed themselves as vehemently opposed to the introduction of Negroes as telephone operators, either individually or in groups. The union representatives felt that it was almost certain that there would be violent opposition to the introduction of Negro workers on to the company's switchboards if attempted at this time. They said, however, that they would be willing to undertake an educational campaign among the operators to convince them that their fears were ungrounded. They suggested that we secure the cooperation of religious groups in furthering such a program of education.[69]

The union never established an educational programme, which indicated a rhetorical rather than genuine commitment to integration. Formed after the Wagner Act granted the right to organize independent unions in 1935, this union's constitution contained no anti-discrimination clause.[70] Union officials disavowed discrimination on their part, claiming that they represented blacks employed by the company and that they were in the process of revising their constitution to include a non-discrimination clause. Indeed, the Telephone Employees Association, like other telephone unions, denied having any control over the company's hiring policy.

Despite union disavowals, there is evidence that the Bell System had reason to fear work stoppages or other union actions against the employment of African Americans. For example, there is a foreboding

tone in a resolution adopted by the National Federation of Telephone
Workers of Pennsylvania. At its annual convention in 1945, the delegates acknowledged the existence of the FEPC but reiterated the
union's duty to 'safeguard the interests of all workers'. Accordingly,
they resolved that 'in that connection that the Council be consulted
and its written consent be obtained before any change in the status of
workers be effectuated by the Company through arrangements with
the FEPC or any other Government Agency'.[71] Union officials who
generally denied having power over hiring practices when black
workers demanded an end to discrimination, asserted authority over
that same process when white workers believed their exclusivity was
in jeopardy. And they sought to enforce their authority.

Union officials and union members threatened various companies
with disruption during the entire war period. Evelyn N. Cooper,
Hearing Examiner of the Legal Division of the FEPC, reported that 'a
strike is reported to have been threatened by some of the national officers of the union at the time Negro operators were first employed in
New York, and in Baltimore it is claimed that there is now more
tension among the white operators than before'.[72] George M. Johnson,
Deputy Chairman and Acting Chief of the Legal Division of the FEPC,
who had investigated hundreds of complaints and corresponded with
dozens of managers, stated that 'in every instance refusal to hire black
women has been based on the alleged possibility of a strike among
white operators if Negroes were brought into work with them'.[73]
White women accounting clerks had participated in a one-day wildcat
strike in Camden, New Jersey on 3 May 1943 when the New Jersey Bell
Telephone company announced that it would hire African American
women clerks. The company refused to capitulate and the strike failed
but white women had demonstrated their willingness to strike against
the employment of African American women.[74]

Even though the operators' job paid less than some clerical work
and required longer and irregular hours, operators continued to resist
integration. Evelyn N. Cooper explained that 'the real reason for the
separate treatment of the operator job category … seems to lie in a
long standing Bell System policy … the companies have provided the
operators with exceptionally nice rest rooms, recreational and eating
facilities, thereby giving them a sort of compensatory "social status"
among telephone company workers'.[75] 'Compensatory social status'
required the continuance of racial exclusivity.[76]

There is ample evidence that these notions about racial exclusivity
prevailed throughout the Bell System despite AT&T claims that the

associated companies enjoyed total independence in the selection of personnel. A study of 44 cities conducted by the Urban League concluded that 'available information is sufficient to substantiate the fact that Negro workers have been systematically excluded from employment in this industry in many cities'.[77] Consequently, the report continued, 'prior to 1940, no Negro switchboard operators were employed in any of the exchanges' investigated. And, 'in fact, there is no record of the employment of Negro operators in any city in the country before that date'.[78] New York Telephone Company hired the first African American operators in November 1944.

Within twenty years, a trend towards hiring black women only as operators and mostly in urban industrial centres had clearly emerged.[79] Management's reversal of its hiring policy in the largest Northeastern and Western cities nearly transformed traffic workforces from white to black.[80] Black women's struggles to obtain the operator's job had succeeded at a time when operators' work lost its attractiveness to white women, who now had alternative opportunities.[81] This factor, the post-Second World War influx of black women to the cities, high turnover and the general expansion of telephone usage all combined to create an economic motivation for the Bell System to hire African American women as operators.[82] In New York City, for example, 54.9 per cent of all operators were African Americans in 1970.[83] By the end of the same year, 34.2 per cent of all Bell System operators and their low-level supervisors were black.[84] Southern Bell and Southwestern Bell excluded blacks from all except the most menial jobs until the early 1970s when they duplicated the segregated work patterns practised in the North.[85]

The Southern delay in hiring African American women as operators and the partial redefinition of telephone operating as black women's work further demonstrates that the reproduction of whiteness is a continuous process shaped by contemporaneous social, political and economic conditions. In the post-Second World War era, Southern operating companies were able to stall integration by using a single 'moral' standard in addition to academic and voice qualifications to bar African American women as operators. As 'part of the effort to maintain a work force of persons of high moral character', Southern Bell and later South Central Bell refused to hire women with 'illegitimate' children.[86] Even women whom personnel evaluators deemed 'co-operative', 'industrious' and in good 'health' with an appropriate 'appearance', were rejected for a 'lack of integrity' if they were unwed mothers.[87]

Despite management's statement that they had 'never applied this practice in order to discriminate with regard to either sex or race', this policy never was applied to men.[88] And the EEOC investigation conducted during the late 1960s found that 'throughout the South ... the policy has tended to exclude Negro females to a far greater extent than whites. Indeed, the Commission has never been presented with evidence of any white woman being rejected on this ground.'[89] Relentless pressure by the EEOC and civil rights organizations forced Southern Bell and South Central Bell to 'reconsider' the 'moral' requirement in 1970.[90]

As telephone operating opened to African American women, the telephone industry abandoned the image of the 'white lady' operator. In the large cities, the Bell System initiated a practice of hiring only African American women for available operating positions.[91] Management pursued this policy because African American women provided a large pool of inexpensive labour and because implementation of plans for the introduction of new labour-saving technology were in progress. The telephone industry had no reason to fear resistance to the impending job displacement. Despite the 'white lady' image, white women operators had never received union protection against technological displacement, and in the context of white male-dominated union assaults on affirmative action, certainly African American women would not.[92] Control over the workplace and the work process continued to motivate Bell managers to reproduce 'whiteness' by segregating black women into basically one job.

Telephone operating became a black woman's job in many large urban areas not only because of changing demographics and Bell System managerial interests, but also because the job lost its prestige and white women, with more abundant opportunities, would no longer work for low wages when there was no 'social compensation' associated with the job. After integration, management continued to privilege white workers by deliberately recruiting and confining black workers to operating and other low-level entry jobs which became stigmatized as black.

This 'psychological' wage translated into a hefty economic advantage as well. A survey of thirty cities at the end of 1970 found that '78.7 per cent of all black employees were in jobs paying a maximum basic annual wage of $7,000 or less; only 39.5 per cent of all white employees were in jobs having such a low salary'.[93] When the actions of the EEOC and a variety of civil rights organizations forced the Bell System to establish equal opportunity programmes, white workers felt threatened and their unions challenged these initiatives by alleging seniority violations and reverse discrimination.[94] Ironically, integration had forced white telephone workers and their unions to participate more actively in the creation of whiteness.

Consequently, there is a history of telephone unions failing to represent black workers especially during the 1960s and 1970s period of bureaucratization when the CWA officials centralized their power but also won major economic benefits particularly for white male workers. Many of the EEOC complaints filed against AT&T included black women's charges against the unions. Barbara S. Gray of Memphis, Tennessee, for example, filed a charge against South Central Bell and CWA Local 3806 in which she claimed that the union '(a) Fails to represent Negroes properly, (b) Fails to give Negroes equal opportunity to be union representatives. (c) Union has taken no action to see that Negroes get the training or advancements they are entitled to.'[95] In many instances, after blacks had been hired, white male *and* female union leaders, protective of their power bases, did not encourage non-white union participation. This was especially true in those places where the membership had rapidly changed from white to black and where the leadership consisted of long entrenched white union bosses. Lavie Bolick, an assistant to a District vice-president in 1970, referring to Atlanta and other Georgia offices confirmed that

> the old administration don't want to stress organizing in those offices because they foresee that the power is going to be there, and *they* ain't going to be able to set on their asses and hold their jobs down because they're going to be threatened by a union member. And as long as he's a nonmember, he's not a threat to their reign, and I hate to put it that way, but as I see it from where I sit. In a lot of our large offices, this is about the way it would sum up if the people would tell the truth.[96]

Although the traffic department had been better organized than the plant twenty years earlier when it was all white, most of Atlanta's black operators remained non-union in 1970 because local leaders would not ask them into the union.[97] Union policies based on racial prejudice and exclusion, like company policies, were not peculiar to the South.

In the Northern cities, white female union leaders fought against non-white leadership and participation while they also neglected to represent the non-whites fairly. New York City operators belonged to

Telephone Traffic Union (TTU) whose white leadership, according to Lessie Sanders, never sent the operators out on strike.[98] TTU membership resorted to wildcat strikes at the end of their contracts because their leadership did not fight for operators' demands. 'We didn't wait for our union,' according to Sanders. 'When we had a fight we went out to try to force the company to see our position because the union would never do it.' For the seven years she worked in Directory Assistance, Sanders recalled 'no elections' and believed that the leaders 'were appointed'.[99] Unfortunately, the white unionists had viewed black women's inclusion not only as potential job competition but also as threats to their 'white lady' identity.

This picture, of course, would not be complete without some mention of those unionists who did abandon their racism and fought racist company hiring practices and working conditions. Indeed, these cases were rare, exceptional and isolated, but they happened. Scott Stephens, a retired CWA International Representative, acknowledged that racism existed in Indiana but that the union there had fought it. He asserted:

> under the direction of Mae Mann, we constantly argued with the telephone company for better positions for the black people, better understanding of their needs, and that there were well-educated people among them. So in the plant department there were jobs created by negotiations, upgraded jobs, for colored people. In the traffic group, girls were interviewed for operators. And in one of our most southern cities, Evansville, Indiana, the company introduced the first colored operators.[100]

Stephens and Mae Mann followed through with the company and the local presidents. Mae Mann, according to him, guaranteed that the local presidents would not give the company any trouble. Stephens and Mann personally introduced the first black operator in Evansville, and they also convinced the reluctant local leaders that this was the way of the future.

Other examples of individual unionist, local or even national union leadership initiatives can be cited, but telephone workers and their unions in general throughout the 1960s and most of the 1970s, never pursued strong equal opportunity goals. Without concerning themselves with unfair racist and sexist hiring and promotion practices, most union leaders maintained that African Americans and other 'minorities' received the same union protections and benefits won by national contractual provisions for all workers. However, most of these contracts had been bargained in the interests of white workers, who did not hesitate to call upon their leaders to use seniority clauses, grievances and even lawsuits to block the entrance of blacks into jobs believed to be the exclusive domain of whites.

## Conclusion

The history of telephone operators over the course of the twentieth century illustrates quite clearly how employers and employees continuously reproduced the privileges and advantages of white identity. Bell System managers maintained control over the workplace by establishing exclusive hiring policies, welfare programmes, employee associations and other paternalistic practices that diverted white women's attention away from issues that would lead to resistance. White women consciously participated in the projections of racist stereotypes and other racist activities in exchange for the economic benefits of these company programmes and the racially closed labour pool. The model operator's white 'lady' image also compensated working class women for their exclusion from the upper classes where race privileges were greatest. Even though these women worked in machine-paced and monitored environments, many had no choices, and it was true that these conditions were better than those in factory and domestic work. Hence, in each generation, white operators demanded and received 'psychological' and economic wages for their participation in the perpetuation of whiteness.

By accepting the 'psychological wage', white women also accepted a wider ideology based on capitalist, racist and sexist domination. Their history in the telephone industry until well after the Second World War reflects an agreement with both male unionists and male employers on black women's place in the industry. For the privilege of condescending to blacks, telephone operators conceded part of their power to resist low wages and extremely stressful working conditions, thereby contributing to management's increasing capacity to control them as the technology became available to do so.[101] By the late 1970s when white and black women were united in their national union, technology had virtually destroyed the occupation of telephone operating.

The implications of this history resounds in the entire labour force. The significance of documenting female whiteness is neither simply to accuse white women of racism nor to 'blame the victim'. Rather, it is to demonstrate the very real obstacles to working-class unity that many labour historians choose to minimize. When scholars argue that workers blindly accept a racial ideology handed down by their employers, the complexities and contradictions of whiteness are obscured. For example, when operators identified with the white 'lady' image, they knew that their working conditions were poor and that they faced job loss due to automation. Yet, neither the operators nor their union leadership rejected the image as a part of a larger strategy for resisting the technological devastation of operating jobs.[102] We know why white workers accept the advantages of whiteness. Future research must answer why they accept the disadvantages. Of course, this new knowledge should lead to the goal of rejecting both.

## Notes

1　D.C. Williamson, General Commercial Manager, Southern Bell Telephone and Telegraph Company, Charlotte, North Carolina to L.P. Morgan, General Personnel Manager, 4 November 1965. National Archives, Record Group 403, Box 35.

2　Although class, regional and urban/rural conditions shaped specific attitudes about work and social place for the 'white lady', notions of 'domesticity' and 'privilege' needing protection and seclusion were adhered to nationally. See Nancy F. Cott, *The Bonds of Womanhood: 'Woman's Sphere' In New England, 1780–1835* (New Haven, Conn., 1977) for the Northeastern manifestation of 'domesticity', and Elizabeth Fox-Genovese, *Within the Plantation Household: Black and White Women of the Old South* (Chapel Hill, NC, 1988) for southern slaveholding women. For the rise of the late nineteenth- and early twentieth-century myth of the black rapist, see Vron Ware, *Beyond the Pale: White Women, Racism and History* (London and New York, 1992) and Gail Bederman, *Manliness and Civilization: A Cultural History of Gender and Race in the United States, 1880–1917* (Chicago, 1995). It is important to note that the concept of the 'white lady' has middle- and upper-class origins, but still represented an ideal for all white women. Certainly, there is a strong element of control in this image of white womanhood, but that discussion is well beyond the scope of this essay.

3　Barbara Jeanne Fields has argued that race and racial ideology are created, recreated and ritualized constantly in 'social life'. Her work pre-dates the 'whiteness' literature and in some ways forms the point of departure for many labour historians engaged in the race vs. class debate. The origins of this debate stem from criticism of the new labour historians who have been accused of either seeing inter-racial labour solidarity where it did not exist or completely ignoring race as a category of analysis. See Barbara Jeanne Fields, 'Slavery, Race and Ideology in the United States of America', *New Left Review* 181 (May/June 1990), 95–118. The attempt to include race as a part of working class formation and identity gave rise to the 'whiteness' literature as typified by David R. Roediger's seminal work *The Wages of Whiteness: Race and the Making of the American Working Class* (London and New York, 1991).

4 They argue that capitalists keep control over the workplace by using race as a method of splitting the working class. According to these historians, class is the most important analytical concept to apply to the American working class. Although she is not explicit in this position, Barbara J. Fields, 'Ideology and Race in American History', in *Region, Race and Reconstruction: Essays in Honor of C. Van Woodward*, ed. J. Morgan Kousser and James M. McPherson (New York, 1982), 150–7, is the point of departure in the most recent literature. She argues that race and class are not 'analytic alternatives'. Class is a 'material reality', whereas race 'is purely an ideological notion'. Because white supremacy is a 'slogan' that means different things to different classes of whites, it is an effective means of obscuring class differences among whites.

5 Although this essay will not address this topic, it is important to note that whiteness also privileges whites over Native Americans, 'Hispanic' Americans and Asian Americans. In important ways, their histories are vastly different than African Americans but many of their experiences as 'others' are quite similar. Equally noteworthy is the process by which whites achieve whiteness (i.e. immigrants) and the extent to which it is possible for some whites to enjoy all of the advantages (i.e. 'white trash'). Despite these constraints European immigrants do become white and 'white trash' still enjoy the fact that at least socially (if not economically) blacks are beneath them on the basis of skin colour.

6 For a theory of how the labour market is divided by education, skill, sex and gender, see David M. Gordon, Richard Edwards and Michael Reich, *Segmented Work, Divided Workers: The Historical Transformation of Labor in the United States* (Cambridge, 1982).

7 For an example of how white workers systematically and sometimes violently excluded blacks from certain jobs on the railways see Eric Arnesen, '"Like Banquo's Ghost, It will Not Down": The Race Question and the American Railroad Brotherhoods, 1880–1920', *The American Historical Review* 99 (December 1994), 1601–33.

8 W.E.B. Du Bois traced the origins of the 'psychological' wage back to the ante-bellum period when Northern capitalists and Southern planters successfully obscured the almost 'identical' interests of white and black workers with appeals to racial solidarity and threats of job competition. Du Bois argued that employers maintained low wages for white workers by 'compensating' them with 'public deference and titles of courtesy because they were white'. Du Bois, *Black Reconstruction in America, 1860–1880* (New York, 1935), 3–31, 700–1. Roediger, drawing on this work, concluded that white workers receive an economic wage (higher pay) and a 'psychological' wage (social status and social gains). See Roediger, *Wages of Whiteness*, 10–13. For a more thorough explanation of how economic wages are realized not only in pay but in housing, transportation and education, see Steven Shulman, 'Racism and the Making of the American Working Class', *International Journal of Politics, Culture and Society* 2 (Spring 1989), 361–6; Karen Brodkin Sacks, 'How Did Jews

Become White Folks?', in *Race*, ed. Steven Gregory and Roger Sanjek (New Brunswick, 1994), 78–102; George Lipsitz, 'The Possessive Investment in Whiteness: Racialized Social Democracy and the "White" Problem in American Studies', *American Quarterly* 47 (September 1995), 369–87; and Noel Ignatiev, *How the Irish Became White* (New York and London, 1995).

9  Roediger states that 'working class whiteness ... [is] a gendered phenomenon, particularly expressing and repressing male longings and the perils and pride of republican citizenship among *men* [my emphasis].' *Wages of Whiteness*, 11. In his most recent book, he calls for the inclusion of women in the analysis of whiteness but his focus remains centred on men. See David R. Roediger, *Towards the Abolition of Whiteness: Essays on Race, Politics, and Working Class History* (London and New York, 1994).

10 See Bederman, *Manliness and Civilization* and Ruth Frankenberg, *White Women, Race Matters: The Social Construction of Whiteness* (Minneapolis, 1993) for white middle/upper-class women's participation in the construction of whiteness. Working women's history also requires a different periodization from middle/upper-class women and male workers.

11 This is not to imply that telephone operators did not join unions or participate in strikes and other forms of dissent. The 'white lady' identity helped to determine the issues over which operators would protest. For telephone operator militancy, see Stephen H. Norwood, *Labor's Flaming Youth: Telephone Operators and Worker Militancy, 1878–1923* (Urbana, Ill., 1990); and Venus Green, 'The Impact of Technology Upon Women's Work in the Telephone Industry, 1880–1980' (PhD dissertation, Columbia University, 1990).

12 John J. Carty quoted by R.T. Barrett in Cecil W. MacKenzie, 'Early Days of Telephone in Buffalo, 1878–1926,' typescript, p. 29, AT&T Archives, box 1127.

13 Katherine M. Schmitt, 'I Was Your Old "Hello" Girl', *The Saturday Evening Post* 12 (July 1930), 121.

14 For the feminization of telephone operating as a method of winning over subscribers, see Green, 'The Impact of Technology Upon Women's Work in the Telephone Industry'. Studies of telephone operators and unionism include: Maurine Weiner Greenwald, *Women, War, and Work: The Impact of World War I on Women Workers in the United States* (Westport, Conn., 1980); Norwood, *Labor's Flaming Youth*, for the United States; Michele Martin, *'Hello Central?' Gender, Technology, and Culture in the Formation of Telephone Systems* (Montreal, 1990) for Canada; and Alan Clinton, *Post Office Workers: A Trade Union and Social History* (London, 1984) for England.

15 B.E. Sunny at the 1887 Switchboard Conference, p. 207, Proceedings found in AT&T Archives.

16 Nathaniel W. Lillie, 'Reminiscences of the Telephone in Boston, 1877–1914', typescript, p. 32, AT&T Archives, box 1116.

17 National Convention of Telephone Companies held at Niagara Falls, NY, 7–9 September 1880. Record of the Organization and first Meeting of the National Telephone Exchange Association (hereafter the proceedings of the meetings of this group referred to as NTEA). Report by Henry W. Pope,

General Superintendent, Metropolitan Telephone and Telegraph Company, p. 160, AT&T Archives.

18  Frank Rozzelle quoted in Fred DeLand, 'Telephone History, 1877–1908', Volume I, Book III, typescript, p. 4, AT&T Archives, box 1109.

19  Delaware and Atlantic Telegraph and Telephone Company, ' Rules and Regulations, 1890', p. 6, AT&T Archives, box 1028.

20  F.H. Bethel, Vice President, New York Telephone Company, Transcript of an address before the Albany Chamber of Commerce, 22 March 1915, *Telephone Review* 6 (April 1915), 134.

21  In 1900, 93.7 per cent of the 21,980 telegraph and telephone operators were native-born white women whose parents were either both native-born (54.6 per cent) or one or both parents were foreign-born (39.1 per cent). Over two-thirds (71.7 per cent) of them were between 16 and 24 years old. Another 22.2 per cent were between 25 and 34 years of age. US Bureau of the Census, *Statistics of Women at Work* (Washington, DC, 1907), 34, 168.

22  H.D. McBride, Superintendent of Traffic, Boston Massachusetts, 'Selection and Training of Operators', paper delivered at the 1905 Traffic Conference, 41, Proceedings found in AT&T Archives.

23  Under extremely rare conditions blacks worked in isolated circumstances in non-custodial positions. For example, Charles L. Smith, a black man and President Vail's protégé, was hired in the late 1880s and worked as the receptionist for the executive offices in Boston for over twenty years. See Joseph A. Gately, 'Telephone Reminiscences', 1939, pp. 20, 59, AT&T Archives, box 1013.

24  A good English speaking voice and enunciation epitomized Bell System operator qualifications. During the application process, the interviewer had to determine the applicant's desirability based upon 'clear and agreeable tone of voice, distinct enunciation, abruptness or impertinence in manner of speaking [or] foreign accent'. McBride quoted at the 1905 Traffic Conference, p. 41.

25  Norwood, *Labor's Flaming Youth*, 42. Incorrectly, Norwood asserts that 'not a single black was employed in the entire Bell System in any capacity higher than that of janitor until the late 1930s'.

26  W.F. Cozad, Superintendent of Traffic in the Colorado Telephone Company made a trip east in 1904 and kept a journal of his impressions of each large city. He observed in New York City 'a goodly number' of foreign born operators. W.F. Cozad, 'Notes on a Trip East', 1904, p. 55, AT&T Archives, box 1044.

27  There is a picture of a black operator in Pittsburgh dated 1891 in the AT&T Archives and the 1900 census lists eleven 'Negro' telephone and telegraph operators, a decrease from 56 listed in 1890. It is probable that these 'Negro' telephone and telegraph operators worked for the Independents. Black telephone operators could also have been working in black firms as PBX operators. US Department of Commerce and Labor, Bureau of the Census, *Statistics of Women at Work*, 158, 159.

28  US Congress. Senate. *Investigation of Telephone Companies*. S. Doc. 380, 61st Congress, 2nd session, 1910, p. 20. The largest groups of women rejected included those who were too small (544), too old (53), too young

(436), insufficient education (519) and poor appearance (169). Doctors only refused one for hearing but excluded 151 for poor sight and 43 for physical defects. Six applicants refused vaccination, 82 had poor voices, seven refused night work, 36 were not willing to wait and 74 others were rejected for miscellaneous reasons.

29  Miss Schmitt opened the New York Operator's School on 13 January 1902 and other large city exchanges soon copied its structure and methods. Katherine M. Schmitt, 'I Was Your Old "Hello" Girl', 121.

30  See Bethell, Transcript of an address before the Albany Chamber of Commerce, 22 March 1915, 134.

31  *The Telephone Review* 4 (April 1911), Cover; and *The Telephone Review* 10–11 (October/November, 1911), Cover.

32  *The Boston Post*, quoted in Norwood, 112.

33  *The Boston Globe*, quoted in Norwood, 112.

34  John J. Carty to President Thayer, 1 March 1909, AT&T Archives, box 1357.

35  Elizabeth Beardsley Butler, *Women and the Trades, Pittsburgh, 1907–1908* (New York, 1909), 285.

36  J.D. Ellsworth detailed the reasons for establishing an Employee Benefit Plan:

> ... for business reasons, viz.:- because some provision for employes [*sic*] is the logical concomitant of a functional organization and increasing specialization [*sic*]; because provision for employes [*sic*] makes it easier to maintain freedom from Labor Unions; because of the increased efficiency which may be expected, because it would help secure the right sort of advertising from our 100,000 employes [*sic*]. (J. D. Ellsworth to Theodore Vail, 6 April 1910, AT&T Archives, box 47)

37  'Rest Room – 195 Broadway Building', an announcement issued 1 November 1916, AT&T Archives, box 2019.

38  F.H. Bethell, Transcript of an address before the Albany Chamber of Commerce, 22 March 1915, 134.

39  Due to high turnover, the majority of operators rarely met the seniority requirements to reach the top of the wage progression schedule (5–7 years) or to receive sickness/disability benefits (at least two years). Operators who averaged $30 monthly, would not remain with the company simply to be able to purchase a $110 share of stock at a contribution limited to $2 monthly or to receive a pension after 25 years at a fixed salary.

40  See Norwood, *Labor's Flaming Youth* for a history of the Telephone Operators' Union.

41  'Constitution of Association of Employees', Long Lines Department, American Telephone and Telegraph Company, p. 6, AT&T Archives, box 6.

42  This clause acknowledged the need to assert racial exclusivity at a time when there were no black operators in the Bell System. However, black women were demanding access to these jobs, especially in New York City.

43  The plans incorporated and re-enforced patronizing, sexist and condescending myths about women. Referring to the complexity of the female

employment problem, one manager stated that in addition to their youth, these women were 'subject to all the peculiarities, both mental and physical, that are characteristic of the sex'. For him 'Temperament [was] one of the chief heritages of the Traffic Department.' A.C. Stannard, 'Personnel Work in the Traffic Department of the Southwestern Bell Telephone Company', a paper delivered at the Personnel Conference, October 1923, 3–4. Proceedings found in AT&T Archives.

44 *Ibid.*

45 For example, operators in Boston resisted 'employee associations' until 1923 when they were defeated in a strike in which New England Telephone and Telegraphy Company had the full support of AT&T.

46 Vernal Black, 'What I Did Today', quoted in A. C. Stannard, 'Personnel Work in the Traffic Department of the Southwestern Bell Telephone Company', paper delivered at the Personnel Conference, October 1923, 45–6.

47 See, 'The Minstrelettes at the Richmond Hill, Virginia and Cleveland Central Office Party', *The Telephone Review* 3 (March 1928), 97; '"Gentlemen ... Be Seated!"', *The Telephone Review* 4 (April 1949), 4–5; and 'Sorry, Wrong Number', *The Telephone Review* 11 (November 1949), 20–1. Male performances and demeaning images of African Americans can also be found in *The Western Electric News*, the *Bell Laboratories Record* and other Bell System journals. See 'We Ask to Know', *Western Electric News* 13 (February, 1925), 1; and 'Deal-Holmdel Party', *Bell Laboratories Record* 27 (July, 1949), 280. See also American Telephone and Telegraph Company, 'Fun 'N' Games: AT&T International Quiz', *Focus* (September 1993).

48 'Would Be Minstrels' Amuse Buffalo Toll Party-Goers', *The Telephone Review* 1 (January 1939), 21.

49 'Sodus Minstrels', *The Telephone Review* 9 (September, 1955), 17.

50 One does wonder what these representations meant to these women in light of Eric Lott's suggestion that white male minstrels were 'inhabiting ... black bodies as a way of interracial male-bonding'; or David R. Roediger's notion that 'white crowds repeatedly colored *themselves*, replacing excluded Blacks from within their own ranks'. Roediger also postulates that 'the *content* of blackface performances identifies their particular appeals as expressions of the longings and fears and the hopes and prejudices of the Northern Jacksonian urban working class, especially the artisanate.' See Eric Lott, 'White Like Me: Racial Cross-Dressing and the Construction of American Whiteness', in Amy Kaplan and Donald E. Pease, eds., *Cultures of United States Imperialism* (Durham, NC, 1993), 475; and Roediger, *Wages of Whiteness* 104, 115.

51 'Phone Co. Won't Hire Negroes to Meet Shortage', *New York Call* (March 1920), 2.

52 Quoted in article 'Phone Co., Won't Hire Negroes to Meet Shortage', *New York Call* (March 1920), 2.

53 *Ibid.*

54 George S. Schuyler, 'Negro Labor and Public Utilities', *The Messenger* (January 1927), 4.

55 *Ibid.*

56 The Mayor's Commission on Conditions in Harlem, 'The Negro in Harlem: A Report on Social and Economic Conditions Responsible for the Outbreak of March 19, 1935' (New York, 1936), 24.

57 New York State Temporary Commission on the Condition of the Urban Colored Population, 'Report to the Legislature of the State of New York'. (New York, 1937), 64.

58 New York State Temporary Commission on the Condition of the Urban Colored Population, Public Hearings, 1937. See for example the testimonies of Walter D. Williams, General Traffic Manager, New York Telephone Company, New York City and Peter D. Lowrie, Auditor of the Bronx–Westchester area, New York Telephone Company, Bronx, New York.

59 *Ibid.*, 1512–15.

60 *Ibid.*, 1514.

61 *Ibid.*, 1522.

62 The FEPC received complaints against Bell System companies including New Jersey Bell Telephone Company (Atlantic City), Pittsburgh Telephone Company, Chesapeake and Potomac (Baltimore), Ohio Bell (Columbus, Ohio), Southern Bell Telephone Company (Louisville, Kentucky), The Southwestern Bell Telephone Company (St. Louis, New Orleans), Southern California Telephone (San Diego, Los Angeles), Pacific Telephone and Telegraph Company (San Francisco and Palo Alto, California and Spokane, Washington).

63 These positions were occupied by women in the Traffic, Accounting and Commercial Departments. Black men were usually hired in the Plant Department 'as garage men, clerks, elevators operators, janitors, porters, cleaners, and floor men'. Edward Lawson to Will Maslow, Director of Field Operations, 17 October 1944, 4, National Archives, Record Group 228, Entry 8, box 71. However, the lifting of the colour bar in these low-level positions did not represent a true widening of opportunity in a large number of jobs. Telephone operators numbered over half of the 750,000 Bell System employees in 1944.

64 *Ibid.*, 2.

65 *Ibid.*, 4.

66 *Ibid.*

67 *Ibid.*, 5. This agreement was allegedly between Stanley Isaacs, Adam Powell, Charles Collier, Benjamin Barnett and the company. FEPC investigators checked with each and reported that 'all four of these persons vehemently denied that they had given their approval to any such plan'.

68 *Ibid.*

69 *Ibid.*

70 Membership qualifications for telephone workers' organizations changed over time. In most cases, company unions explicitly limited membership to whites. After the creation of independent unions and the formation of the Federation of Telephone Workers (NFTW, 1937–39), local affiliates determined their own membership qualifications. I found no anti-discrimination clauses in any of their constitutions. When the Communication Workers of America formed (1946–47) there was an antidiscrimination clause in their constitution from the beginning.

71 *FTWP News*, 'Resolution No. 1 FAIR EMPLOYMENT PRACTICE COMMIT-
   TEE', February 1945, 4.
72 Evelyn N. Cooper to Committee Members, Confidential Memorandum, 7
   March 1945, 2. National Archives, Record Group 228, Entry 25, Box 94.
73 George M. Johnson, Deputy Chairman and Acting Chief of Legal Division
   to Clarence M. Mitchell, Associate Director of Field Operations, 8 March
   1945, National Archives, Record Group 228, Entry 25, Box 94.
74 In this period of American hate strikes, white male telephone workers at
   the Western Electric Point Breeze manufacturing plant outside of
   Baltimore, Maryland, stopped working when the company refused to
   provide separate toilet facilities for black and white workers. When war
   production was affected by the strike the US Army seized control of the
   plant, ended the strike and defeated the demand for separate facilities.
   John N. Schacht, *The Making of Telephone Unionism, 1920–1947* (New
   Brunswick, New Jersey, 1985), 114–15.
75 Evelyn N. Cooper to Committee Members, Confidential Memorandum, 7
   March 1945, 2. National Archives, Record Group 228, Entry 25, Box 94.
76 The significance of compensatory social status is highlighted when we
   realize that many of the Catholics who objected to integration were probably the nativeborn children of white ethnic groups (immigrants) who
   could now enjoy the privileges of whiteness. By the Second World War,
   social and political conditions had changed to the point that religion
   (Protestant, Catholic, Jew) and ethnicity (Jew, Italian, Irish, etc.,) were
   subordinate to whiteness.
77 National Urban League, Department of Industrial Relations, '"Number
   Please?": Employment of Negro Workers in the Telephone Industry in 44
   Cities' (New York, 1946), 1–2. The cities covered the entire United States
   and included Boston, Atlanta, Detroit, Chicago, Little Rock, Memphis,
   Minneapolis, Newark, New Orleans, New York City, Philadelphia,
   Omaha, Portland, Oregon, and Seattle, Washington.
78 *Ibid.*, 5.
79 Bernard E. Anderson, 'Equal Opportunity and Black Employment in the
   Telephone Industry', in *Equal Employment Opportunity and the AT&T Case*,
   ed. Phyllis A. Wallace (Cambridge, Mass., 1976), 183.
80 The Bell System hired 53,903 black employees between 1965 and 1971
   while the entire industry had only hired 54,000 between 1950 and 1960.
   *Ibid.*, 189–90. These black operators were concentrated in New York,
   Chicago, Newark, Washington, DC, Cleveland, Los Angeles, Philadelphia,
   Detroit and San Francisco.
81 Black people began protesting against Bell System discrimination in the
   1920s. Afterwards, they participated in boycotts, all-night vigils, mass bill
   pay-ins (sometimes in pennies), mass phone-ins to tie up the equipment,
   applying protest stickers to phone bills, demonstrations and legal
   complaints (filed with the FEPC and the EEOC). For examples, see the
   March on Washington Press Releases and newspaper clippings *The St.
   Louis American*, 27 May 1943, 17 June 1943, 5 August 1943, 2 and 16
   September 1943; *The Chicago Defender*, 19 June 1943, 25 September 1943;
   *The St. Louis Argus*, 28 May 1943, 2 June 1943, 6 August 1943; *The
   Pittsburgh Courier*, 5 and 26 June 1943) in the Brotherhood of Sleeping Car

Porters Scrapbook located in the Chicago Historical Society. Complaints to the FEPC (Record Group 228) and the EEOC (Record Group 403) can be found in the National Archives.

82 David Copus, Lawrence Gartner, Randall Speck, William Wallace, Marjanette Feagan and Katherine Mazzaferri. 'A Unique Competence: A Study of Equal Employment Opportunity in the Bell System', 183–4. A paper written in 1971 by the lawyers who participated in the Equal Employment Commission investigation into the employment practices of the Bell System operating companies. Submitted as 'EEOC Prehearing Analysis and Summary of Evidence' before the Federal Communications Commission.

83 Copus et al., 236.

84 Copus et al., 242.

85 A look at their record during the 1960s is illustrative:

'In the entire state of Mississippi, Southern Bell employed no blacks in any entry level job above service worker or laborer until June, 1965. In New Orleans, Southern Bell hired its first black above service worker or laborer in November, 1963, and its first black Operator one year later. The Company hired its first black Operator in Florida in March, 1964; and in South Carolina in July, 1964. Southwestern Bell hired its first black Operator anywhere in Kansas in 1963. The first black Installer employed in Kansas was hired in June, 1969. No black above service worker or laborer was hired in Arkansas until 1964. The first black Operator in Oklahoma was hired in March, 1964. (*ibid.*, 195)

86 D.C. Emerson, Vice-President, American Telephone and Telegraph Company to Bernard Strassburg, Chief, Common Carrier Bureau, Federal Communications Commission, 9 December 1969, 4. National Archives, Record Group 403, Box 35. Southern Bell became two companies in 1968 after white women and black women and men had filed hundreds of discrimination complaints against Southern Bell. Lawyers for the National Organization of Women believed that this was a tactic to frustrate the EEOC investigations.

87 See the interviewers' reports in the National Archives, Record Group 403, Box 35.

88 W.R. Carter, Vice-President, South Central Bell to Vice-President (Louisiana), Vice-President and General Managers, 20 May 1969. National Archives, Record Group 403, FCC Staff Exhibit 48, Box 16.

89 EEOC, Report, 'EEOC Compliance Experience with Southern, Southwestern and Pacific Bell,' typescript, no date, 4. National Archives, Record Group 403, Box 37.

90 W.R. Carter, Vice-President, South Central Bell to Vice-President (Louisiana), Vice-President and General Managers, 20 May 1969. National Archives, Record Group 403, FCC Staff Exhibit 48, Box 16.

91 For example, during an eleven-month period in Chicago, '71.3% of all Operators hired were black', and within three months in 1970 92.2% of the operators hired in Washington, D.C. were black. Copus et al., 258.

92 Black women hired into the Bell System during the late 1960s momentarily reversed the decline in operators due to the introduction of

automatic dialling equipment. In 1970, the Bell System operating forces had increased to 165,628 from 139,347 in 1963. Due to the rapid introduction of computerized machinery after 1970, the number of operators declined to 88,599 in 1981. See Venus Green, 'Race and Technology: African American Women in the Bell System, 1945–1980', *Technology and Culture* supplement to Vol. 36 (April 1995), S101–S143. Instead of US Census figures which include operators from independent companies, these figures are taken from: American Telephone and Telegraph Company, 'Bell System Statistical Manual, 1920–1964' (New York, 1965), 708; and 'Bell System Statistical Manual, 1950–1981' (New York, 1982), 705.

93  Copus et al., 239.
94  For the Communications Workers of America (CWA) challenges to the EEOC Consent Decrees signed in 1971 see Phyllis A. Wallace, 'The Consent Decrees', in *Equal Employment Opportunity and the AT&T Case*, 276.
95  EEOC, NA box 109, Case File No. 9-0220 dated 19 March 1969. Sex discrimination charges included failure to represent, unequal pay schedules, unequal job classifications based on sex and that the Union upheld State Female Hour Laws in states where such laws applied. Hundreds of the charges are dispersed throughout these records but boxes 82–4 and 107–11 contain most of them.
96  Lavie Bolick, Assistant to vice-president of District 3, CWA. Interviewed by John Schacht at District 3 Headquarters, Atlanta, Georgia, 17 February 1970. Oral History Project, CWA Archives, Washington, DC, 34 (Hereafter OHP, CWA Archives).
97  Martha Moudy, CWA Representative in District 3. Interviewed by John Schacht at District 3 Headquarters, Atlanta, Georgia, 17 February 1970. OHP, CWA Archives, 16.
98  Lessie Sanders interviewed by Venus Green (telephone) on 14 October 1989, New York City.
99  *Ibid.*
100 Scott Stephens, Retired International Representative, CWA. Interviewed by John Schacht at Stephen's home in Anna Maria, Florida, 23 February 1970. OHP, CWA Archives, Washington, DC, 16.
101 Alice Kessler Harris, *Out to Work* (New York, 1982), 148.
102 For white women, the loss of jobs was due to the introduction of automatic dialling from the 1920s through to the 1960s. Black women lost jobs after the 1960s as a result of the introduction of computerized call processing machines.

# 4
## The Elusive Irishman: Ethnicity and the Postwar World of New York City and London Dockers

*Colin J. Davis*

Patrick Hanshaw, a long-time London resident in the dock area of Wapping, writes in his autobiography, 'Your average docker was a born punter [gambler]', and during the 1940s the 'Irish trait of being willing to bet on two flies crawling up or down a wall still held good with Wapping's dockers'.[1] Such a statement illuminates the continuing residue of an Irish inclination among London's dockers. A form of Irish identity was also evident along the waterfront communities of the west-side of Manhattan during the same period where Irish-Americans dominated the docks and the representative trade union. To a large extent the Irish influence in New York City was even greater. As one-time longshoreman Larry Sullivan explained, 'The dock gangs were mostly all Irish'.[2] Hanshaw's more ambiguous use of the term 'Irish trait' to define the existence of Wapping dockers, compared to Sullivan's description of west side longshoremen as 'Irish', conjures up a series of questions enveloping self-definition of ethnicity and the role assimilation has played in loosening the ethnic cord.

What explains such lingering notions of Irish identity among London dockers in the late 1940s, while in New York City it remained a strong and vibrant part of self-definition? The purpose of this essay is to arrive at an answer for the differing conceptions of ethnicity. My contention is that continuing ethnic and racial division in the United States labour force encouraged the New York Irish longshoremen to retain a defensive form of ethnic identity, thereby holding on to lucrative dock jobs and trade union offices. The London Irish dockers, on the other hand, had virtually been assimilated into the English working-class by the late 1940s. Their jobs, however, still imbued London dockers with a sense of separateness from surrounding working-class communities, creating a form of town or almost village perspective on life.

An examination of Irish-American longshoremen and London Irish dockers comes at a most exciting time. The dynamic of ethnicity is a topic that has long attracted the attention of social, urban and labour historians, and recently it has been energized by new approaches that utilize notions of social construction and group interdependence. The debate concerning ethnic identity and assimilation has been framed, in the observation of Russell A. Kazal, by three groups in the United States. These are 'scholars of ethnicity', 'of racial identity' and 'labor historians'.[3] John Bodnar is a representative historian of ethnic identity, whose work has focused on eastern European immigrants. For Bodnar, such immigrants had a dual 'desire to become American' while at the same time retaining an ethnic self. Bodnar, however, confined his study to the turn of the twentieth-century experience.[4] Labour historians recently have attempted to drive the story forward to the Second World War. James Barrett, Lizabeth Cohen and Gary Gerstle have argued that the American labour movement and the national state during the 1930s began to break down ethnic identity and replaced it with a more class-based, inter-ethnic assimilation.[5] David Roediger's work on the Irish in America moved the discussion beyond nationhood to one of 'whiteness'. In his study, *The Wages of Whiteness*, Roediger argues that Irish-Americans' yearning for social acceptance encouraged them 'to equate whiteness with Americanism', thus allowing them to separate from African-Americans, while simultaneously joining white America.[6] Theodore Allen parallels Roediger in his argument regarding the construction of race. Allen argues the 'white race' is an 'invention' conceived by 'emigrant population[s]' to ensure acceptance into the host society.[7]

Moving beyond the definition of race based primarily on skin colour, these scholars have voiced a more concrete identification grounded in the construction of race. Although providing a more sophisticated appraisal of identity, one of the major criticisms levelled at Roediger et al. is that their studies are statically imbedded in the nineteenth century leaving the postwar period relatively unploughed.[8] Studies of London dockers with an Irish heritage also tend to concentrate on the mid- and late nineteenth-century. Many of the studies are framed by a colonial or imperial backdrop, wherein the Irish either segregate themselves or were segregated from the larger English working-class culture. As Lynn Hollen Lees argues, 'They lived close to the English, but they remained apart ... Although neighborhoods were shared, neither geographic nor social assimilation took place.'[9] Such a view of Irish settlement has recently come under attack. David Fitzpatrick, for example, forcefully argues that the Irish in Britain were not a monolithic group but rather created three forms of identity: one a replanted Irish identity, another a more 'hybrid immigrant culture', and a third, which chose to move away or 'forget' that they were Irish.[10]

These authors, although providing insightful discussion, do not necessarily 'bring in' the notion of construction. Laura Tabili's work, building on that of Paul Gilroy, Eric Hobsbawm, Terence Ranger and others, highlights how ethnicity is not only constructed by subjects and societies alike, but also is in a state of continual flux.[11] Just as important, the experience of the London dockers highlights how identity can also be discarded. Fixation on 'construction', then, is only half the story. Only through a rigorous appraisal of what it meant to be 'Irish' and how it transformed over time can a more intricate and complete picture be obtained. For this essay the necessary quantitative research has not been done to provide such a 'complete picture'. None the less, its purpose is to suggest how ethnicity among New York and London dock workers underwent transformation before, and particularly after, the Second World War.

None of the above studies has used the comparative method to investigate the changing nature of ethnic identification. Generally, one specific national group is examined and held up as the mirror of the lived experience. The comparative approach can bring in a more fine-tuned assessment of time and space, and the structural and cultural determinants of human behaviour. The advantages of the comparative method is that it can provide connections and disconti-nuities, ushering in a more complex evaluation of ethnicity. As Theda Skocpol has argued, historical sociologists have long used the compar-ative method 'for the specific purpose of highlighting the particular features of each individual case'.[12] Hopefully such cross-fertilization can provide important insights into the connectedness across time and space of ethnic and class identification. By comparing two groups of workers who share an ancestral path, that is, New York Irish long-shoremen and London Irish dockers, a more complete examination of ethnicity framed by work can be achieved. Comparative history can allow us to ask questions as much about silences as about the more visible self-definitions of ethnic identity. In addition, the unique qual-ities of each case can be judged by comparing the sociopolitical conditions in which dockers laboured. Though having much in common with their respective Irish pasts, by the postwar period they had undergone significant transformations. While the New York long-shoremen's Irish identity continued to be plainly visible, London dockers diverged dramatically in their self-definition.

## London

Both groups entered dock work at approximately the same time during the mid-nineteenth century. The Irish famine certainly was a defining moment for both groups, leading to emigration to their respective cities. Also unifying the two groups was the region or counties of Irish origin. The Irish who emigrated to London were predominately from Munster and the counties of Cork and Kerry. By 1861, 107,000 had moved to London, creating an Irish community of 178,000, 'the largest settlement in Great Britain'.[13] Pre- and post-famine migration patterns also need evaluation. Certainly more research is required on these respective movements into the dock areas of London.[14] Most of the migrants in London moved into cheap lodgings, generally in communities bordering the River Thames. Because of this riverside settlement and their rural status, men were attracted to the casual labour of dock work. Employers also came to prefer Irish labourers because of their tendency to accept hard work and low wages. As one employer remarked, 'without the aid of the Irish ... the business of the docks would be seriously impeded'.[15]

By the end of the nineteenth century, what is certain is that dockers with an 'Irish' heritage dominated the dock trades. Nurturing such authority were familial relationships. London-Irish dockers commonly brought their sons into the trade. Thus a continuum was established whereby the Irish dominated the work and thereby the union. This was particularly true of the Stevedores Union. Stevedores ranked themselves as the more skilled of the waterfront workers because they loaded cargo, a more practically skilled job. Hoping to dominate such work, the Irish created what John Lovell has termed a 'close hereditary corporation'.[16] This command of dock work and the union was particularly evident in the 1889 'docker's tanner' strike. Ben Tillett, the strike leader, was the son of Irish immigrants, while James Tooney, who was born in Ireland, was President of the Strike Committee.[17] Another important example of the overwhelming Irish influence was that it was Cardinal Manning who helped settle the strike, while Protestant clergy stood indifferently on the sidelines. According to Gareth Stedman Jones, even following the success of the

1889 strike, 'casual workers ... of Irish extraction' listened more to the 'homilies of Cardinal Manning than to the torrent of speeches from the Social Democratic Federation'. The dockers thus accepted leaders such as Tillett 'not because of their socialism but in spite of it'.[18]

Placing Catholicism as the primary identifier, however, does not fully recognize the complexity of Irish and British-Irish identity. To emphasize Catholicism over class and ethnicity betrays a simplistic notion of lived experience. In his recent study on the Manchester Irish, Steven Fielding argues that the migrants and the generations that followed were 'neither simply Irish, Catholic, or working class, but an amalgam of all three'.[19] Although Fielding's appraisal may hold true for the late nineteenth and early twentieth centuries, following the Second World War, class appears to have taken the upper hand among London dockers. Additionally, in identifying the amalgam, most authors have examined only northern cities where the sectarian divide was more in evidence. As Sam Davies has found in Liverpool, attachment to religion rather than social democratic principles was more prevalent.[20]

But this allegiance to the Church was being broken down by the end of the First World War. Many Irish customs were being adapted to suit a more anglicized context. The English Roman Catholic Church did much to transform the more Irish Catholicism of Celtic magic and religion. The Irish language was also subsumed, but the wake did transfer to England and was the 'one major folk ceremony brought to London'. Yet by the end of the 1940s even this ritual had undergone change in London's East End. According to Patrick Hanshaw, 'The deceased still lies at home in state for at least four or five days. ... However, the body is always segregated in another room, so if there are those who are a little bit squeamish or nervous at looking at a dead body, they don't have to.'[21] The wake was also a site where Irish identity was reaffirmed through song. Stevedore John Donovan related how as a child in the early 1920s his father would sing. 'Dear Homeland, Far across the Sea, Do They Wonder if I'm at Peace, Do They Think of Me?' According to Donovan a melancholic atmosphere prevailed following the singing of the song. Only after his mother punched some of the mourners in the arm and began singing, 'Lets all be happy again ... and battle our cares away' did the sad interlude pass. Interestingly, Irish-Americans also sang songs at wakes that mixed 'sorrow and hilarity'. Although Irish-American wakes included singing, dancing and drinking, in London during the 1940s such frivolity had fallen out of favour. According to Patrick Hanshaw when the wake of his grandmother became rather rowdy with singing and playing of musical instruments, his Aunt Noah yelled, 'Shut that f***ing racket down. And if you don't piss off out of this flat in the next few minutes, you will be wearing that f***ing accordion like a dog collar.' This exchange, according to Hanshaw, 'was a marked division between the old and new', that is, his grandmother's generation as opposed to that of his aunt.[22]

Increasingly during the end of the nineteenth century, the Irish identity of dockers was being undermined by their allegiance to the trade union, the National Transport Workers' Federation and the Labour Party. Although Irish Nationalists tried to instill a feeling of Irishness, creating such organizations as the Gaelic League, London dockers of Irish descent looked more to their union and the burgeoning Labour Party as their representative economic and political organizations. As Lynn Hollen Lees argues, 'Occupational loyalties helped to break down ethnic separatism.' This was particularly evident in the 1920s once the partition of Ireland had occurred. Correspondingly, according to David Fitzpatrick, 'Irish Nationality would never again be the focus of political activity for Britain's Irish population.'[23] Additionally, economic expansion discouraged much of the earlier anti-Irish violence. As Roger Swift has argued, by the late nineteenth century 'economic growth ... may have helped to reduce ethnic rivalries'.[24]

London's dockers of Irish descent increasingly identified with their occupational and English class. John Donovan's generation perceived themselves therefore as members of the London working class. As he pointed out, we were 'just Londoners'. Unlike in the segregated Liverpool docks, the work gangs in the 1940s were also mixed. That is, not only with dockers of English and Irish heritage, but there were 'no Catholic or Protestant gangs', according to Donovan.[25] This was also attested to by dockers of non-Irish ancestry. Joe Bloomberg, who worked in the docks in the 1940s up until the 1960s, explained, 'you had the [Irish] names' but the gangs were 'all mixed'. As he explained, dockers of Irish descent 'thought no more about the Irish [than the Irish] thought about them'. It was residential and class quality that brought the dockers together. As Joe Bloomberg pointed out, 'We were all brought up together ... it was Wapping or Stepney ... and it was what you'd done during that time' that provided character or identity.[26]

By the end of the Second World War a dramatic transformation had taken place among East London docker communities. Although retaining a Catholic identity, their Irishness was fast disappearing. The generation that had grown up in the 1920s and 1930s, although cognisant of their Irish past, regarded themselves as Londoners. To be more exact, when asked for their identification they invariably described themselves as 'Eastenders' or even more specific, as from 'Wapping' or the 'Island' (Isle of Dogs). Like other Londoners, they defined themselves by the borough or even neighbourhood in which they lived. There continued a sense of being apart, but it was not necessarily one based on ethnicity but class. By the late 1940s it was dock work that separated dockers from other working-class neigh-bourhoods. As one stevedore from the Isle of Dogs remarked, 'we were different ... a clannish big family ... couldn't talk about anybody at a bus stop' for fear of being overheard. This sense of being apart was reaffirmed when on many occasions bus conductors refused entry to dockers returning from work because of their dirty, and at times foul-smelling, clothes.[27]

It would be wrong, however, to suggest that all traces of Irish iden-tity had disappeared. For some in the East End there still remained a sentimental or strong imaginative vision of their Irish past. An ideal-ized image was (and is) conjured up to describe or validate certain behaviours or outlook. Ted Johns, who worked as a waterman along the docks, claimed his militancy in the union and community was tied to his 'Celtic background', although he was third-generation London-Irish. Just like the Irish, according to Johns, London dockers were regarded by employers as 'expendable', and when British troops unloaded cargo during postwar strikes the army was perceived as 'an occupying power'. But although there was evidently 'a strong sense, not of Irishness, but Irish influence', according to Johns the 'class issue overlaid everything else'. It was a powerful class issue of us against them. As Johns explained, it was like the 'attitude that all coppers are bastards ... same in the dock industry all employers are bastards'.[28]

Patrick Hanshaw, the son of a docker and also third generation London Irish, echoed Ted Johns in his sentimental attachment to Irishness, while at the same time voicing an overarching class appraisal of dockers' lives. In his autobiography, *Nothing is Forever: Growing up in Wapping in the Post-war Years*, Hanshaw highlights his sentimental veneration by explaining, 'I am true to my Irish ancestry and tend to be a dreamer, going off at tangents into things that happened in other times and places.' After spelling out his formative years and the continuing Irish influence of song and religion, just like

Bloomberg, Hanshaw pinpoints the village quality of Wapping. Comparing his area to that of neighbouring Shadwell, he relates a common ditty of the time, 'Wapping for wit, Shadwell for shit.' Again, it is not that Wapping is any more Irish than Shadwell, rather, Hanshaw is reflecting a common cockney parochial sense of place. As with Ted Johns, the enemy is not English culture or other working class neighbourhoods *per se*, but employers. As Hanshaw explains it, the docker was at 'constant war against the "guvnor" ... To the "guvnor", the docker was just one in a sea of faces ... Somebody to be used and discarded when he had outlived his usefulness. Attitudes that had developed over a period of generations would never die ... For the docker, the guvnor was the only opponent. He had to be engaged in mortal combat every working day.'[29]

## New York

The Irish who settled in New York also came to dominate the dock or longshore industry. Like London, the migrants originated from the Munster counties of Cork and Kerry. They clustered in Manhattan, although in Brooklyn the migrants were from Donegal and Mayo.[30] As with the London Irish, the New York Irish worked where they lived. Along the west side of Manhattan the Irish congregated in specific neighbourhoods including Chelsea and Hells Kitchen. As Cal Winslow argues, 'The Irish lived there, cramped in between streets and ware-houses, in neighbourhoods known for big families and saloons.'[31] Until the early 1890s the Irish were by far the predominant group on the New York waterfront. After a series of strikes when employers brought in Italian and African-American strikebreakers, Irish control of the docks was first challenged. The Irish longshoremen tried to counter the increasing numbers of Italians and blacks by refusing to work on the same ships. In his 1912 study, Charles Barnes related incidents when 'If a gang of "Ginnies", or "Dagoes", as they were called was put in the hold with the Irish, the latter would quit.'[32] Such tactics, however, failed and soon Italians came to control the dirtier jobs of handling coal, and the piers in Brooklyn.

   Although unable to stop the rapid influx of Italians and other ethnic groups, the Irish reserved for themselves the better jobs in and around the docks. By the turn of the century, Irish-Americans controlled the easier dock and deck jobs, leaving the more strenuous and dangerous hold jobs to new arrivals from Ireland or other immigrant groups. The Irish-American longshoremen held on to a more ethnicized class identity simply as a response to ethnic succession and the extraordinarily ethnic character of New York working-class life.[33] Thus much of the Irish cohesion was predicated on keeping other ethnic and racial groups out of their areas of operation. Such a strategy reaffirmed their Irishness. Along the west side of Manhattan, then, Irish work gangs dominated the waterfront. From as far north as Hells Kitchen to the southern tip of Manhattan, the piers became a series of Irish fiefdoms. Such control continued through the 1940s. In Brooklyn some Irish activity continued along Third and Fourth Avenues, but as longshoreman Paul O'Dwyer pointed out, 'The Irish were dying out really and the Italians were becoming more numerous.'[34]

Irish control of Manhattan docks was predicated on the generational transfer of jobs. As with other dockers throughout the world, familial relations played a key role in getting and reserving jobs.[35] Larry Sullivan is good example of this phenomenon. He first started working in an easier dock job in 1942 for the US Lines Shipping Company. Although, as he explained, many got jobs because the hiring boss knew their fathers, in his case he followed two older brothers. As he pointed out, 'they got me hired as part of a gang. I was extra. You shaped up every day and you went to work or you didn't go to work.' As in other ports, the longshoremen lived near the waterfront. As Sullivan explained, 'That's what it was, Chelsea was Irish American.' The ease of walking to work was the common denominator: 'At one time, when I started there was 80 per cent walked to work and 20 per cent traveled.'[36]

Irish control of the union, the International Longshoremen's Association (ILA), solidified dominance along the waterfront. Under the leadership of Joe Ryan, the ILA succeeded in having a union official present at the shape-up where men literally were picked out of the crowd to work. The advantage for the Irish union officials was that they controlled who got work. Anyone who questioned the union's actions easily could be overlooked for employment. An attorney representing rank-and-file longshoremen testified in 1948 to the Senate Committee of Labor and Public Welfare that a union leader successfully maintained his power 'because he is able to discipline any man who dares to raise his voice in a union meeting ... That man does not work anymore.'[37] The power of hiring then ensured that a particular ethnic group would be picked for work. This exclusionary control particularly affected African Americans. Appearing every day for the shape-up exposed the black longshoremen to the racism of the hiring boss and attendant union official. One black longshoreman described the humiliating experience: 'Sometimes standing on the pier with my union button and my union book, the hiring boss acts like he hates me ... It happens all the time.'[38]

For African-Americans rampant discrimination by the hiring bosses and the ILA made for an insecure existence. But Irish-American longshoremen were not the only ethnic group that excluded African-Americans. In Brooklyn, where larger numbers of blacks worked, Italian-Americans invariably reserved the good (better paying) jobs for themselves, whether it be cargoes or the centre holds of the ships. Banana shipments, for example, were generally considered black cargo because of their odious quality. Additionally, while Italian-American union locals dominated certain piers, the Jim Crow Local 968 did not enjoy such a privilege. Thus blacks had to shape-up as extras, and only rarely as gangs. To some extent the ILA's relative acceptance of blacks was tactical to protect against strikebreakers. As one black union official testified, 'We are in the union today because the white man had to take us in for his own protection. Outside the organization the Negro could scab on the white man. Inside he can't.'[39] What existed in New York City was a combination of biracial unionism and free-floating black members. Mirroring the ethnic locals of Italians and Irish, blacks either were forced to create their own or accept what was available. What separated black locals, however, was embedded racism and their inability to control a pier to ensure regular employment.[40]

By the 1940s, the pattern of ethnic and racial exclusion was beginning to break down. On the Grace Line piers Italian and black gangs laboured. Even traditionally Irish gangs were being transformed. As Sullivan pointed out, 'all the members picked were mostly Irish with a mixture of Italian'. In these mixed gangs it was the Italian and black members who invariably worked in the hold. Interestingly, even native-born Irishmen were hired. As with the other ethnic groups they worked in the hold or hatch because 'Irish Americans did not want to go down in the hatch'. Thus 'Irish' identity was a qualified concept. It was one thing to be from the neighbourhood or 'American', but quite another if you were an immigrant. Longshoreman Angelo Pacifico explained a similar phenomenon in the Hells Kitchen area of Manhattan. Hells Kitchen was a 'mixed neighborhood. Strong Italian, Irish was the biggest nationality.' A similar ethnic hierarchy was in place where 'Predominately on the dock was Irish ... and hold jobs they were predominately Italian, Yugoslav, Polish, Czech'.[41] So even though controlling the easier dock jobs, over the decades since the nineteenth century the Irish hold on the waterfront jobs was being gradually broken. Correspondingly, they tended to move up the occu-pational ladder to the easier dock or deck jobs. Their grip on the west side and Brooklyn piers was also being undermined by the appearance of regular gangs of other ethnics.

These Irish fiefdoms also reinforced ethnic solidarity because of the influence of gangsters. The loading and criminal rackets attracted a slew of tough guys, usually Irish, who battled among themselves to reap huge profits from organized theft, gambling, loan sharking and shake-downs. On the West Side of Manhattan, the Bowers gang had gained tenuous control by the 1940s. Their inability to dominate the area led to widespread bloodshed as the respective gangs fought for control, causing one West Side union local to gain the infamous nick-name the 'Pistol Local'. The 'waterfront priest' John Corridan, testifying to the widespread criminal activity on the waterfront, noted that the standard joke on the docks was that when longshoremen read of murderers in the local newspapers they remarked: 'If he can beat that rap he has a good job down here.'[42]

Other ethnic groups were present in Manhattan but in smaller numbers, and they worked as extras or on dirty jobs in the hold. Although dominating the port in the early twentieth century, the Irish-Americans were eventually forced to share power with Italian-Americans. The arrangement was based on raw power. Italians came to control union locals in Brooklyn, Staten Island, the Lower East Side and on the New Jersey shore. To a certain extent such an arrangement reflected the changing political complexion of the city. As the Irish grip on City Hall loosened, such was also the case in the city's labour movement.[43] But as power shifted from the established Irish groups to others vying for control, it did not necessarily lead to the loosening of Irishness or Irish identity; indeed, it led to the strengthening of such an identification.

Such was the case of Irish control of the ILA. Even by the late 1940s, the Irish on the west side of Manhattan continued to control the major offices of the ILA. Joe Ryan was elected President of the ILA for life, and retained his control even when threatened with a series of wildcat strikes in 1945, 1948 and 1951. Just as important, major Manhattan Irish locals, such as Local 791, continued to set the stan-dards of wages and work rules. Highlighting the importance of Local 791, Joe Ryan continued to maintain his membership in the local. According to Larry Sullivan, 'So he came to our meetings. He would take a blasting at the meeting and he answered the best he could and stuff like that.'[44] Local 791, commonly known as the 'Mother Local' and led by Gene Sampson (an Irish-American in the mould of Joe Ryan), was the leader in taking unofficial strike action in the port throughout the early postwar years. It was invariably the first local to walk out and was quickly followed by others throughout the port.

Local 791's militancy also affected the rhythm of work. As Angelo Pacifico explained, 'It was the Mother Local. It set precedent like what to do, how to work.'[45] Such work standards were reinforced when travelling gangs were dispatched into Manhattan from outlying piers. In one case a Brooklyn Italian-American gang was unloading a ship on the West Side when they were approached by Manhattan longshoremen. Sebastian DiFazio a member of the Italian gang explained what followed: 'we'd made a good showing. But they'd come back and they'd tell you, "Bring everything back" ... We had to do it their way.' A Brooklyn hatch boss, Leonard DiFazio (brother of Sebastian), had a similar incident after he sent dockmen in his gang down into the hold. He related how he was asked, '"Are you the hatch boss?" I says, "Yeah". He says, "Over here, dockmen don't go down the hold." I says, "I'm with you fella".'[46]

The different approach to the work rules and establishing the rhythm of work had much to do with the strength of the Irish locals. As Angelo Pacifico pointed out, 'In Brooklyn, yeah. And these people wouldn't speak back. Why they wouldn't speak back is they were predominately all Italian, they had an Italian boss, and you just don't do this you know ... That wasn't the situation on the west side of Manhattan ... It was more respect ... They respected you as a man you know ... It's just that we tried to keep conditions more humane.'[47] There were structural reasons why the west side of Manhattan was more militant. These included steady work and better opportunities to make extra money. However, as Larry Sullivan points out, 'being mostly Irish' helped solidify a collective response. Since the nineteenth century, the west side Irish had created a tradition of fighting for the proper scale of wages and improvement of working conditions. Such action reflected through to the generations that followed. As Larry Sullivan explains, 'Our rank and file members they were more independent ... Then if they thought something was right, they thought so. You see other places they would more or less allow something ... [but] once we started, they would follow us out. We had quite a few [strikes] we started.'[48]

It also must be pointed out that the Irish were a generation older than the Italian longshoremen. Invariably third or fourth generation, the New York Irish had rejected a sense of insecurity that might accompany being new to the country. Encapsulating the notion of 'ethnic succession' the Irish had created a stronger sense of working class solidarity, while the Italians, who were more likely first and second generation, thought twice before confronting their poor working conditions and gangsters along the Brooklyn waterfront.

Although created and led by the Irish locals, the west side long-shoremen, regardless of ethnic group, generally followed an independent course. This was especially the case of those longshore-men from the relatively mixed area of Hells Kitchen. Just like their East End counterparts in London, Hells Kitchen longshoremen were unified by their class position. Angelo Pacifico related his experience with his best friend who was a longshoreman with an Irish back-ground: 'No matter where we were, wherever we went out, wherever we socialized, wherever we drank, he was never going to leave me, I was never going to leave him. I don't care if we are in an Irish neigh-borhood, or he was on the East Side in the Italian neighborhood. I don't care. I don't turn my back on him. He was like my brother. We grew up together, we went to school together.'[49] So even in New York, ethnicity no longer exclusively defined friendship and job control by the late 1940s. Although it is plainly evident that ethnicity continued to determine getting a job and holding union office, the gradual with-drawal of the New York Irish from the waterfront was undermining their power base.

What can be learned from this comparison of similar ethnic and worker groups? The comparative method of investigating New York longshoremen and London dockers has highlighted the differences and similarities between the two groups. In each case Irish identity was directly related to the contextual milieu in which both groups lived and worked. Initially for the London Irish dockers, their alle-giance was to their ancestral homeland, but during the twentieth century this attachment was transferred to trade union, the Labour Party and local community. Such a transfer ensured a submergence into the London working class, and thereby a self-definition as Londoner or Eastender. By the late 1940s such a phenomenon had virtually cut the cord with Ireland. What remained was a thin connec-tion for some based on sentimental attachment, while others had severed the link completely. For most dockers of Irish ancestry their association was with other members of the English working class, and on occasion with dockers throughout the world. Although at times separated from the London working class by a sense of place and community, none the less, the primary identification was one of class.

Thus the experience of the London dockers says as much about being unmade, as opposed to constructed. That is, by constructing a London or East End identity, these dockers discarded their Irish background. While self-conscious construction and the discarding of ethnic identity was prevalent, just as vital were outside forces. In the London case it was the job, trade union and Labour Party that continually played a prescriptive role, reinforcing a class identity.

In the New York case, the Irish identity remained strong. Such a state of affairs was based on a traditional segmented racial and ethnic labour force, and on a conscious construction of identity. First by controlling all jobs along the waterfront and then of certain positions that enveloped better working conditions, the New York Irish longshoremen came to hold a position of predominance. Constructing an 'ethnicized class identity' ensured control over the better dock jobs and the trade union. Just as vital, the same sub-group also controlled the leadership of the rank-and-file movements. Such dual control of movement culture ensured supremacy until the 1960s. But also by the 1950s friendships developed in the community and at work were pulling apart ethnic identity and control. Just as in London, it was the local community that played a greater role in determining self-definition. When it was a mixed ethnic neighbourhood, friendships could cross the ethnic divide.

In sum, the elusive Irishness on the London docks was more than made up for on the west side of Manhattan. Each group struggled to define themselves first as Irish and then as workers. How far they would go to reinforce their ethnic identity depended on local sociopolitical conditions. In the New York case it was more a sense of being 'white'. Such reactions should warn us to avoid sweeping statements concerning ethnicity when placed in the context of shifting political and social forces. These workers, while tied to a common ethnic identity, took different roads to maintain power within the workplace. For both sets of workers there was a calculation based upon power and opportunity. Each perceived that their position within their communities and workforces was dependent on the symbiotic desires of accommodation and resistance. What was at stake was job control and placing food on the table. Other than the importance of providing for the family was a continuing sense of separateness, one based on ethnicity and race, whilst the other more firmly grounded in class relations. The respective workers then either relied on ethnic cooperation or placed constraints on their ancestral past when it interfered with communal and class solidarity.

# Notes

1 Patrick Hanshaw, *Nothing is Forever: Growing Up in Wapping During the Post-War Years* (London, 1993), 165.
2 Interview, Larry Sullivan, 13 July 1995.
3 Russell A. Kazal, 'Revisiting Assimilation: The Rise, Fall, and Reappraisal of a Concept in American Ethnic Identity', *The American Historical Review* 100 (April 1995), 438.
4 John Bodnar, *The Transplanted: A History of Immigrants in Urban America* (Bloomington, 1987). See also Kathleen Neils Conzen, et al., 'The Invention of Ethnicity: A Perspective from the USA', *Journal of Ethnic History* 12 (Autumn 1991).
5 James R. Barrett, 'Americanization from the Bottom up: Immigration and the Remaking of the Working Class in America, 1880–1930', *Journal of American History* 79 (December 1992): 996–1020; Lizabeth Cohen, *Making A New Deal: Industrial Workers in Chicago, 1919–1939* (Cambridge, 1990); and Gary Gerstle, *Working Class Americanism: The Politics of Labor in a Textile City, 1914–1960* (Cambridge, 1989); 'Liberty, Coercion and the Making of Americans', *Journal of American History* 84 (September, 1997), 524–58.
6 David Roediger, *The Wages of Whiteness: Race and the Making of the American Working Class* (London and New York, 1991).
7 Theodore W. Allen, *The Invention of the White Race, Volume 1: Racial Oppression and Social Control* (London and New York, 1994), 22.
8 For an excellent critique, see David Brundage, '"Green over Black" Revisited: Ireland and Irish-Americans in the New Histories of American Working Class "Whiteness"', paper presented at the 'Racializing Class, Classifying Race Conference on Labour and Difference in Africa, the USA, and Britain', University of Oxford, July 1997.
9 Lynn Hollen Lees, *Exiles of Erin: Irish Migrants in Victorian England* (Ithaca, NY, 1979), 19, 46.
10 David Fitzpatrick, 'A Curious Middle Place: The Irish in Britain, 1871–1921', in *The Irish in Britain, 1815–1939* (Savage, MD, 1989), 30, 34.
11 Laura Tabili, '*We Ask for British Justice:' Workers and Racial Difference in Late Imperial Britain* (Ithaca, NY, 1994); Paul Gilroy, *There Ain't No Black in the Union Jack*; Eric Hobsbawm and Terence Ranger, eds. *The Invention of Tradition* (Cambridge, 1980).
12 Theda Skocpol, 'Emerging Agendas and Recurrent Strategies in Historical Sociology', in Theda Skocpol, ed., *Vision and Method in Historical Sociology*, (New York, 1984), 369.
13 Lees, *Exiles of Erin*, 19, 46.
14 Kathleen Paul, 'A Case of Mistaken Identity: The Irish in Postwar Britain', *International Labor and Working Class History* 49 (Spring 1996), 116–42. More research is also needed on English migration into the dock areas of London. See D. Mathews, '1889 and all that: New Views on the New Unionism', *International Review of Social History* 36 (1991).
15 Harrington W. Benjamin, 'The London Irish: A Study in Political Activism, 1870–1910' (PhD dissertation, Princeton University, 1976), 54. Similar occupational concentration in low-wage jobs was evident in nineteenth

century Lancashire and Cheshire. Neville Kirk, 'Ethnicity, Class and Popular Toryism, 1850–1870', in Kenneth Lunn, ed., *Hosts, Immigrants and Minorities: Historical Responses to Newcomers in British Society, 1870–1914* (Folkstone, 1980).

16 John Lovell, 'The Irish and the London Dockers', *Bulletin* No. 35 (Autumn 1977), The Society for the Study of Labour History.

17 John Archer Jackson, *The Irish In Britain*, 119.

18 Gareth Stedman Jones, *Outcast London: A Study in the Relationship Between Classes in Victorian Society* (New York, 1984), 348.

19 Steven Fielding, *Class and Ethnicity: Irish Catholics in England, 1880–1939* (Buckingham, 1993), 2.

20 Sam Davies, *Liverpool Labour: Social and Political Influences on the Development of the Labour Party in Liverpool, 1900–1939* (Keele, 1996); See also John Belchem, 'The Irish in Britain, United States and Australia: Some Comparative Reflections on Labour History', in Patrick Buckland and John Belchem, eds., *The Irish in British Labour History* (Liverpool, 1993).

21 Lees, *Exiles of Erin*, 186–8; Patrick Hanshaw, *"Nothing is Forever": Growing up in Wapping During the Postwar Years*, 18; For an excellent study of how religion and education played in homogenizing the London Irish, see Mary J. Hickman, *Religion, Class, and Identity: The State, the Catholic Church, and the Education of the Irish in Britain* (Brookfield, VT, 1995).

22 John Donovan, Interview, 9 July 1996. Kerby A. Miller, *Emigrants and Exiles: Ireland and the Irish Exodus to North America* (New York, 1985), 557. Patrick Hanshaw, *Nothing is Forever*, 17.

23 Lees, *Exiles of Erin*, 242; Fitzpatrick, 'A Curious Middle Place', 44.

24 Roger Swift, 'Heroes or Villains?: The Irish, Crime, and Disorder in Victorian England', *Albion* 29:3 (Autumn 1997), 420.

25 John Donovan, Interview, 9 July 1996. For religious segregation of Liverpool gangs, see Eric Taplin, 'The History of Dock Labour: Liverpool: circa 1850–1914', in *Comparative International History of Dock Labour, c.1790–1970* (Amsterdam, 1997), 14.

26 Joe Bloomberg, Interview, 8 August 1996.

27 George Pye, Interview, 14 August 1996.

28 Ted Johns, Interview, 11 July 1996.

29 Hanshaw, *Nothing is Forever*, 27, 42, 144.

30 John T. Ridge, 'Irish Counties Societies in New York, 1880–1914', in Ronald H. Baylor and Timothy J. Meagher eds., *The New York Irish*, (Baltimore, 1996), 275–300.

31 Calvin Winslow, 'On the Waterfront: Black, Italian and Irish Longshoremen in the New York Habour Strike of 1919', in John Rule and Robert Malcolmson eds., *Protest and Survival: Essays for E.P. Thompson*, (London, 1995), 369.

32 Charles Barnes, *The Longshoremen* (New York, 1977), 8.

33 Such a strategy was also used by hard rock miners in Butte, Montana. David Emmons, *The Butte Irish: Class and Ethnicity in an American Mining Town, 1875–1925* (Urbana, Ill., 1989).

34 Paul O'Dwyer, Oral History Collection of Columbia University, 42.

35 Recruitment of sons, daughters, nephews, cousins and sons-in-law was a common policy used by both employers and dockers around the world

during the casual period (generally up to the Second World War) and the
later decasualization period. Colin J. Davis, 'Formation and Reproduction
of Dockers as an Occupational Group', paper presented at the Conference,
Comparative International History of Dock Labour, 1790–1970,
Amsterdam, November 1997.

36  Larry Sullivan, Interview, 13 July 1995.
37  'Testimony of Julius E. Bagley', Senate Committee on Labor and Public
    Welfare, *Fair Labor Standards Act, Amendments, Part 1*, 80th Cong,. 2nd sess,
    p. 994. The second quote is from Charles P. Larrowe, *Shape-Up and Hiring
    Hall: A Comparison of Hiring Methods on the New York and Seattle Waterfronts*
    (Westport, Conn., 1976), 74.
38  Malcolm Johnson, *Crime on the Labor Front* (New York, 1950), 116.
39  Sterling Spero and Abrahm L. Harris, *The Black Worker: The Negro and the
    Labor Movement* (New York, 1931), 199.
40  For excellent discussion of bi-racialism among longshoremen, see Eric
    Arnesen, *Waterfront Workers of New Orleans: Race, Class and Politics,
    1863–1923* (New York, 1988). For the mix of ethnic and racial groups, see
    Cal Winslow, 'On the Waterfront'.
41  Sullivan, Interview; Angelo Pacifico, Interview, 12 July 1995.
42  'Testimony of Edward A. Heffernan', *NYS Crime Commission, Vol. 5,
    1548–1559*; Larrowe, *Shape-Up and Hiring Hall*, 22–3; Johnson, *Crime on the
    Labor Front*, 210–13, 165–82; 'Testimony of Father John Corridan', Senate
    Committee on Interstate and Foreign Commerce, *Waterfront Investigation.
    Part 1: New York-New Jersey Waterfront*, 83rd Cong., 1st sess, 569.
43  Stephen P. Erie, *Rainbows End: Irish-Americans and the Dilemmas of Machine
    Politics, 1840–1985* (Berkeley, 1988); Roy Peel, *The Political Clubs of New
    York City* (Port Washington, NY, 1935), Theodore J. Lowi, *At the Pleasure of
    the Mayor: Patronage and Power in New York City, 1898–1958* (London,
    1964). For connection between the Irish and the US labour movement, see
    David Montgomery, 'The Irish and the American Labor Movement', in
    David Noel Doyle and Owen Dudley Edwards, eds., *America and Ireland,
    1776–1976: The American Identity and the Irish Connection* (Westport,
    Conn., 1980).
44  Sullivan, Interview.
45  Pacifico, Interview.
46  Sebastian DiFazio, Interview, 10 July 10 1995; Leonard DiFazio, Interview,
    12 July 1995.
47  Pacifico, Interview.
48  Sullivan, Interview.
49  Pacifico, Interview.

# 5
# A Racialized Hierarchy of Labour? Race, Immigration and the British Labour Movement, 1880–1950

*Kenneth Lunn*

A significant proportion of the published work on ways in which issues of 'race' and immigration have impacted on the British labour movement has continued to plough an already deep and increasingly unproductive furrow.[1] The framework essentially focuses on a 'native' labour movement, composed largely of white males, which has viewed 'others' as challengers to the hard-won rights of trade unions and their associated political parties. This presents, therefore, a history of negativity, of opposition and of hostility.[2] Such work may occasionally acknowledge the contributions of certain groups, such as the Irish, to British labour politics. There are also examples of the toleration of others, particularly those with defined legitimate claims to citizenship status, although they remain essentially beyond the pale of white British male identity. In the main, however, the model remains fixed and static.

In some cases, this approach has produced the most basic and distorting of generalities. For example, Panikos Panayi's 1994 survey of 'race' and immigration for the period 1815–1945 has only a few references to the labour movement in any form. What little there is either comments on trade union hostility to migrants or on the formation of separate Jewish unions at the turn of the century.[3] This volume, deemed to be at the cutting edge of the historical study of 'race' in Britain, defines the responses of labour as simplistically reactionary and exclusionist. Such a categorization does little justice to a far more complex history.

Other studies, particularly those that focus on specific migrant groups, have tended to be based around empirical detail rather than contextual analysis.[4] Studies on the Irish from the mid-nineteenth century onwards and on the phase of Jewish immigration from the

1880s to the early twentieth century fall largely into this pattern.[5] Much of the existing literature on so-called 'ethnic' seafarers – men of Chinese, African, West Indian, Arab and Lascar origin – has seen them as essentially cheap labour exploited by shipowners and resented by white crews.[6] Similar perspectives are taken as the starting point for the consideration of the reception of various groups of European nationals who arrived in Britain during and immediately after the Second World War. The same applies to those studies that are still defined as central to British immigration history: the arrival of substantial numbers from the 'New Commonwealth' from the 1950s onwards.[7]

Of course, not all the work in this now substantial literature conforms to this blanket classification. There are those who have at least sought to identify complexities within such an approach, to see both positive and negative responses from the 'host' labour movement, at national and local level. However, they still react to the essential format identified and deviations from the defined norm of responses are identified as exactly that. Thus, the dominance of this overarching framework effectively determines the nature and structure of historical writing in this area.

In contrast, therefore, the argument presented in this essay is based on the need to move away from such a limited and narrowing perspective. There has been little contact between the rethinking of 'race' which has taken place in much of the academic world and the ways in which the subject has been dealt with by historians both of the labour movement and of 'race' and immigration in Britain. This is particularly unfortunate, given that some of the most effective writing from social scientists such as Paul Gilroy and Robert Miles[8] has urged the importance of a more-telling consideration of historical forces in the construction of 'race' in Britain. That their own work has sometimes simplified that history should have provided even more incentive to historians working in this field. In reality, what has happened is that some token recognition of the theoretical debates is made, but the empirical seams are then returned to, in much the same way as before. This has inevitably meant that the historical study of 'race' in Britain has failed to keep pace with shifts in a general methodology and thus any significant consideration of the labour movement's engagement with 'race' has suffered from this kind of insular approach.

One significant exception to this critique, and a work which has raised the issues identified above, is Laura Tabili's '*We Ask for British Justice*',[9] essentially a study of black[10] seafarers in the interwar period.

This volume has been relatively neglected in the British historiography, an omission at first puzzling but perhaps on reflection understandable. Tabili is critical of much of the existing literature and, in a fairly trenchant introduction, focuses on its naivety and lack of structural analysis. She identifies the need for a reconstruction of the historical contexts within which racial conflict or racial cooperation occurred and the ways in which such contexts, and with them the meaning of racial difference, altered over time.[11] Other dimensions of her argument, such as the need to identify material as well as ideological underpinnings of racial stratification, and to focus on a properly historicized approach to the discussion of 'race', are beginning to be explored in the literature and form the basis of the points in this chapter.

Tabili's study, however, is perhaps too narrow, concentrating on one specific group of workers over a couple of decades, to provide the detailed evaluation required to move the debate onto new ground. Nevertheless, one of the considerable gains from her work, and this may well be a major reason for its relative neglect in Britain, is its awareness of American debates. Her background and current location have clearly contributed significantly to her arguments, and the value of transposing these theoretical concerns is very apparent. For this reason alone, Tabili's volume deserves greater attention. Indeed, it is the contention of this chapter that concepts such as 'whiteness', drawn from an American perspective, have considerable relevance for the British situation and are of particular importance in any analysis of labour movement attitudes in the nineteenth and twentieth centuries.

My aim here is to offer some attempts to shift the terms of engagement in this sub-field, and I will suggest that four areas might repay closer attention.

## Ethnic and labour history

Perhaps still the most problematic of areas in this research agenda is the perception of ethnic minorities as having easily definable and fixed characteristics, of corresponding to the systematic racializing and identification of the stereotyping trends of British cultural discourses. It is still the case that texts make reference to 'the black experience', 'Jewish history', the 'Asian response' as if any of these descriptions corresponded to an undifferentiated and unproblematic narrative. Any simplistic notion of groups or individuals slotting naturally into the role of passive victim of capitalism, or indeed of having any automatic set of values or ideological concerns, needs to be challenged. What is required here is a more detailed evaluation of the cultural, political, social and economic divisions within the various ethnic 'communities' in Britain during these years, and the complexity of their engagement with trade union and labour politics.

Already, a more sophisticated approach towards the evaluation of Jewish immigration and settlement in Britain has produced such analysis. The work of writers such as Bill Williams, Bill Fishman, Joe Buckman and Colin Holmes[12] has not simply demonstrated the range of political viewpoints within different Jewish communities from the 1880s onwards, it has also attempted to locate these within a wider setting. Thus, for example, Williams's work on Manchester and Buckman's on Leeds have, amongst other things, identified the social and economic forces which concentrated Jewish workers into particular sectors of the economy, such as tailoring and shoe-making. They note a very uneven degree of commitment to labour organization by Jewish immigrants, combined with significant phases of militancy and challenge. Separate unions were sometimes formed, although these were constructed not merely from a sense of ethnic identity but as a consequence of hostility from established unions. Both authors also emphasize the general weakness of labour organization in these sectors of the economy – as a consequence of the forms of employment and control – and thus draw us away from an 'ethnic' explanation of labour relations towards one which is rooted in a wider setting. They also identify the historical dynamics of relationships and attitudes, noting different patterns and evolving attitudes, both from sections of the immigrant community and from 'native' workers. As Tabili has argued, it is vital to understand 'race' relations as a dynamic process, not as 'the inevitable if deplorable response to economic or sexual competition between two mutually exclusive and naturally antagonistic groups of working men'.[13] The need to acknowledge the complexities of situations 'fissured by class, gender, skill, and other dynamics'[14] was perceived by Williams and Buckman, and their approach reflected this awareness, something which Tabili's all-encompassing critique perhaps failed to recognize.

Until very recently, studies of few other immigrant groups had taken cues from this earlier material. Any work on African and Asian migration before 1945 tended to discuss the experiences of these groups in terms of their passive reception of hostility, relieved only by white Christian sympathy and lodging houses in the main seaport towns. Ethnic seafarers, the largest single identifiable cohort, were often seen as being exploited by shipowners, officers and government officials, and as objects of hatred by white British seamen and their union. They were, in short, merely the objects of discrimination.[15] However, new work by a number of scholars has increasingly drawn attention to the richness of organizational and cultural challenge displayed by the various groups employed within the merchant marine in the first half of the century. Within many of the seaport towns, very effective and supportive community and labour networks provided resistance to institutional forms of racism and the exclusionary practices of the National Union of Seamen.[16] Organizations such as the Coloured Seamen's Union, the Liverpool Negro Association, the Free Yemeni Movement, the Chinese Seamen's Union and the Indian Seamen's Union all made a significant impact at one point or another in the period under consideration. Such findings reinforce the need for historians to look beyond the territorial boundaries of Britain for an understanding of the social, political and cultural forces shaping imperial relations and to re-examine the ways in which traditional labour history sources have failed to provide this wider picture.

Perhaps the most valuable of the recent studies, and the model for further work, has been that carried out by Richard Lawless.[17] His detailed analysis of the Arab community which became established in South Shields, in the north-east of England, has provided a wealth of evidence on the origins of that community, continuing links with Aden and the Yemen, and the ways in which Arab seafarers and their dependants sought to establish lines of negotiation, where possible, with British political and legal institutions. He also demonstrates amply the ways in which these communities maintained and adapted existing cultural patterns to the demands of living in a new country. In this respect, Lawless has matched the challenge of breaking the stranglehold of 'problem and victim status' by 'representing a black presence outside these categories'.[18] Any notion of a submissive and indeterminate immigrant group is challenged very effectively by Lawless's identification of strong political and cultural leadership within the community. The exposure of the implications of British imperialism and the debates around citizenship – particularly in the 1930s, when the anti-Arab campaigns mounted at local and national level by union and government were at their peak – is clear. They were highlighted in published material, such as local newspapers, and in general discussion, and provide evidence that many Arab seamen were only too aware of the issues at stake. They also indicate that 'race', in its narrow conception, was only one element in the debates, and that questions of Arab and British identity involved much more complex political and cultural issues.

It is studies such as this which are essential to a wider understanding of 'race' in labour relations. They will often require the evaluation of sources outside Britain and language skills which are, perhaps, still too reluctantly acquired by British historians. In this respect, Buckman's study of Leeds Jews was greatly enhanced by his control of Yiddish material. Earlier studies on Lithuanians employed in Scottish coalfields in the late nineteenth century were significantly developed by subsequent work using the Lithuanian language press.[19] Work which attempts to unpack the notions of the heterogeneity of ethnic groups and which moves away from 'race' as a deterministic perspective will aid the emergence of a more sensitive history of ethnic and labour relations. Without these essential dimensions, we will remain locked into a somewhat myopic and ultimately unhelpful perspective.

## The legacy of empire

A second area worthy of exploration is the way in which 'race' and racism in Britain have been explained through the formulaic phrase 'the legacy of empire'. This theme has been dealt with elsewhere,[20] so what follows is a brief summary of arguments and suggestions. As a substitute for significant historical analysis and an evaluation of the processes of ideological inheritance and construction, the concept of 'legacy' has been used somewhat randomly as a standard introduction to the study of essentially postwar immigration. Indeed, as Gilroy pointed out, such a loose use of the term, and the assumptions behind it, fundamentally misrepresent the conceptual importance of 'race' as a social construct:

> Racism is not a unitary event based on psychological aberration nor some ahistorical antipathy to blacks which is the cultural legacy of empire and which continues to saturate the consciousness of all white Britons regardless of age, gender, income or circumstances. It must be understood as a process ...[21]

More recently, Mary Hickman and Bronwen Walter have criticized sociologists for their 'invention' of 'new racism', a concept which relied heavily on notions of inclusion and exclusion based on skin colour and which was constructed around analyses of post-1945 immigration. Such notions paid little attention to the longer-term formation of 'race' as a category based on more complex criteria. As they argue, '[t]he "race relations" paradigm has rather unquestioningly accepted the myth of British homogeneity prior to the 1940s.'[22] However, not all sociologists have taken such a blinkered view of the importance of history. Some twenty-odd years ago, Michael Banton and John Harwood suggested that the relationship between what might be termed 'the legacy of history' and 'contemporary political affairs', which gave birth to the popular imagery of 'race', required a recognition of a long and complex history of attitudes and processes for the transmission of values.[23] The argument, therefore, is that any unquestioning notion of 'the legacy of empire' both distorts this sense of dynamic construction and foregrounds the importance of a national perspective, one which is equally shared by all. Attitudes and cultures were often formulated in a local context, whether it was through the influence of the local state, or community and workplace networks. This is not to argue for the absence of a national input, politically, culturally or economically – which, as John MacKenzie and others have shown, could be significant[24] – but to suggest that this had to compete with a number of alternative pressures, whose origins were from a more localized setting. In ideological terms, the national state has often found it difficult to create a common voice. As Charles Husband argues:

> There is no single monolithic ideology shared by all Britons. The interlocking imagery and values which dominate the experience of any one group defined by class, region, ethnicity or gender is not the same as that prevailing in another group. And the same image or value found to be present in two different groups does not necessarily have the same range of meaning . . .[25]

With regard to the labour movement and the legacy of empire, therefore, it is vital to emphasize that any account of that history needs to take cognisance of the fragmented nature of these influences. Whilst that legacy clearly does involve the construction of racialized stereotypes and hostility at national and local level, there are also examples of positive images and of a recognition of common interests, as Tabili's work has shown.

## The formation of 'race' in British labour history

From the discussion above, it is evident that the essential argument, that 'racial conflict in Britain was and is a legacy of imperialism',[26] needs to be clarified. A simplistic reading of this phrase might present a vision of 'race' in British history as one based essentially on black/white relations and on movements and identifications of 'others' based upon the immediate imperial experience, whether in mainland Britain or in its subject territories. With this in mind, due recognition ought to be given to patterns of acquired responses – other ways in which labour became racialized. In this respect, the comments of Diana Kay and Miles on the long history of such a process, drawing on the experiences of the Irish in the nineteenth century and on Jewish immigration, are a starting point.

> While skin colour is a particularly easy human characteristic to signify in order to exclude, and particularly difficult to hide, there are other physical, as well as cultural, characteristics that are equally open to signification for the purposes of defining the Other. And the discourse of 'race' can be easily utilized to this end whatever the origin of the migrant population and whatever its somatic characteristics.[27]

This is not to argue for the immutability of racial stereotypes, nor for the acceptance of 'race' hostility as inevitable and somehow 'natural', but to recognize, within many dimensions of the British working-class experience, that there are sets of ideas and attitudes on 'race' and immigration which are transmitted across generations. These may not be the most influential voices in any particular situation, and they may be significantly altered by the conjuncture of forces at any given time, but they do demonstrate the vitality of cultural traditions in debates around 'race'. An unwillingness to acknowledge this historical inheritance, and the possibilities of its operation in a particular situation, would suggest a lack of understanding of the functioning of many aspects of British social, political and cultural history.

It is possible to refer to any number of incidences whereby such a process has been vital. Indeed, this is one of the most significant gains from the largely empirical work of Holmes and others. For example, attempts to move the study of Irish workers into the twentieth century, an area much neglected in 'race' research,[28] almost inevitably confronts the importance of persistent stereotypes given force by nineteenth-century immigration. This is despite the alleged waning of interest in the Irish as a migrant group, overtaken by Jewish immigration and subsequently a range of other ethnic groups.[29] At worst, a myth of assimilation is created, a model rejected by a number of recent contributors to the historiography of the Irish in Britain.[30] Whilst these negative Irish stereotypes may have originated in the nineteenth-century context of labour migration (with even earlier antecedents), they retain a telling constancy throughout the period under consideration here. Arguably, they have served to provide a formative notion of 'immigrant worker' in the modern British labour market. As Edward Hunt has argued with regard to Irish immigration in the nineteenth century, 'there are three ways in which immigrants are thought to reduce living standards: by taking work, by reducing wages, and by weakening trade unionism.'[31] These images of the Irish as economic competitors became a component part of a labour culture which retained a vitality into the twentieth century, and they were significant in shaping responses not only to subsequent elements of Irish migration but also towards other groups. The language and imagery of trade union and popular culture in the later period demonstrates this legacy.

Some of these apparently uniquely Irish characteristics, such as images of hard drinking and lack of personal hygiene, were also drawn into play in later years. Thus, attempts during the Second World War to recruit Irish workers for the British war effort were hampered by a re-invocation of these long-held stereotypes. With scant regard for evidence, Irish males were defined as hardened drinkers with a liking for methylated spirits, and were ruthlessly searched on their arrival at British ports. It was often difficult to obtain lodgings in private homes for these workers, despite their contribution to the Home Front, as many communities drew upon older traditions of hostility. There were accusations, subsequently found to be unsubstantiated, that Irish women were responsible for spreading lice in some Midlands munitions factories.[32] All of these instances seem to have been based on inherited patterns of thought, on the anticipation of incidence, rather than any material evidence.

A similar argument could be constructed around labour movement attitudes towards Jewish immigration. Here, the connection with empire is less clear, except in chronological coincidence. The formative influence of the last quarter of the nineteenth century and the early years of the twentieth have had an enduring impact, and has already been identified here. Whilst the unevenness in levels of response has been noted, the formative reaction was one of overt hostility and the reworking of a powerful range of anti-Semitic images within many dimensions of British culture. This subsequently impinged on later phases of Jewish immigration. For example, Tony Kushner's work on the reception of Jewish refugees in the 1930s indicates very powerfully the extent of institutionalized responses from the TUC leadership and from rank-and-file trade unionists.[33] Whilst such a response could be explained away by the economic circumstances of the Depression years and subsequent fears of unemployment, Kushner's detailed analysis suggests less the 'rational' reaction to the immediate crisis of the 1930s and far more an acquired cultural identification of Jews within the labour market, an historical acquisition. Yet, as another of his pieces shows, such stereotypes could be discarded or simply not invoked. His overview of Jew and non-Jew relations in the East End of London provides a thoughtful survey of the ways in which direct community experience of common identities and perceptions sought to undermine a vaguer ideological or cultural baggage.[34]

To continue the illustration of this general argument, we can turn to studies of postwar immigration and in particular to commentaries surrounding the employment of Poles and European Volunteer Workers. John Tannahill's study, published in 1956, noted:

> In most industries there was, no doubt, a background of suspicion of the foreign worker, arising partly from ignorance and partly from the old fear of unemployment. Foreign workers are, even now, sometimes told to 'go home and stop taking our jobs away from us.' There is a vague feeling that there is only a fixed quantity of money and goods to be shared, and anything given to the foreigner means less for the British.[35]

Tannahill's comments, whilst part of a very specific study on white European labour, also seem to reflect responses to the developing migration from the Caribbean in the immediate inter-war period. In addition, however, they signify a longer history of such attitudes. The emphasis is on the importance of a set of memories, which had become part of a discourse within labour culture. This could be invoked in particular circumstances, such as those in the years following the war. It is the combination of these generalized values and images, combined with a more direct and specific historicization, which deserves closer attention.

## Identity, whiteness and Britishness

The final issue to be examined is one which seeks to identify the relative slowness of this sub-field of history to pick up on some of the more recent discussions in analytical approaches elsewhere in history and in other disciplines. In this case, attention to such notions as 'identity', 'Britishness' and 'whiteness', conceptually developed in response to contemporary experiences, has clearly impacted on historical studies and demonstrated their potential for significant developments within the discipline. The singular emphasis on 'race' as the sole or major determinant is now seen as a dangerously distorting perspective. As Miles and others have warned, being locked into a 'race' paradigm can obscure the conjuncture of forms of identification which constitute any given situation. This is particularly apposite in the case of British history, where a focus on 'race' is largely synonymous with 'black'. Indeed, as has already been suggested, this concentration on black immigration has led to a distortion of the nature and construction of 'race' in Britain. Formative influences, in labour movement culture in particular, were often drawn from situations involving white immigrants.

What is often striking in the empirical research on these kinds of labour market situations is the way in which it appears that clashes over jobs, conditions of work, pay and union membership were the basis for much broader questions of identity. For example, from the work that has been done on the National Union of Seamen and the struggles over the employment of 'foreigners' and 'aliens', it is the issue of British identity which is a contested area. As Tabili has emphasized in this particular instance, from the late nineteenth century, what was being debated was not merely the protection of British jobs but the consequences of British imperialism. It was, after all, the establishment of an empire and the possibilities of colonial status which placed many ethnic groups across the world in a situation where they were competing directly and indirectly with 'white British' workers. The day-to-day language of the union and its membership may not have articulated this in so clear a fashion, but innumerable examples suggest a consciousness of the position. It was well illustrated by a speech in the House of Commons by David Logan, a Liverpool MP, in 1934, deploring the impact of unemployment on white British seafarers.

> Is it a nice sight, as I walk through the south end of the city of Liverpool, to find a black settlement, a black body of men – I am

not saying a word about their colour – all doing well and a white body of men who faced the horrors of war walking the streets unemployed? Is it a nice sight to see Lascars trotting up the Scotland Road, and round Cardiff, and to see Chinamen walking along in the affluence that men of the sea are able to get by constant employment, while Britishers are walking the streets and going to the public assistance committee?[36]

Representatives of the British state and the NUS focused on questions about the identity of 'alien' or 'foreign' seamen. A persistent refusal to recognize citizenship as merely a legal status, and attempts to imbue it with racial and/or cultural characteristics, were key elements in the union's campaigns over some fifty years. In this way, arguments about place of origin took on more than a formal significance. To be entitled to employment rights, colonial subjects had to prove place of origin in precise territories. Thus, Hong Kong and Aden took on even more significance for Chinese and Arab seafarers. Evidence of some forgery of documents, in some cases to back up *bona fide* claims, exists. However, the union, aware of the possibilities of this kind of legalized deception, sought to argue that, even where legal proof of birth could be presented, it was no qualification for British status. The Chinese, Arab or Lascar seaman could never be the equivalent of the British (i.e. white) sailor. Much of the legislation designed to deal with this perceived economic competition was built around increasingly precise definitions of what constituted 'British' and 'alien', as the titles of various statutes suggests.[37] Agreements between shipping lines and the union – validated by the National Maritime Board on behalf of the state – structured inequalities based on a racialized hierarchy of labour. Different manning levels for different ethnic groups were implemented, with higher numbers being required for Chinese or Lascar stokers than for whites. In addition, an elaborately defined system of wage scales also differentiated between the various groups.[38] The boundaries could be renegotiated from time to time – as for example in the case of Lascar seamen, where pressure from India saw the relaxation in 1939 of restrictions on the waters in which Lascar crews could be deployed[39] – but essentially the components of the structure remained intact, benefiting all those parties who had been in agreement to its original purposes.

It might be thought that this argument was an isolated one, dealing with the very specific circumstances of the merchant marine in these years. However, there was a wider context within these discussions, for the processes of racialization were taking place. 'British' identity was as much at stake as 'alien' status. Indeed, it was frequently the case that the definition of 'alien' was based on being 'non-British', hence the increasingly precise formulation of these categories in the legislation relating to merchant seamen. But was 'British' an unchallenged and unchallengeable identity?

Arguably, this is one of the areas of weakness in Tabili's approach. Its narrow focus misses engagement with the wider picture. Late twentieth-century concerns about the decline of Britain as a world power, and the concomitant lack of confidence in what it means to be British, have awakened an academic interest in the historical formation and restatement of that identity.[40] Kathleen Paul's recent study of 'race' and citizenship in post-1945 Britain has drawn attention very effectively to the active processes of definition and redefinition of 'Britishness' and the informal hierarchies both constructed by and imposed upon conceptions of citizenship.[41] Such a process was also at work during the interwar period and, although white British seafarers may have taken the immediate lead from their work situation, the broader cultural references of earlier years must have contributed to patterns of thought identifiable in the 1920s and 1930s.

Perhaps it is at this point that some reflection on the value of debates around the notion of 'whiteness' is appropriate. The implications of this for writing the history of ethnic groups and ethnicity are marked, yet have only just begun to make any impact. Most (white, male, middle-class) historians have continued to discuss 'race' and ethnicity in terms of the construction of 'others' and have thus tended to accept and to reinforce the influences of racism. For example, in the edited volume *Ethnic Labour*,[42] the concern was to focus on the experiences of non-white seamen in the British merchant navy. It offered a number of studies which have advanced our awareness of the various themes highlighted throughout this chapter. However, in its exclusive use of the term 'ethnic' to refer to non-white seamen, it tended to dilute the significance of the constant making of a sense of white and British identity in the process of racialization. This is not to question the intentions of the various authors who have proceeded from this starting point. It is simply that, by implicitly defining these 'ethnic' seamen as such, we have paid insufficient attention to the ways in which a 'white' sense of identity was a crucial aspect of the various situations – economic, political and social – which helped to shape the experiences under consideration.

Indeed, in looking at the ways in which the labour movement in

Britain has engaged with the politics of 'race', the relevance of the 'whiteness' debate seems even more relevant. In particular, it is important to recognize the dangers of simplifying a notion of 'whiteness', as in the past notions of 'black' or 'Asian' have been reduced to homogeneous categories. Alastair Bonnett has identified these tendencies, but also noted the subtlety of 'more historically informed, social constructionist, interpretations of "whiteness"', and its value in stressing the 'hybridity' of identity.[43]

As has already been suggested, it has been involvement with 'white' immigration which has played a significant part in much of the labour movement's conceptualisation of 'race'. In the case of Irish migration, the nineteenth century saw attempts to create an image of the Irish working man as not only an economic competitor but also a morally and culturally inferior human being. Arguably, this stereotype continued into the twentieth century. With the formation of an independent Irish state, legal notions of citizenship could enter the equation and reinforce the 'British'/'other' aspect. At times, this dominant imagery had to be reversed, as for example when the British state needed Irish labour to meet the needs of war in 1939–45. Having spent the 1930s constructing mechanisms to control, and in some cases reverse, the flow of migrants from Eire, it now sought to recruit from the Republic, much against the prevailing sentiment of many local communities and to the distinct unease of labour organisations. In this situation, opposition was frequently constructed around hostility towards alleged Irish characteristics, defined as non-British and irrevocably so. Here was the employment of a conscious sense of ethnicity, constructed against the ethnicity of the Irish, and being reasserted at a time of national crisis, when images of the nation were a significant dimension of the war effort.

One further illustration of this theme was the experience of European refugees and immigrants after the Second World War. As 'whites', it has sometimes been suggested (as implied by the Tannahill quote earlier), that whilst they faced opposition from other workers, this was nothing that might have been described as racist. Other studies suggest something very different.[44] Kay and Miles have drawn attention to the ways in which European Volunteer Workers (EVWs) were racialized, but in ways rather different from a growing unease about the impending immigration from the Caribbean.

It should therefore be stressed that notions of 'stock', 'blood' and 'breeding' were embedded in official discourses about the EVWs ...

The EVWs were, therefore, racialized in the course of assessing their suitability as suppliers of labour power and therefore as migrants ... There was also concern, within and outside the state, that collectively, all EVWs were likely to become a problematic presence, living in 'ghettos' and unable to speak English.[45]

Here again we see the dimensions of 'whiteness' and of 'Britishness' being brought into play, but Kay and Miles go further in indicating the complexities of 'whiteness'. They note the ways in which differentiations were made between categories of these European workers and in which racialized hierarchies were constructed.[46] In a number of situations – from recruitment in the camps of Europe, to the placement of workers in particular jobs, to the explanations for the suicides of numbers of these newcomers – a racialized language distinguished between groups of 'whites'. Degrees of assimilability were assessed upon the particular 'stock' or 'blood', and characteristics, most notably differences between Baltic and Slav 'races', were attributed. Any study of this phase of European migration to Britain clearly now has to take on board the implications of these wider discussions on ethnicity, identity and whiteness.

## Conclusion

It is difficult to draw together coherent conclusions from such a tentative piece of work. The major concern here has not been to produce massive empirical detail or to attempt to catalogue the wide variations within the pronouncements and strategies of the British labour movement on matters of 'race' over the period under consideration. That work has been done effectively by others and continues to form the basis of much scholarship in the field. However, this does seem to be rooted still in a particular approach which makes it difficult to move beyond narrow, empirically self-selecting studies. Whilst accepting that such work is essential and is the bedrock of any wider historical analysis, there seems little indication that any broader synthesis is taking place. This chapter has attempted to indicate some possible ways of shifting the terrain of discussion and of opening up arguments about labour movement attitudes at both an institutional and a workplace and community level. It will hopefully offer ways of implementing a more genuine basis for comparative study with other national and international experiences and of incorporating a wider reception of new conceptual and methodological approaches.

# Notes

1  For examples of such work, see C. Holmes, ed., *Immigrants and Minorities in British Society* (London, 1978); C. Holmes, *John Bull's Island: Immigration and British Society, 1871–1971* (London, 1991); K. Lunn, ed., *Hosts, Immigrants and Minorities* (Folkestone, 1980); K. Lunn, ed., *Race and Labour in Twentieth-Century Britain* (London, 1985). My own published work is certainly open to this kind of critique.

2  For the universality of this model, see the positional conference paper of Jan and Leo Lucassen, cited in J. and L. Lucassen, eds., *Migration, Migration History, History: Old Paradigms and New Perspectives* (Bern, 1997), 344.

3  See P. Panayi, *Immigration, Ethnicity and Racism in Britain, 1815–1945* (Manchester, 1994), 95, 102–27.

4  For example, R. Ramdin, *The Making of the Black Working Class in Britain* (London, 1987) served a useful purpose in its collation of detail but, despite its title, lacked a wider contextual framework.

5  On the Irish, see the extensive bibliography in R. Swift and S. Gilley, eds., *The Irish in Britain, 1815–1939* (London, 1989). On Jewish immigration, the best summary remains Holmes, *John Bull's Island*.

6  An indication of more recent work will be found in D. Frost, ed., *Ethnic Labour and British Imperial Trade: A History of Ethnic Seafarers in the UK* (London, 1995); this also appeared as a special issue of *Immigrants and Minorities* 13:2 & 3 (1994).

7  For a survey of existing literature, see Holmes, *John Bull's Island*. K. Paul, *Whitewashing Britain: Race and Citizenship in the Postwar Era* (Ithaca, NY, and London, 1997), is a valuable addition to the literature.

8  P. Gilroy, *'There Ain't No Black in the Union Jack': The Cultural Politics of Race and Nation* (London, 1987); R. Miles, *Racism After 'Race Relations'* (London, 1993).

9  L. Tabili, *'We Ask for British Justice': Workers and Racial Difference in Late Imperial Britain* (New York, 1994).

10  On Tabili's use of 'black', see *ibid.*, 9.

11  See *ibid.*, 1–14.

12  B. Williams, 'The Beginnings of Jewish Trade Unionism in Manchester, 1889–1891', in Lunn, ed., *Hosts, Immigrants and Minorities*, 263–307; W. Fishman, *East End Jewish Radicals, 1875–1914* (London, 1975); J. Buckman, *Immigrants and Class Struggle: The Jewish Immigrant in Leeds, 1880–1914* (Manchester, 1983); C. Holmes, *Anti-Semitism in British Society, 1876–1939* (London, 1979).

13  Tabili, *'We Ask for British Justice'*, 6. A. Kershen, *Uniting the Tailors: Trade Unionism Amongst the Tailors of London and Leeds, 1870–1939* (London, 1995) has some detailed material but perhaps lacks this kind of critical evaluation.

14  Tabili, *"We Ask for British Justice"*, 7.

15  See here the very insular approach of A. Marsh and V. Ryan, *The Seamen* (Oxford, 1989).

16  For details, see Frost, ed., *Ethnic Labour*.

17  R. Lawless, *From Ta'izz to Tyneside: An Arab Community in the North-east of England During the Early Twentieth Century* (Exeter, 1995).

18  Gilroy, *'There Ain't No Black'*, 12.

19  See M. Rodgers, 'Political Developments in the Lithuanian Community in Scotland, c.1890–1923', in J. Slatter, ed., *From the Other Shore: Russian Political Emigrants in Britain, 1880–1917* (London, 1983), 141–56.

20  K. Lunn, 'Immigration and Reaction in Britain, 1880–1950: Rethinking the "Legacy of Empire"', in J. and L. Lucassen, eds., *Migration, Migration History, History*, 335–49.

21  Gilroy, *'There Ain't No Black'*, 27.

22  M. Hickman and B. Walter, 'Deconstructing Whiteness: Irish Women in Britain', *Feminist Review*, 50 (1995), 7.

23  M. Banton and J. Harwood, *The Race Concept* (Newton Abbot, 1975), 9.

24  See J. MacKenzie, *Propaganda and Empire: The Manipulation of British Public Opinion, 1880–1960* (Manchester, 1984); J. MacKenzie, ed., *Imperialism and Popular Culture* (Manchester, 1986).

25  C. Husband, 'Introduction: "Race", the Continuity of a Concept', in C. Husband, ed., *'Race' in Britain: Continuity and Change* (London, 1982), 19–20.

26  Tabili, *'We Ask for British Justice'*, 183.

27  D. Kay and R. Miles, *Refugees or Migrant Workers? European Volunteer Workers in Britain, 1946–1951* (London, 1992), 175.

28  See comment in S. Fielding, *Class and Ethnicity: Irish Catholics in England, 1880–1939* (Buckingham, 1993), 127.

29  Statistically, the Irish constituted the largest single 'immigrant' group in Britain until the 1970s. See Holmes, *John Bull's Island*, 216.

30  For details, see Hickman and Walter, 'Deconstructing Whiteness'.

31  E. Hunt, *British Labour History, 1815–1914* (London, 1981), 167.

32  For details, see K. Lunn, '"Good for a Few Hundreds at Least": Irish Labour Recruitment Into Britain During the Second World War', in P. Buckland and J. Belchem, eds., *The Irish in British Labour History* (Liverpool, 1993), 102–14.

33  See T. Kushner, *The Holocaust and the Liberal Imagination: A Social and Cultural History* (Oxford, 1994), 61–118.

34  T. Kushner, 'Jew and Non-Jew in the East End of London: Towards an Anthropology of "Everyday" Relations', in G. Alderman and C. Holmes, eds., *Outsiders and Outcasts* (London, 1993), 32–52.

35  J. Tannahill, *European Volunteer Workers in Britain* (Manchester, 1956), 63–4.

36  *Parliamentary Debates*, vol. 295, 4 December 1934, col. 1458.

37  For details, see Frost, ed., *Ethnic Labour*.

38  For details, see M. Sherwood, 'Strikes! African Seamen, Elder Dempster and the Government, 1940–42', in Frost, ed., *Ethnic Labour*, 130–45.

39  For background and details, see F. Broeze, 'The Muscles of Empire – Indian Seamen and the Raj 1919–1939', *The Indian Economic and Social History Review* 18:1 (1981), 43–67.

40  See L. Colley, *Britons: Forging the Nation 1707–1837* (New Haven, Conn., 1992); K. Lunn, 'Reconsidering "Britishness": The Construction and Significance of National Identity in Twentieth-century Britain', in B. Jenkins and S. Sofos, eds., *Nation & Identity in Contemporary Europe* (London, 1996), 83–100.

41 Paul, *Whitewashing Britain*.
42 Frost, ed., *Ethnic Labour*.
43 A. Bonnett, 'Anti-racism and the Critique of "White" Identities', *New Community* 22:1 (1996), 97.
44 See Kay and Miles, *Refugees or Migrant Workers?*; K. Lunn, 'The Employment of Polish and European Volunteer Workers in the Scottish Coalfields 1945–1950', in K. Tenfelde, ed., *Towards a Social History of Mining in the 19th and 20th Centuries* (Munich, 1992), 582–92.
45 Kay and Miles, *Refugees or Migrant Workers?*, 124–5, for example.

# 6
# Racism and Resistance in British Trade Unions, 1948–79[1]

*Satnam Virdee*

## Introduction

This essay provides a critical analysis of the relationship between black[2] labour and British trade unions between the years 1948 and 1979. Specifically, it has three main aims. First, it discusses why, following mass immigration from the Caribbean and the Indian subcontinent, elements of organized labour colluded with employers to restrict the job opportunities open to black workers. Second, the essay investigates the nature of resistance to such exclusionary practices offered by black workers themselves. Third, it analyses what impact the changing industrial relations climate of the early 1970s had on working-class consciousness, and in particular on white trade unionists' attitudes and practices towards black workers.

## Racism and the position of migrant labour in class relations in postwar Britain

The demands of an expanding postwar economy meant that Britain, like most other European countries, was faced with a chronic shortage of labour.[3] The demand for labour was met by a variety of sources including 500,000 refugees, displaced persons and ex-prisoners of war from Europe between 1946 and 1951 and a further 350,000 European nationals between 1945 and 1957.[4] However, the overwhelming majority of migrants who came to Britain were from the Republic of Ireland, the Indian subcontinent and the Caribbean.[5]

On the whole, the labour migration from the Indian subcontinent and the Caribbean proceeded by informal means with little 'effort made to relate employment to vacancies. Instead it was left to the free market forces to determine the size of immigration.'[6] However, those industries where the demand for labour was greatest actively recruited black workers in their home countries.[7] Employers such as the British Transport Commission, the London Transport Executive, the British Hotels and Restaurants Association, and the Regional Hospitals Board all established arrangements with Caribbean governments to ensure a regular supply of labour.[8] Overall, Smith[9] has estimated that 12 per cent of Caribbean men, 9 per cent of Indian men, 7 per cent of Pakistani men and 2 per cent of East African Asian men already had a job arranged before they came to Britain. By 1958 and a decade of black labour migration, there were 125,000 Caribbean and 55,000 Indian and Pakistani workers in Britain.[10]

Despite the heterogeneous class structure of the migrating populations,[11] they ended up occupying overwhelmingly semi- and unskilled positions in the British labour market.[12] The explanation for this was two-fold. First, the growth of new jobs offering relatively higher rates of pay and improved conditions of employment in industries such as light engineering resulted in a significant shift of white labour out of older sectors of industry and into these jobs. Second, the exclusionary practices of employers, motivated in part by racism, prevented black workers from competing equally for these relatively more attractive jobs, which forced them to take up jobs in those older sectors of industry such as textile production which large numbers of white workers had recently left.[13]

Importantly, research suggests that elements of organized labour colluded with employers to exclude South Asian and Caribbean workers from key forms of employment, especially skilled work.[14]

## Existing theoretical approaches to understanding the relationship between trade unions and black labour

On the whole, there has been a distinct paucity of theoretically informed analyses investigating the reasons why elements of organized labour colluded with employers to restrict the job opportunities open to black workers. One group of notable exceptions have been those scholars writing within what may be termed the black radical tradition.[15] Broadly speaking, scholars such as Sivanandan from the Institute of Race Relations,[16] Darcus Howe[17] and the Race Today Collective[18] and later Paul Gilroy[19] contend that elements of skilled, white organized labour instituted racially motivated exclusionary practices against migrant labour because they accrued both economic and ideological benefits. Hence, for Sivanandan,[20] the white worker

> is a party to his oppression. He too benefits from the exploitation of
> the black man, however indirectly, and tends to hold the black
> worker to areas of work which he himself does not wish to do, and
> from areas of work to which he himself aspires, irrespective of skill.

This enforced location of black workers in the semi- and unskilled
positions in class relations contributed to skilled white labour maintaining its strong bargaining position in the labour market, whilst
simultaneously exacerbating the racism of semi- and unskilled white
labour 'forced' to work alongside black labour in jobs offering relatively poorer and insecure terms of employment:

> the profit from immigrant labour had not benefited the whole of
> society but only sections of it (including some sections of the white
> working class) whereas the infrastructural 'cost' of immigrant
> labour had been borne by those in greatest need.[21]

Such material gains accrued by skilled white labour, it was contended,
were accompanied by the perception of ideological benefits which
served to fracture working class solidarity in Britain so that:

> the attitude of racial superiority on the part of white workers rele-
> gates their black comrades to constitute a class apart, an
> under-class: the sub-proletariat. And the common denominator of
> capitalist oppression is not sufficient to bind them together in a
> common purpose.[22]

Following on from such an analysis was a second conclusion: the
racist fracture of the working class, instituted by skilled white labour,
was deemed to be permanent in nature. That is, it could no longer be
assumed that the working class was capable of undertaking its historical role as an agency of progressive social change. Hence, Gilroy
contends:[23]

> The proletariat of yesterday, classically conceived or otherwise,
> now has rather more to lose than its chains. The real gains which it
> has made have been at the cost of a deep-seated accommodation
> with capital and the political institutions of corporatism. Its will, as
> Calhoun has also pointed out 'is apt be a reformist will'.

If the white working class were unlikely to challenge the racism faced by the black working class, a strategy, founded upon an alternative agency, had to be developed if racist exclusionary practices were to be effectively combated. According to the black radical perspective, this alternative strategy was 'black self-organization' built around the construction of a political solidarity between African-Caribbean and South Asian workers. As Howe[24] makes clear: 'The black working class will be in charge ... the black struggle has an independence, validity, and vitality of its own'.

The work of Robert Miles and Annie Phizacklea[25] provides an important counter to the conclusions reached by those from the black radical tradition. On the basis of their work, the suggestion made by black radicals that the white working class and the trade unions were incapable of combating racism in their ranks has to be seriously re-examined. Whilst acknowledging the racism faced by black workers from white workers and trade unions, Miles and Phizacklea[26] point out how, by 1973, the TUC (the federation of British trade unions) was already being forced to recognize the need to combat racism in the trade unions. This development had arisen due to three interrelated factors:

> First, there occurred in the early 1970s a number of industrial disputes which were distinguished by ... complaints by black workers of discrimination made against trade union officials ... Secondly, since the 1950s, there has been a current of internal trade union criticism, voiced regularly at the annual congress, and this increased following these disputes. Thirdly, there has been increasing trade union concern about the apparent growth of the National Front which is regarded as a neo-fascist organisation.[27]

Despite the undoubted importance of Miles and Phizacklea's work, their analysis does have limitations. They argue that the change in TUC policy towards black workers in the early 1970s arose due to the growing recognition amongst black and white workers of the need to combat racism and fascism.[28] While no doubt correct, this conclusion begs the question, why did growing numbers of white workers begin to believe this in 1973 and not earlier or later? By failing to place this change of policy in the context of the wider industrial relations developments of the time, in particular the growing class conflict between worker and employer and its impact on working-class consciousness, their explanation remains a partial one.

By undertaking an analysis of key events during this period, I argue that existing explanations have only limited power when it comes to understanding the relationship between organized labour and the black worker during this thirty-year period. First, this essay argues for the importance of understanding the primary role that trade unions play as organizations of sectional working-class interests and the forms of class consciousness they engender if we are to offer a more comprehensive explanation of their response to migrant labour. Second, the paper assesses how a particular set of economic, political and ideological factors influenced the strategies trade unions employed to defend their members' interests in the two decades after the Second World War. Third, it goes on to analyse how the dominant form of class consciousness which such strategies engendered was key to understanding the racist attitudes and actions of some trade unionists to black labour. Finally, I explore how changes in these economic, political and ideological factors during the late 1960s and early 1970s, forced changes in the types of strategies trade unions employed, which in turn was accompanied by a change in the dominant form of class consciousness, reflected also in their attitudes and actions towards black labour.

## Trade unions as organizations of sectional working-class interests and its implications for class consciousness

As well as being inaccurate in arguing that the response of the trade union movement was almost entirely racist in nature throughout this thirty year-period (which I will directly address later),[29] writers from the black radical tradition have argued that elements of organized labour instituted racist exclusionary practices against black workers because of the economic and ideological benefits they would accrue. For black radicals, this amounted to a 'betrayal' of the objective class interests of the white working-class. Hence, their suggestion that in the absence of white working-class support, black self-organization was the only viable strategy of resistance to combat such practices effectively.

Implicit within these conclusions and analytical framework is the assumption that somehow, prior to the arrival of postwar migrant labour, the British working class were not internally divided and instead existed as a unitary structural and ideological entity.[30] Such an assumption ignores a large body of historical work demonstrating that apart from a few, highly exceptional periods, the British working class has been internally divided by gender, skill levels, industry and occupational location since its formation in the late eighteenth and early nineteenth centuries.[31]

It is against this backdrop that the role of trade unions must be understood. Historically, trade unions organized groups of workers around markers of difference such as skill levels created by the changing labour process and thereby reflected them in their organisational forms. As Kelly[32] argues:

> The contours of trade unionism were shaped by the contours of capitalist industrialisation, with unions arising separately in one trade after another, each organising the various occupations created within the division of labour. In other words, the historical evolution of trade unionism imparted to it a sectional character as workers were organised in terms of their specific employment, not their general class position.

Such sectionalist forms of organization gave rise to sectionalist forms of action. On the whole, a trade union did not seek to represent the interests of the whole working class but rather the 'short-term interests of particular groups of workers'.[33] This it did through the negotiation of higher wage levels and improved terms and conditions of employment for its membership.

To advance this primary aim of improving the pay and conditions of their membership, postwar British trade unions have had available to them a range of strategies. Amongst the most prevalent were free collective bargaining with employers at either industry or plant level; utilizing restrictive practices to limit the supply of labour available to an employer to ensure that the price of labour of those workers already employed in an industry remained relatively high; or, usually in the final instance, undertaking strike action, mainly involving workers in the same workgroup or industry but in some cases workers from other industries.[34]

Which particular strategy is deployed during any one moment in time is dependent upon several sets of factors, including the following: the state of the labour market in which the trade union organizes; the politics of trade union leaders at both a national and local level; employer strategies towards the union and its membership; the extent of state intervention in labour–employer relations; and finally, labour–employer relations more generally, or, as some would contend, the state of the 'class struggle'.[35]

It is the strategy adopted by trade unions and their members under these economic, ideological and political factors that strongly determines the forms of class consciousness that emerge. Kelly[36] defines class consciousness as referring to two things: first, the perceived relation between an individual and his/her own class; and second, the perceived relation between his/her own class and the other class. A three-fold analytical distinction is utilized to understand variations in people's identification with their own social class. These are a sectional class consciousness where workers identify themselves and their interests primarily with a section of their class with whom they have an immediate interest (e.g. colleagues at work); a corporate class consciousness where workers identify themselves and their interests with the corporate body and the interests of the working class as a whole within capitalism; and, finally a hegemonic class consciousness where workers identify the revolutionary interests of the working class with the interests of society as a whole.

Additionally, the relations between classes are conceptualized in the following three ways. Relations between workers and employers may be seen as complementary where both parties perform different, but essential and interdependent functions within the enterprise of the economy; they may be seen as conflictual, with conflicts of interest over wages, workloads and other issues underpinned by a shared interest in procedural agreements; finally, relations may be seen as fundamentally antagonistic where elements of conflict in the relationship such as capital's exploitation and domination of labour constitute its most salient feature. Hence, the strictest definition of a revolutionary class consciousness would require the attainment of hegemonic consciousness coupled with a belief in the fundamental antagonism between the two major social classes.

The next section investigates how these economic, ideological and political factors influenced the types of strategy that trade unions employed to defend their members' interests and why this was important in understanding the response of parts of organised labour to black labour in the two decades that followed the Second World War.

## Trade union strategies in Britain, 1945–67

Due to the prevalence of tight labour market conditions, the two decades that followed the war were characterized by full employment and rising real wages for many sections of the British working class. This contributed to the development of what Crouch[37] has referred to as the 'Welfare Compromise' where both Conservative and Labour governments committed themselves to using Keynesian economic policies to regulate demand and smooth trade cycles by controlling public expenditure. Along with employer representatives, the national leaderships of the large trade unions were strong supporters of such policies because they served to strengthen their power over their own members as well as achieving greater influence over economic and industrial policy formation.[38] By delivering real wage increases to their members through the negotiation of national/industry-wide agreements with employers, these trade union leaders hoped that the need to undertake industrial action – a strategy that trade union leaders had far less control over – would become increasingly unlikely.[39]

However, parallel to this development was the growing importance of the 'informal system' of industrial relations based on the actual behaviour of managers, shop stewards and workgroups at the place of work.[40] With the supply of labour scarce, many groups of skilled workers found themselves in a strong bargaining position. Facilitated by the growth of lay union representatives – the shop stewards – groups of workers were able to wrest from employers improved pay and conditions at plant level that were far in excess of that agreed at the national level for the industry. By the 1960s, collective bargaining at plant level had become 'the most important level of bargaining over pay in manufacturing'.[41]

With the increasing importance of devolved forms of collective bargaining, the shop steward also had greater independence to employ other strategies to improve his members' interests. One of the most important in the immediate postwar era of full employment and scarce labour was the use of restrictive practices to control the supply of labour entering a particular plant thereby ensuring that the price of labour already working in the plant remained relatively high. Many different criteria were used to restrict the supply of labour, including most importantly, skill levels.

If the strategies of free collective bargaining or restrictive practices were unsuccessful in achieving their goal of improved pay and conditions, then shop stewards led short, unofficial strikes, commonly known as 'wildcat strikes', often involving only the local workgroup.[42] However, contrary to public opinion at the time, a relatively small proportion of workers actually engaged in strike action during this period. Kelly[43] shows that in the 1950s, over 80 per cent of days lost in officially recorded disputes were accounted for by less than 20 per cent of the workforce. Further, those groups of workers who engaged in strike action did so for relatively short periods of time and, moreover, there was little evidence of secondary strike action.[44] As a result, the form of strike action that may have been the first step towards the formation of a class consciousness that transcended sectional interests was largely absent during this era. Similarly, research has also shown that the shop stewards responsible for pay bargaining and leading strike action at the local level articulated highly 'restrictive, sectionalist attitudes and the defence of local rather than general [working-class] interests'.[45]

There is little doubt that during the two decades following the Second World War, the strong bargaining position that elements of skilled organized labour found themselves in as a result of the tight labour market conditions enabled them to secure significant improvements in pay and conditions for their members.[46] However, the strategies adopted by trade unions to wrest improved pay and conditions also had important consequences for the development of a particular form of class consciousness. Precisely because sectionalist action was normally sufficient to ensure better pay and conditions, this period was characterized by a sectionalist class consciousness where, on the whole, workers identified their interests primarily with other members of their workgroup or those who worked in the same industry. Additionally, labour–employer relations were, on the whole, complementary, with an acceptance of the roles played by management and workers in the industry. It was on very rare occasions that this situation of industrial peace was punctuated by short strikes and the development of a conflictual relationship between workers and employers.

It was the prevalence of such a sectionalist class consciousness which was key to understanding how a racist ideology was able to gain an audience amongst some groups of workers during this period as I shall demonstrate below.

## Sectionalist action and consciousness and its importance in explaining the response of organized labour to black labour

Even prior to the postwar mass migration from the Caribbean and the Indian subcontinent the prevalence of racist imagery and sentiment was widespread amongst all sections of British society.[47] Drawing its images from slavery and then colonialism, it viewed racialised social groups first as 'inferior', 'sub-human' and then as 'child like' and 'in need of civilisation'.[48] When the postwar migrants began to arrive, such racist stereotypes were transcended by the development of an 'indigenous racism' whereby

> the cruder, historically specific ideas of inferiority and lack of civilisation [were] replaced by feelings of cultural difference, of 'Britishness', of 'whiteness' ... White colonial and cultural supremacy was being threatened 'on the streets' in Britain as well as in the former colonies. In response, the black person was defined as 'alien', a threat to 'Britishness', a person with no right to be here.[49]

On some occasions, such imagery and sentiment translated into racist political mobilisation and violence towards black migrants. Some of the more notorious incidents in the 1950s included the racist riots against blacks in Nottingham, Dudley and Notting Hill.[50] The established political parties, Conservative and Labour, did little to combat such racism and on some occasions actively courted the racist vote.[51] During the October 1964 general election in Smethwick (a small industrial town near Birmingham), the Conservative Party candidate, Peter Griffiths, publicly endorsed one of the racist slogans circulating in the town at the time: 'If you want a nigger neighbour, vote Labour'.[52] Similarly, the Labour Party, the 'moulder of working class opinion', offered little resistance to such racism and indeed were party to it, as evidenced by their refusal to commit themselves to a principled policy of decolonization and their support for measures to control further immigration from 'non-white' countries.[53] Hence, there was little political will to tackle the racism faced by racialized social groups and racial discrimination in housing and employment remained legal until 1968.[54] This constellation of racist sentiment and imagery had a strong hold over significant elements of the white working class population in the 1950s and 1960s. This was further reinforced by the almost total absence of organized opposition to such racism from within the working class itself. As Joshi and Carter make clear:[55]

> when black workers began to arrive here in some numbers in the 1950s, there was no progressive, anti-racist political ideological framework which would have enabled the working class to 'make sense' of a black presence in Britain.

The dominant sectionalist class consciousness so widely prevalent amongst the white working class enabled this racist ideology to gain a wide acceptance amongst them. One of the central components of this negative racialization of black workers was that they represented a source of cheap labour that threatened the newly improved living standards of skilled white workers if they were employed in the same industries in large enough numbers.[56] Hence, one branch secretary of a craft union reported:

> We are continually on the look-out for employers who seek to use coloured workers for cheap labour to the detriment of their countrymen; also employers who allow coloured workers to work unlimited overtime opposed to local and national agreements between federated firms and the union.[57]

Similarly, another writer highlighted the concern felt by many trade unionists about the threat posed by the potential employment of racialized labour: 'in the branches and factories the problem of jobs and wages is more directly felt and that many workers ... quite genuinely feel immigrants to be a danger'.[58]

With little sense of a corporate class consciousness constructed around a notion of working-class solidarity but rather a sectionalist class consciousness characterized by the primary concern of protecting the terms and conditions of their immediate membership, elements of skilled organized labour at individual plant level, fearful of the perceived threat posed by migrant labour, colluded with employers to ensure that the trade union strategy of restrictive practices took on an added racist dimension by excluding migrant labour from skilled jobs.[59] This practice was particularly evident in those industries that were in decline such as textiles and foundry work where white workers felt particularly threatened.[60] According to Fryer,[61] 'in many industries, white trade unionists resisted the employment of black workers, or insisted on a "quota" system limiting them to ... about 5 per cent'. When such racist practices came under threat of being breached, white workers took industrial action to defend them. In February 1955, in the West Midlands, white workers at the West Bromwich Corporation Transport system began a series of Saturday strikes in protest against the employment of an Indian trainee conductor. Similarly, and also in 1955, white transport workers in Wolverhampton decided to ban all overtime from 1 September in protest against the increasing employment of black recruits. The local union contended that the 5 per cent quota which had been informally agreed with management had been breached because 68 of the 900 total workforce were black workers.[62]

There were also other racist exclusionary practices agreed between white trade unionists and employers which served to impact adversely on black workers: the principle of 'last in first out' was not applied at a time of redundancy if it meant that white workers would lose their jobs before black workers.[63] Hence, Stephens[64] found that one 'official of a general union thought that in the event of redundancy occurring his members would insist on coloured workers going first'.

On the whole, individual trade unions at a national level failed to counter the racist views and actions of some of their members:

> all national trade union bodies do not exert sufficient drive to combat this confusion among certain of the rank and file, and all too often confine themselves to a declaration of where they stand without attempting to carry all their members with them.[65]

A survey carried out in the mid-1950s of 61 trade union branches demonstrated that trade union action to challenge racism at an individual branch level was also minimal and very much at the level of policy formation: of 22 trade union branches that had 'coloured' workers, only five were found to have passed resolutions in favour of equal treatment.[66] Instead, motions from transport workers to the TGWU annual conference demanding that black workers be banned from the buses were passed, while hospital branches of COHSE passed resolutions objecting to the recruitment of Caribbean nurses.[67]

One might have expected that an important source of opposition to such disunity in the organized labour movement may have been the Trade Union Congress (TUC). However, the TUC's powers of intervention over the specific policies of affiliated unions are limited,[68] reflecting their status as 'the servant of the affiliated unions and not their master'.[69] As a consequence, the TUC and its executive body, the General Council, faithfully reproduced the dominant views of the major affiliated unions on the subject and thereby

> failed to acknowledge that there existed considerable hostility towards black workers amongst white trade unionists and increasingly came to adopt the position that the problems arose from the immigrant's refusal to 'integrate'.[70]

Apart from isolated cases such as the campaign mounted by black community organizations and some individual whites against the operation of a 'colour bar' introduced by white bus workers in Bristol in 1955,[71] there is little evidence of organized resistance to such racist practices from either black or white workers during this period. As Sivanandan argues[72] 'resistance to racial abuse and discrimination on the shop floor was more spontaneous than organised'.

Overall, then, the sectionalist class consciousness so dominant during this era where workers would identify their interests narrowly with other workers in their local workgroup or with workers in the same industry rather than the working class generally greatly facilitated the hold of a racist ideology over some elements of organized labour. It was the interaction of these factors that explains why some white trade unionists colluded with employers to restrict the job opportunities open to black workers.

## Black self-organization as a strategy of resistance to racism, 1965–73

The second conclusion drawn by those writing from a black radical perspective was that the division between elements of white organized labour and the black working class was permanent in nature. This in turn implied that the white working class and the organized labour movement was written off as an agency of progressive social change and black self-organization was put forward as the only viable alternative to combat the racism and exclusionary practices that black workers were subjected to.[73]

The evidence from the mid-1960s showed that while a sectionalist class consciousness continued to facilitate the hold of a racist ideology over large elements of white organized labour, black labour began to organize collective resistance to such exclusionary practices. An important catalyst in the development of such organized and independent black resistance was the arrival in Britain, in late 1964 and early 1965 respectively, of the two leaders of the American anti-racist movement: Malcolm X and Martin Luther King met representatives of the black British community and encouraged them to establish organizations to combat racism. Two national anti-racist organizations were established: the Racial Action Adjustment Society (RAAS) influenced by the ideas of Malcolm X and the philosophy of revolutionary black nationalism, and the Campaign Against Racial Discrimination (CARD) influenced by the teachings of Martin Luther King.[74]

The first evidence of such organized resistance to racism and exclusionary practices in the workplace emerged shortly afterwards. In May 1965, Asian and Caribbean workers went on strike at Courtauld's Red Scar Mill in Preston, Lancashire. This was a large rayon mill which produced industrial textiles. About one-third of the total workforce of 2,400 were of Caribbean or Asian origin. However, they were overwhelmingly located in the tyre-cord spinning department where they formed two-thirds of the total workforce; the rest being Italian and East European migrants.

Towards the end of 1964, TGWU officials entered into negotiations with management about a new productivity agreement for workers in the tyre-cord spinning department. By spring 1965, management, the TGWU official and the four local stewards representing the tyre-cord spinning department came to an agreement whereby workers had to work more machines for proportionately less pay; specifically, a 50 per cent increase in work for a 3 per cent increase in pay. The workers were furious and refused to accept the agreement. Eventually, the Caribbean and Asian workers walked out in protest leaving only the European workers to carry on working. However, not only did the TGWU fail to support the black workers by refusing to make the strike official, they actively colluded with management by refusing to recognize that the strikers had a legitimate grievance. The vice-chair of the factory-wide shop stewards organization using racist imagery told a reporter that the dispute was 'tribal' in nature, while another steward claimed that 'several hotheads are stirring up trouble for their own selfish interests'.[75] Although there was no support forthcoming from white trade unionists, the black workers were able to continue the strike for three weeks through the active support of RAAS and individual white radicals.

Another strike by black workers quickly followed which again illustrated both trade union inaction and racism. In 1967, at a Coneygre Foundry in the West Midlands, management precipitated the strike by Asian workers through the use of racially discriminatory redundancy procedures: management refused to operate the generally accepted trade union principle of 'last in first out' and selected 21 Indians – and no whites – to go. However, the Asian workers' trade union, the Transport and General Workers Union (TGWU), refused to make the strike official and rejected the idea that racial discrimination was involved. Moreover, white workers in another trade union, the Associated Union of Foundry Workers (AUFW), refused to support the strike and continued to cross the Asian workers' picket line, encouraged by the local AUFW official, who explained that his members were not involved in the redundancies. Despite the obvious lack of solidarity shown by white trade unionists, the strike was sustained by the support provided by other Asian workers and the Indian Workers Association (IWA). It was this support from the community that eventually forced management to take back all 21 Asian workers made redundant who wished to return.[76]

Whilst Asian and Caribbean workers were beginning collectively to resist the racist exclusionary practices that had served to exclude them from skilled work, elements of the white working class were being mobilized by racist politicians to consolidate further such divisions within trade unions. When Enoch Powell, a former Conservative Health Minister who had been responsible for the recruitment of Caribbean nurses to Britain in the 1950s,[77] made an inflammatory speech in Wolverhampton in April 1968, warning of the threat posed by black immigration to the traditional British way of life, 'London dockers struck work and marched on parliament to demand an end to immigration. Three days later they marched again, this time with the Smithfield meat-porters.'[78]

Strikes by black workers continued into the early 1970s[79] with the high-point of black self-organization as a strategy to combat racism and exclusionary practices being the Mansfield Hosiery Mills dispute which took place in the East Midlands in October 1972. Mansfield Hosiery was a company that made pullovers. The process involved three groups of workers: the 'knitters' who earned the most and who were all white, and the 'runners-on' and the 'bar-loaders' who earned the least and were overwhelmingly of Asian origin. The 500-strong Asian workforce had effectively been denied access to the best-paid jobs on the knitting machines over a long period of time. In October 1972, a strike was called over this and other anomalies in the payment system. Management responded by agreeing to train two Asian knitters and so the strike was called off. However, almost immediately the white workers on the knitting machines, fearing that their jobs were under threat, came out on strike. According to Moore,[80] 'This strike had been promised by the local union leadership if the whites were, in his words, 'flushed out of the knitting jobs'. Under pressure from the local union, the National Union of Hosiery and Knitwear Workers (NUKW), management backtracked on its promise to train Asian knitters and instead offered them a small increase in pay. This resulted in the escalation of the dispute with 400 Asian workers, including Asian workers from another company factory, coming out on strike in sympathy. The company immediately dismissed these workers and began to recruit white trainees for the knitting jobs. It was at this point that the union was forced to request that management stop recruiting 'scab' labour. However, it was not until the strikers occupied the union offices that the union finally made the strike official, although it still refused to call out its white membership. Again the Asian strikers had to rely on the support they received from the Asian community rather than the trade union movement to sustain the strike. Eventually, they succeeded in winning all their demands and 28 Asian workers were selected for training as knitters.[81]

This strike had important repercussions within the trade union movement. After almost a decade of organized resistance to racism by black workers, the first indications of a change in attitude within parts of the labour movement appeared. The Mansfield Strike Committee born out of the dispute but comprising representatives of black political organizations, Asian workers from different areas as well as the strikers themselves was central to the organization of a major conference for trade unionists which was held in June 1973. Three hundred and fifty delegates from all the major unions, as well as representatives from the black community organizations, came together in Birmingham and from this emerged the 'National Committee for Trade Unions Against Racialism' (NCTUAR).[82]

However, this growing recognition of the need to challenge racism in the trade union movement was not solely attributable to the industrial struggles being waged by black workers; rather it also reflected the growing radicalization of important elements of white organized labour. It was these two factors taken together which helped to create the political conditions which enabled the ideas of anti-racism to gain at least a foothold in the trade union movement. The next section analyses the reasons that motivated such a change in attitude amongst elements of white organized labour.

## Government attempts to curb shopfloor trade union activity

Parallel to the beginning of organized black resistance to racist exclusionary practices in the mid-1960s was growing state concern about unofficial shopfloor trade union activity. It is commonly agreed that the late 1960s and early 1970s represented an era of continual government attempts to curb such trade union activity.[83] Political debate had come to focus on the trade unions and the development of industrial relations at the workplace level, in particular the increasing ability of shop stewards (unpaid trade union officials) to carry out bargaining in an informal manner at plant or workgroup level. The government contended that such a development encouraged disorder, and especially 'wildcat' strikes. As a result, the 'shop steward became a symbol of trade union irresponsibility, and workplace conflict came to be seen as *the* major problem underlying poor productivity performance and Britain's economic problems'.[84]

Although the Donovan Commission reported in 1968 that shop stewards were not the problem but poor management, the Labour government continued to seek a legal resolution to the 'problem' of 'wildcat' strikes. In 1969, the government published a white paper called 'In Place of Strife' which outlined its proposals for curbing such activity. However, the bill was defeated due to the pressure brought to bear on the government by the trade union movement. Nevertheless, the Conservative government which took office in 1970 was able to successfully introduce an Industrial Relations Act in 1971 which replaced the collectivist laissez-faire industrial relations with a comprehensive legal framework intended to restrict conflict.[85]

The response of the trade union movement to such proposals for change could not have been expected. The growing intervention by the state in employer–labour relations forced a major change in trade union strategy. According to Callinicos,[86] 'attempts by the government and employers to ... control the shop stewards led ... to the biggest class confrontations for half a century'. The number of strike days lost increased dramatically: from an average of under four million days a year during the 1950s and 1960s to 24 million days lost in 1972 alone.[87] According to Kelly,[88] a significant proportion of these strikes were qualitatively different from those of the 1950s and 1960s: in the 1950s over 80 per cent of days lost in officially recorded strikes were accounted for by less than 20 per cent of the workforce ... By the mid-1970s a wide range of traditionally moderate and peaceful workers, many of them women, had embarked on strike action, many for the first time in their lives'. Additionally, attempts to curb unofficial strike activity saw the return of the political strike for the first time since the 1920s. A series of one-day stoppages against the 1971 Industrial Relations Bill culminated in the TUC instructing all its members not to comply with the Act by refusing to register themselves as trade unions when the bill became law. Finally, over 500 occupations and sit-ins took place during this period.[89]

These developments contributed to an uneven shift in class

consciousness taking place amongst key elements of organized labour: in particular there was a growing move beyond the sectionalist class consciousness of the 1950s and 1960s to a form of corporate class consciousness which recognized the importance of working-class unity and collective action if resistance to state attempts to regulate the role of trade unions were to be successful. Critical to the organization of this resistance were socialist trade unionists who had a political outlook that was internationalist in character. Verberckmoes[90] argues that, 'The relative strength of left-wing tendencies in the trade union movement definitely played a mobilising role in the explosion of strike activity between 1968 and 1974.' By the mid-1970s, it was estimated that 10 per cent of all trade union officials were communists.[91] The formation of a corporate class consciousness during this period was further evidenced by the significant leftward swings in the leadership of several major trade unions including the AEU, TGWU and the GMWU.[92]

This growing politicization of key elements of the white working class based around the ideology of working-class solidarity coupled with ten years of independent struggle by black workers against racist practices created the political and ideological conditions necessary for the ideas of anti-racism to seep into the trade union movement and open up the possibility of white organized labour beginning to resist racism because it harmed the development of a corporate class consciousness. However, it was the fear of growing far-right influence in the trade unions that finally resulted in a qualitative shift in the policy and the practice of the affiliated trade unions and the TUC from the 'problem of integration' to the 'problem of racism'.[93]

The dispute that caused widespread concern about far-right influence in trade unions took place in a firm called Imperial Typewriters in Leicester in 1973. One thousand one hundred of the 1,650 workforce were Asians, a large proportion from East Africa. Against a background of long-standing grievances over low pay, bad conditions and racial discrimination, a strike began involving 40 Asian workers. Management however, refused to recognize their grievances. Accompanying the general dissatisfaction with working conditions was the strikers' concern that there was only one Asian member of the shop stewards committee. Therefore, they also demanded the right to elect their own steward. However, the strikers' union, the TGWU, publicly declared its opposition to the dispute and refused to make the strike official, arguing that the Asian workers had not followed the correct negotiating procedures. The TGWU convenor in the factory refused to speak to the strike leaders on the grounds that union members were only eligible for election as shop stewards after two years' membership. This lack of support from the union merely served to solidify Asian worker unity and over 400 workers were now out on strike. A critical factor in the dispute was the involvement of the far-right political party, the National Front, whose members regularly came to the factory gates to intimidate the picketing strikers and support the white workers who continued to work. Despite such intimidation and the refusal of the trade union to support the striking workers, the Asian workers were sustained throughout their action by support from the Asian and Caribbean communities. After three months on strike, management conceded to their demands.[94]

## Tackling racism through collective working-class action, 1974–9

Change followed quickly after the dispute. In particular, those groups of activists who emphasized the importance of working-class solidarity now began to mobilize more forthrightly on the issue of racism. The decade of struggles by black workers coupled with the fear of the rise of the National Front made this part of the organized labour movement acutely aware that racism hindered the formation of working-class unification which was so critical to the defence of working-class interests in the face of state and employer measures.[95] A document produced by the International Socialists, a far-left organisation, in the mid-1970s for use within the workplace argued that racism 'threaten[s] the strength of trade union organisation inside the factory, and so tip[s] the balance of class power still further towards the employers'.[96] Similarly, a document released by a rank and file docker in the TGWU and endorsed by Jack Jones, the leader of the TGWU at the time, argued that

> The harsh reality is that the working class is divided by racialism to a damaging degree. An urgent responsibility falls upon trade union activists to seek those remedies which can unify our class and meet head-on the racialism embedded in so much of our society.[97]

This growing change in mood amongst some groups of activists was quickly reflected in the TUC. At the 1974 TUC Annual Conference, the General Council announced that it had submitted oral evidence and a memorandum to the Select Committee on Race Relations and Immigration where it acknowledged for the first time that black workers were subject to racism and discriminatory practices. Moreover, this evidence went on to state that 'trade unions should actively oppose racialism within their own ranks', both from the organised far-right and rank-and-file white trade unionists.[98]

At the 1975 TUC Annual Conference delegates from several affiliated unions made speeches denouncing the racism and the activities of the National Front and called upon trade unionists to warn their members of the dangers of racism to working-class solidarity. Although a minority current of opposition to racism in the trade union movement had existed since the late 1950s,[99] this current grew rapidly in the mid-1970s with local committees and trades councils becoming increasingly concerned about the need to tackle racism in the labour movement.

To further this aim, the General Council announced just after the 1975 TUC Annual Conference the establishment of a new sub-committee of the General Council, the Equal Rights Committee, whose main responsibility would be to develop policies to promote equal opportunity. Additionally, in 1975, the TUC General Council established the Race Relations Advisory Committee to work with the Equal Rights Committee on issues relating to 'race relations'.[100] In July 1976, the General Council issued a press release which called for the trade union movement to actively tackle racial discrimination:

> Much needs to be done to eliminate the discrimination and disadvantage facing ethnic minorities and for their part the General Council are advising affiliated unions about steps they should take to strengthen the organisation among immigrant and black workers and unity between work people.[101]

Hence, by the mid-1970s, there was a recognition amongst increasing elements of white trade unionists that working class solidarity could only be built by actively opposing the racism and disadvantage faced by black workers. This was demonstrated in practice in the Grunwick dispute.[102] Grunwick Film Processing Laboratories Ltd was a firm that developed and printed colour films. There were two factories in Willesden, in north-west London, which employed about 440 people. The dispute lasted from August 1976 to July 1978 and was led by Asian women who worked long hours in appalling conditions for low wages.

An argument with a manager led to the dismissal of one worker, which in turn led three others to walk out in protest. From this, the strike rapidly escalated with nearly a third of the 440 workers out on strike. The strikers decided to establish a union and after advice from the local Trades Council, joined the Association of Professional, Executive and Computer Staff (APEX). Once they had become members, APEX immediately made the strike official by announcing that strike pay would be given to the strikers. Grunwick's management responded by dismissing all the strikers. However, the strikers refused to concede and responded by stating 'If you refuse to talk to us, we will turn off all the taps, one by one, until you have to.'[103] To do this, they required support from other workers and according to Ramdin,[104] 'Support for the strike from sections of the British labour movement was quick and widespread.'

At the 1976 TUC Annual Conference, Roy Grantham, General Secretary of APEX, called on the entire trade union movement to give its support. He explicitly raised the issue of racism, arguing it was central to the exploitation that Asian workers suffered. Similarly, Tom Jackson of the Union of Post Office Workers (UPW) pledged support and agreed to stop the delivery of mail coming in or out of Grunwick which would effectively prevent the business from operating. It was not only senior white trade unionists that offered support to the strikers but also large numbers of rank and file white workers. Ramdin[105] describes how the local people of Brent responded with 'donations from Mulliner Park Ward, Rolls Royce Works Committee, Express Dairies, Associated Automation (GEC), TGWU, the UPW Cricklewood Office Branch'. Importantly, on 1 November 1976, the post office workers in the UPW stopped delivering Grunwick's mail.

Despite such solidarity, Grunwick's management refused to concede to the strikers' demands. As a result, the strike committee responded by calling for the trade union movement to support a mass picket of the firm for one week in June 1976, which they hoped would cause maximum disruption during Grunwick's busiest trading period. The call for support did not go unheeded with up to 20,000 pickets (overwhelmingly white) supporting the Asian women strikers. Additionally, local post office workers continued to stop the delivery of mail coming in or out of Grunwick despite having their strike pay withdrawn by their union, the UPW. Contracted TGWU drivers, working for the police on picket duty at Grunwick, refused to drive them into the firm's premises. Delegations of London dockers and Yorkshire miners came to the picket lines and supported the strikers.[106] The dispute continued for two years until July 1978 when the Asian women workers were eventually forced to go back to work. Nevertheless, it demonstrated clearly that, under conditions of intense class struggle and the growing formation of a corporate class consciousness, it was possible for white workers to undertake collective action in support of black workers.

Throughout the late 1970s, there was a growing recognition amongst key elements of the organized labour movement that racism served only to weaken the trade union movement and that it had to be actively addressed. Several major unions, including the GMBATU, BIFU, NUT, NATHFE, NALGO and the CPSA, issued positive statements against racism and set up bodies to monitor equal opportunity policies. Similarly, a resolution passed at the 1977 TUC Annual Conference called upon the General Council to conduct a campaign against racists in trade unions. This led to the production of a General Council statement on racism in 1978 and in 1979, the TUC sent a circular to all unions that had not adopted policies on tackling racists in their unions to do so.[107]

## Conclusions

For many writers in Britain, organized labour has been written off as an agency capable of combating racism. It has been contended that skilled elements of organized labour were an active social agent in the introduction of racially motivated discriminatory practices which excluded black labour from skilled work because they accrued both economic and ideological benefits.[108] From the evidence provided in this essay, it is clear that such a conclusion represents only a partial reflection of actual events during this epoch.

There is little doubt that during an era of full employment and relatively scarce labour, the dominant strategies deployed by trade unions, especially shop stewards at a local plant level, to defend their members' interests were highly sectionalist and engendered sectionalist forms of class consciousness. While such strategies no doubt secured improved pay and conditions for large groups of workers during this period, they also served to engender a racist division within the working class. The prevalence of a sectionalist class consciousness amongst elements of organized labour meant that some of them, fearful of the threat to their newly improved living standards posed by the arrival of supposedly cheaper migrant labour, instituted racially discriminatory practices against them. In this sense, parts of organized labour were an active social agent in the manufacture of this racist division within some trade unions.

It was not until the mid-1960s that collective resistance to such racist practices emerged. Due to the continued prevalence of a sectionalist class consciousness amongst elements of white labour and the dominance of racist sentiment, it was black workers organizing independently that first began to challenge such practices. However, unlike the black radicals who contended that white workers were unlikely to support black workers and that therefore black self-organization had become the only viable strategy capable of effectively combating such practices, the evidence showed that black self-organization was a rather important precursor to working-class unification.

The attempts to curb unofficial trade union activity in the late 1960s and early 1970s served to politicize key elements of the white working-class and resulted in the formation of an oppositional working-class identity. In particular, there began to take place a significant shift beyond the narrow, sectionalist consciousness of the 1950s and 1960s to a more politicized form of corporate class consciousness which recognized the importance of working-class solidarity and collective action to protect workers interests. This major development, coupled with almost a decade of industrial struggles against racism by black workers and growing fear of far-right influence in trade unions, created the 'preconditions' for the ideas of anti-racism and solidarity between black and white labour to gain a wider audience in the trade union movement. By the mid-1970s, the TUC and some affiliated trade unions explicitly recognized that working-class solidarity could only be achieved through combating racism, and, as a result, policies and practices were introduced to tackle racists in trade unions. However, the most visible manifestation of solidarity between black and white labour came during the course of the Grunwick dispute when thousands of white workers including miners, dockers, transport workers and post office workers actively supported Asian women on strike. This dispute demonstrated that amidst the growing politicization of parts of the organized labour movement, many white workers were able to overcame the ideology of racism and act in solidarity with black workers.

## Notes

1  I would like to thank Peter Alexander, Rick Halpern, Roger Horowitz,

Neville Kirk, Sheila Rowbotham and John Solomos for useful comments on a previous draft of this chapter.

2   I use the term 'black' to reflect the social construction developed by Asian and Caribbean trade unionists during the period under discussion. However, where necessary, I also distinguish between different 'ethnic' groups by using the terms 'Asian' and 'Caribbean'. That all of these terms are social constructions and not 'objective' categories is captured by the controversy in the USA and Britain over self-categorization. See F.J. Davis, *Who is Black? One Nation's Definition* (Philadelphia, 1991) and T. Modood, '"Black", Racial Equality and Asian Identity', *New Community* 14:3 (1988).

3   See S. Castles and G. Kosack, *Immigrant Workers and Class Structure in Western Europe* (Oxford, 1985).

4   See A. Sivanandan, 'Race, Class and the State: The Black Experience in Britain', *Race and Class* 17:4 (1976), 348.

5   See R. Miles, *Racism* (London, 1989).

6   See Sivanandan, 'Race, Class and the State'.

7   See P. Fryer, *Staying Power: The History of Black People in Britain* (London, 1984) and R. Ramdin, *The Making of the Black Working Class in Britain* (Aldershot, 1987).

8   Ramdin, *The Making of the Black Working Class in Britain*, 197.

9   D.J. Smith, *Racial Disadvantage in Britain* (London, 1977).

10   Fryer, *Staying Power: The History of Black People in Britain*, 373.

11   See W.W. Daniel, *Racial Discrimination in England* (London, 1968) and A. Heath and J. Ridge, 'Social Mobility of Ethnic Minorities', *Journal of Biosocial Science* Supplement 8, (1983), 169–84.

12   See Daniel, *Racial Discrimination in England* and Smith, *Racial Disadvantage in Britain*.

13   Miles, *Racism*.

14   See A. Sivanandan, *A Different Hunger: Writings on Black Resistance* (London, 1982); Fryer, *Staying Power: the History of Black People in Britain*; Ramdin, *The Making of the Black Working Class in Britain*; J. Wrench, 'Unequal Comrades: Trade Unions, Equal Opportunity and Racism', R. Jenkins and J. Solomos, eds., in *Racism and Equal Opportunity Policies in the 1980s*, (Cambridge, 1987).

15   See C. Robinson, *Black Marxism: The Making of the Black Radical Tradition* (London, 1983).

16   See Sivanandan, 'Race, Class and the State'; A. Sivanandan, 'The Liberation of the Black Intellectual', *Race and Class* 18:4 (1977); Sivanandan, *A Different Hunger: Writings on Black Resistance*.

17   See D. Howe, 'Enter Mrs. Thatcher: A Race Today Statement for Our Time', *Race Today* 10:3 (March 1978), 57–62.

18   Race Today Collective, *The Struggle of Asian Workers in Britain* (London, 1983).

19   P. Gilroy, 'Steppin' out of Babylon – Race, Class and Autonomy', in CCCS, *The Empire Strikes Back* (London, 1982) and P. Gilroy, *There Ain't No Black in the Union Jack* (London, 1987).

20   Sivanandan, 'The Liberation of the Black Intellectual', 339.

21   Sivanandan, 'Race, Class and the State', 350.

22  Sivanandan, 'The Liberation of the Black Intellectual', 339.
23  Gilroy, *There Ain't No Black in the Union Jack*, 246.
24  D. Howe, 'Enter Mrs. Thatcher', 62.
25  R. Miles and A. Phizacklea, *The TUC, Black Workers and New Commonwealth Immigration: 1954–1973* (Working Papers on Ethnic Relations, 6, Research Unit on Ethnic Relations, University of Bristol, 1977); R. Miles and A. Phizacklea 'The TUC and Black Workers: 1974–1976', *British Journal of Industrial Relations* 16:2 (1978), 195–207; A. Phizacklea and R. Miles, *Labour and Racism* (London, 1980).
26  Miles and Phizacklea, 'The TUC and Black Workers'.
27  Miles and Phizacklea, 'The TUC and Black Workers', 165.
28  Miles and Phizacklea, 'The TUC and Black Workers'.
29  See also B. Pinder, 'Trade Unions and Coloured Workers', *Marxism Today* (September 1961), 282–6, and Miles and Phizacklea. *The TUC, Black Workers and the New Commonwealth Immigration: 1954–1973.*
30  Miles (1982) makes a similar criticism of the work of Castles and Kosak (1985) on which Sivanandan draws. See R. Miles, *Racism and Migrant Labour* (London, 1982) and Castles and Kosack, *Immigrant Workers and Class Structure in Western Europe.*
31  For an overview, see A. L. Morton, *A People's History of England* (London, 1994); H. Pelling, *A History of British Trade Unionism* (London, 1987); E. P. Thompson, *The Making of the English Working Class* (London, 1991); S. Boston, *Women Workers and the Trade Unions* (London, 1980).
32  J. Kelly, *Trade Unions and Socialist Politics* (London, 1988), 55–6.
33  Kelly, *Trade Unions and Socialist Politics*, 57.
34  See R. Hyman, *Marxism and the Sociology of Trade Unionism* (London, 1972) and T. Clarke and T. Clements, eds., *Trade Unions under Capitalism* (London, 1977).
35  See Hyman, *Marxism and the Sociology of Trade Unionism*; P. Anderson, 'The Limits and Possibilities of Trade Union Action', in T. Clarke and T. Clements, eds., *Trade Unions under Capitalism* (London, 1977), 333–50; Kelly, *Trade Unions and Socialist Politics.*
36  Kelly, *Trade Unions and Socialist Politics*, 86–7.
37  C. Crouch, *Class Conflict and the Industrial Relations Crisis* (London, 1977).
38  H. Clegg, *The Changing System of Industrial Relations in Great Britain* (London, 1979).
39  Pelling, *A History of British Trade Unionism.*
40  S. Kessler and F. Bayliss, *Contemporary British Industrial Relations* (Basingstoke, 1995), 12–14.
41  Clegg, *The Changing System of Industrial Relations in Great Britain*, 9.
42  M. Terry, 'Trade Unions: Shop Stewards and the Workplace' in P. Edwards, ed., *Industrial Relations* (London, 1995), 203–28.
43  Kelly, *Trade Unions and Socialist Politics* 107–8.
44  K. Grint, *The Sociology of Work* (London, 1991).
45  J. Verberckmoes, 'The United Kingdom: Between Policy and Party', in P. Pasture et al., eds., *The Lost Perspective? Trade Unions Between Ideology and Social Action in the New Europe*, vol.1 (Aldershot, 1996), 223.
46  See the discussion in W. Brown, *Piecework Bargaining* (London, 1973) and H. Beynon, *Working for Ford* (London, 1984).

47 Fryer, *Staying Power: The History of Black People in Britain*; Ramdin, *The Making of the Black Working Class in Britain*; C. Holmes, *John Bull's Island* (Basingstoke, 1988).
48 Fryer, *Staying Power: The History of Black People in Britain*.
49 S. Joshi and B. Carter, 'The Role of Labour in the Creation of a Racist Britain', *Race and Class* 25:3 (Winter 1984), 53–71.
50 Fryer, *Staying Power: The History of Black People in Britain*.
51 J. Solomos, *Race and Racism in Britain* (Basingstoke, 1993).
52 Cited in J. Solomos and L. Back, *Race, Politics and Social Change* (London, 1995), 54.
53 Joshi and Carter, 'The Role of Labour'.
54 Solomos, *Race and Racism in Britain*.
55 Joshi and Carter, 'The Role of Labour', 55.
56 P. Wright, *The Coloured Worker in British Industry* (Oxford, 1968); L. Stephens, *Employment of Coloured Workers in the Birmingham Area* (London, 1956); Pinder, 1961, *ibid*.
57 Cited in Stephens, 1956, *Employment of Coloured Workers in the Birmingham Area*, 18.
58 Pinder, 'Trade Unions and Coloured Workers', 282.
59 See Sivanandan, *A Different Hunger: Writings on Black Resistance*; Fryer, *Staying Power: The History of Black People in Britain*; Wrench, *ibid*. Ramdin, *The Making of the Black Working Class in Britain*.
60 M. Duffield, *Black Radicalism and the Politics of De-Industrialisation: The Hidden History of Indian Foundry Workers* (Aldershot, 1988).
61 Fryer, *Staying Power: The History of Black People in Britain*, 376.
62 Ramdin, *The Making of the Black Working Class in Britain*, 200.
63 Wrench, 'Unequal Comrades', 165.
64 Stephens, *Employment of Coloured Workers in the Birmingham Area*, 16.
65 Pinder, 'Trade Unions and Coloured Workers', 283.
66 Stephens, *Employment of Coloured Workers in the Birmingham Area*, 18.
67 Wrench, 'Unequal Comrades'.
68 R. Martin, *TUC: The Growth of a Pressure Group: 1868–1976* (Oxford, 1980).
69 Kessler and Bayliss, *Contemporary British Industrial Relations*, 173.
70 Miles and Phizacklea, *The TUC, Black Workers and New Commonwealth Immigration*, 3.
71 M. Dresser, *Black and White on the Buses: The 1963 Colour Bar Dispute in Bristol* (Bristol, 1986).
72 Sivanandan, *A Different Hunger: Writings on Black Resistance*, 5.
73 Gilroy, *There Ain't No Black in the Union Jack*.
74 Sivanandan, *A Different Hunger: Writings on Black Resistance*.
75 Cited in P. Foot, 'The Strike at Courtaulds, Preston: 24 May to 12 June 1965', *IRR Newsletter* Supplement (July 1965), 6.
76 Wrench, 'Unequal Comrades', 166; Duffield, *Black Radicalism and the Politics of De-Industrialisation: The Hidden History of Indian Foundry Workers*, 86–9.
77 Fryer, *Staying Power: The History of Black People in Britain*.
78 Sivanandan, *A Different Hunger: Writings on Black Resistance*, 24.
79 Sivanandan, *A Different Hunger: Writings on Black Resistance*.
80 R. Moore, *Racism and Black Resistance in Britain* (London, 1975), 75.

81  Moore, *Racism and Black Resistance in Britain*, 75–7; Wrench, 'Unequal Comrades', 166–7.
82  Sivanandan, *A Different Hunger: Writings on Black Resistance*.
83  D. Marsh, *The New Politics of British Trade Unionism: Union Power and the Thatcher Legacy* (London, 1992), 33.
84  J. Eldridge, P. Cressey and J. MacInnes, *Industrial Sociology and Economic Crisis* (Hemel Hempstead, 1991), 25.
85  Verberckmoes, 'The United Kingdom'.
86  A. Callinicos, 'The Rank-and-File Movement today' *International Socialism*, 17, (Autumn 1982), 18.
87  Grint, *The Sociology of Work*, 172, Table 7.
88  Kelly, *Trade Unions and Socialist Politics*, 107.
89  Kelly, *Trade Unions and Socialist Politics*, 108–109.
90  Verberckmoes, 'The United Kingdom', 227.
91  Verberckmoes, 'The United Kingdom', 227.
92  Kelly, *Trade Unions and Socialist Politics*, 109.
93  Miles and Phizacklea, 'The TUC and Black Workers'.
94  Miles and Phizacklea, 'The TUC and Black Workers'; Wrench, 'Unequal Comrades'.
95  See Communist Party, *Racism: Action Guide: How to Combat It* (London, no date); International Socialists, *The Black Worker In Britain* (London, 1974); P. Foot, *Workers against Racism* (London, no date); Communist Party, *The Fight against Racialism in Britain* (London, 1974); B. Nicholson, *Racialism, Fascism and the Trade Unions* (London: TGWU Region No. 1, 1974). This current of white resistance to racism in the workplace was also increasingly evident in the wider community. In addition to the longer established black anti-racist groups, by 1973/4, many whites had also begun to establish anti-racist committees supported by local trades councils. The racist pronouncements made by rock stars such as David Bowie and Eric Clapton led to the formation of a national organization called Rock Against Racism in August 1976 (Gilroy, *There Ain't No Black in the Union Jack*, 120–1). 1976 and 1977 were important years which saw growing confrontation between racists and anti-racists which culminated in anti-racists preventing the National Front from marching through Lewisham in south London – an area of high black concentration. In 1977, the National Front polled 119,000 votes in the Greater London Local Council elections and threatened to become the third party in British politics. The Anti-Nazi League (ANL) was established in 1977 to counter this threat and they did so successfully in alliance with other more locally-based anti-racist organisations by exposing the National Front as 'Nazis', which ultimately contributed to their eventual electoral demise. In a celebration of multiculturalism and anti-racism, the ANL and RAR organised two anti-racist carnivals in 1978 – one of which was attended by 80,000 people (Gilroy, *There Ain't No Black in the Union Jack*).
96  Foot, *Workers Against Racism*.
97  Nicholson, *Racialism, Fascism and the Trade Unions*, 7.
98  Miles and Phizacklea, 'The TUC and Black Workers', 199.
99  Stephens, *Employment of Coloured Workers in the Birmingham Area*, 18; Miles and Phizacklea, 'The TUC and Black Workers', 202.

100  Miles and Phizacklea, 'The TUC and Black Workers', 198.

101  Miles and Phizacklea, 'The TUC and Black Workers', 199.

102  For a more detailed discussion of this dispute, see J. Rogaly, *Grunwick* (London, 1977); A. Phizacklea and R. Miles, 'The Strike at Grunwick', *New Community* 6:3 (1978), 268–78; Sivanandan, *A Different Hunger: Writings on Black Resistance*; Ramdin, *The Making of the Black Working Class in Britain*.

103  Phizacklea and Miles, 'The TUC and Black Workers', 270.

104  Ramdin, *The Making of the Black Working Class in Britain*, 289.

105  Ramdin, *The Making of the Black Working Class in Britain*, 292.

106  Rogaly, *Grunwick*; Ramdin, *The Making of the Black Working Class in Britain*.

107  Labour Research 'Race at Work', *Labour Research* (July 1983), 182–3.

108  Sivanandan, *A Different Hunger: Writings on Black Resistance*; Gilroy, 1982, ibid.; Gilroy, *There Ain't No Black in the Union Jack*.

# 7
# Colonial Labour and Work Palaver: Labour Conflict in Britain and West Africa

*Diane Frost*

This chapter aims to examine the role of West African migrant workers in the context of British colonial trade *circa* 1880–1960. In particular, it will explore the issue of labour conflict in the two port cities of Liverpool, in the UK, and Freetown, in West Africa. This occurred at two levels. First, it involved intra-class conflict, both in Britain, between white British labour and West African colonial labour, and in West Africa, between different ethnic groups fighting for control over seafaring and stevedoring work. Secondly, it involved confrontation between labour and capital, and again this occurred in both port cities. The main objectives will be to examine the broader structural factors within which such conflict occurred, and to consider the significance of 'race' for both class and intra-class relations. Empirical data presented here are based on a case-study of one particular ethnic group – the Kru – and its relationship with both the British colonial authorities and with other West African labour involved in shipping.

The Kru people originate from eastern Liberia, where, from at least the eighteenth century onwards, they became economic migrants. As trade and traffic increased on the West African coast, so their mobility grew, and some worked aboard slave ships bound for the Americas.[1] During 'legitimate trade', they were employed on board European ships, a process which marked the beginning of their 'making' as proletarians (to use E.P. Thompson's seminal concept) and the gradual ending of their status as peasant farmers and fishermen. Initially, seafaring and other forms of paid employment were undertaken to supplement farm earnings, and were one way of accumulating 'bridewealth', but, gradually, as shipwork became more lucrative, peasant farming and fishing became less important. This was especially so when Kru began migrating to Freetown, the capital of Sierra Leone, and later to Liverpool.

With the introduction of new and improved ships, particularly with the establishment of the steamship in the mid-nineteenth century, maritime work diversified and new employment opportunities opened up. The Kru came to occupy engine-room positions as firemen, as stokers and as donkeymen (i.e. those who did 'donkey' work, carrying coal to the furnaces).[2] They were also employed as stevedores, or 'krooboys', working up and down the West African coast.[3] By the end of the nineteenth century they were firmly located in an occupational niche in a European system of trade that would transport some of them much further afield, in particular to Liverpool.

Kru labour was subjected to various social processes that derived from work *and* the broader social and economic context of British colonialism. As with other newly proletarianized West Africans, they were engaged by colonial employers because they provided cheap and exploitable labour that could be employed as needed, and laid off when surplus to requirements (as during the interwar years, when engine-room labour was badly hit by unemployment).[4] This relationship was made more complex by the prevailing colonial ideology of 'race' impacting on the nature of work. In part, the employment of Kru as engine-room ratings – and their unemployment in the interwar years – had been prescribed by a racist mythology that ascribed West Africans with physical characteristics more 'suitable' for such work.[5] Thus, race and class were closely aligned with work – all interacted, and were fundamental to the experience of Kru seamen in both Freetown and Liverpool.

## West African labour versus British colonial shipping

Disputes between the Kru and their employers prior to the Second World War mainly emerged from within the ranks of coastwise or stevedoring Kru labour, rather than articled Kru seamen.[6] The latter were more reluctant to go on strike partly because divisions and competition between black and white workers discouraged such action. Yet they did risk action during the Second World War, when their bargaining power was exceptionally strong.

'Palaver' or strife involving stevedoring Kru labour in West Africa was frequent, especially before the Second World War. This tended to revolve around issues such as wage rates, but in one or two cases disputes arose over the use of non-Kru labour. On several occasions, stevedoring Kru labour was able to mount effective strikes, and this was due almost entirely to a Kru monopoly over labour supply. Kru headmen recruited from within their own community to the exclusion of other groups, and this was actively encouraged by the British colonial authorities. Thus, if and when strike action broke out, attempts by the authorities or the employers to bring in non-Kru labour were not always successful. On one occasion, in 1874, in an endeavour to highlight the 'superiority' of Kru labour, Kru headmen deliberately recruited Mende labour during a dispute,[7] knowing full well that they worked at a slower, less efficient pace. A decision by Kru stevedores to take strike action might also be dependent on the support of the headmen. These men acted as a powerful disciplining agent; supervising Kru, taking responsibility for their punishment and, crucially, acting as the sole recruiter. If a Kru worker made 'palaver' with which his headman did not agree, he might never be recruited again, even by other headmen.[8]

Kru stevedores went on strike on numerous occasions in support of higher wages. Sometimes this involved Kru workers going on the offensive when they were in a position of relative strength. More often though, strike action was forced on them by the employers' decision to reduce wage rates. Such defensive action could turn violent, especially if the threat of outside labour was used to undermine the strike. This happened on at least one occasion, in Freetown in 1904, when new rates of pay were introduced for cargo workers. These were 33 per cent below what the workers had previously been paid. The Kru refused to work and several hundred of them assembled along the wharf in Freetown. Stones were reported to have been thrown at the police and, anticipating disorder in Krootown Road (the area where most Kru lived), a number of policemen were dispatched. It seems the situation did not escalate and that a riot was averted.[9]

In another incident, in 1905, Kru stevedores were accused by a ship's officer of broaching (i.e. stealing) cargo and other goods. According to a witness, when the captain of the SS *Aro* deducted a fine from their wages, 'the krooboys refused to do any more work ... the following morning, they were ordered to turn to by Mr. Nelson, but I believe they emphatically declined'. The captain also ordered Nelson, the chief officer, to search the krooboys' boxes, but when he did so they threatened to throw him overboard, whereupon he produced a revolver. He was subsequently convicted and imprisoned in Sierra Leone for his actions, though it seems no one was injured.[10] The incident showed that Kru stevedores would on occasions challenge the authority of the officers, especially when they felt an injustice had been done. To deduct sums of money from all men's wages for alleged thefts on a previous voyage – which is what had been threatened – was both arrogant and provocative.

Available figures for wages paid to Kru firemen on articles suggest that these took a dramatic dip in 1906–7, from around 3/- to 2/-.[11] This reflected general economies being made in the cost of West African coastwise and articled labour. Thus, in 1906, Elder Dempster required kroo labour from Freetown for services at Forcados in Nigeria. Sierra Leonean Kru asked for 45/- a month, since the contract would last 12 months and the work was reputed to be hard. In addition, many were not keen on being in Forcados for such length of time. However, the steamship companies had begun to establish labour bureaux down the coast, to which they could turn as an alternative source of recruitment when the krooboys in Freetown were not 'cooperative'. David Brown, the Kru Tribal Ruler, responded:

> After consideration with my people, they have asked me to communicate with His Excellency, they will not accept less than the sum of 45/- per month for services at Forcados for a period of 12 months, knowing as they do the nature of the work they have to perform, for it means incessant labour night and day. They trust however that Sir Alfred [of Elder Dempster] will think over the matter and if he accedes to their terms they are quite willing to proceed at the shortest notice.[12]

Sir Alfred Jones dismissed the Freetown krooboys' demands as 'absurd', especially, he said, 'when we can get them on the Kroo Coast [Liberia] and Calabar [Nigeria] at 15/-.' From this apparent position of strength, Jones could dispense with the services of the Sierra Leone krooboys and force them into unemployment and considerable hardship. The Kru eventually agreed to accept less favourable conditions.[13]

In another case, also in 1906, Brown supplied the SS *Boulama* with Mende labour, instead of Kru, to work the cargo. The intention was to delay the ship, in which he succeeded by half a day. This could be explained by the fact that the captain had, on two previous trips, treated Kru krooboys unfairly. Allegedly, he had refused to pay them when work had finished, and had taken two of the men to Sinoe, Liberia, against their wishes. These men were forced to make their own way back to Freetown, at great expense and inconvenience, and on hearing this Kru stevedores in Freetown had agreed that Mende, rather than themselves, should be sent to work on the *Boulama*. This also occurred on other ships, such as the SS *Burutu*, in 1907, this time because of discontent with wages.[14]

The Freetown police were responsible for checking that no labour other than Kru went on board ship, but were apparently bribed to allow Mende workers to pass themselves off as Kru. An official of the British and African Steam Navigation Company explained:

> I very much regret the necessity of my having to again complain of having Mendi boys allowed to come instead of Kroomen [Kru]; out of 23, all we could get, no less than 17 were Mendis and though the police assured me he was there to prevent any Mendis from coming on ship, my headman Brown tells me police officers on duty always get 10/- from the headmen of Congo boats for allowing Mendis to go on these boats. I think this will explain matters.[15]

The practice of recruiting non-Kru stevedores by Kru headmen for coastwise work occurred frequently throughout 1906, and especially after Kru stevedores had been forced to accept a wage reduction. Brown explained the situation as he saw it. The steamship companies wanted cheap labour but then quickly discovered that 'cheap labour' could not work to the same standards as experienced labour. Their solution was to obtain skilled labour for cheap pay – hence the cut in Freetown stevedore's wages. At the same time, explained Brown, the steamship companies began employing fewer 'skilled' hands from Freetown and began taking a larger number from elsewhere. In this way they could employ 'unskilled' for less pay, whilst performing the same work under the guidance of 'skilled' labour. Eventually they could do away with the old skilled hands. The problems that the Freetown Kru caused companies such as Elder Dempster led them to dismiss the Kru and provided further justification for the idea of a labour bureau. Jones told the Colonial Secretary's Office in early 1907:

> There is no doubt that the boys from Sierra Leone are a bad lot, and they are promising to get worse. It is a fortunate thing for us that we have been able to arrange Labour Bureaus elsewhere, and in the interest of British trade and shipping, I think it is a wise thing to promote these Labour Bureaus where we can get good labour and be independent of the Sierra Leone Krooboys.[16]

Kru stevedores from Freetown continued to be paid 1/- per day for a number of years. However in 1911, due to worsening economic circumstances, including an increased cost of living in Freetown, labourers recruited to work the cargo of the SS *Sapele* refused to do so at the old rate. They demanded an increase to 2/- per day.[17] Elder Dempster and the Colonial Secretary's Office insisted that the rate agreed with the Kru in 1906 should remain, in spite of the changed economic conditions. Krooboys gave a list of complaints to their headmen and refused to go back to work unless their demand for higher wages was met. They complained of the irregular and spasmodic nature of employment – the number of days worked in a month might be no more than 12–14 – and that the 1/- per day was not sufficient to keep themselves and their families. They pleaded that the cost of living had gone up since wages had been cut to 1/- a day, and absolutely refused to work for less than 2/-.[18] Since Elder Dempster had to admit that the working of ships in the harbour had improved with 'regard to the class of men engaged', they agreed to increase wages. Although the kroo were offered only a 6d increase, with the aid of the labour headman they were persuaded to accept.[19]

West African seamen and stevedores had to find creative ways of supplementing their earnings. Some became involved in trading, buying goods in Nigeria – such as yams, cloth or garri – and taking them to Sierra Leone or Liverpool to sell. Others 'acquired' ships surpluses, such as empty tins or plastic containers, that were collected and recycled as tradeable goods. There were also the 'sweepings' from the hatches, where burst bags of sugar or rice were swept up, sieved and taken home. These 'perks of the job' supplemented daily earnings and made ship work financially more attractive. Supplementary earnings were an important element of overall earnings, and were necessary in order to participate in Kru society in Freetown. The polygamous, patriarchal family structure of the Kru required the male head to take responsibility for the rest of his family. Many used earnings for 'bridewealth' and aspired to have several wives, since this endowed them with high social standing. In addition, stevedores and seamen had to pay a 'customary fee' to the labour headman; this was passed on to the Kru Tribal Ruler for welfare purposes, which included the building of churches and schools and the maintenance of the Kru Tribal Court. Control over Kru custom was taken over by the British colonial authorities in 1905, and under the Tribal Regulations of that year labourers refusing to pay were liable to a fine not exceeding 10/-.[20] Kru seamen and stevedores were also obliged to 'dash' the headman – that is, engage in customary bribery – if they were to secure work. A British officer, who worked on the West African trade in the 1960s commented: 'Everybody who came on board the ship to work had paid somebody off – dockers, seamen, kroo – everybody had paid someone to get that job, whether it was a few days' or even a week's wages.'[21]

The social organisation of the ship underlined very powerfully the lines of demarcation based on class and 'race'. Thus, it was a rare sight to see a black officer on board a British ship before the 1960s. Moreover, since the early 1900s, all ships trading between West Africa and Britain had crews that had been 'Africanized'. In particular, engine-room workers – firemen, stokers, donkeymen and greasers – were recruited from the same ethnic group, the Kru, who were thought to be physically strong, though first, second and third engineers were always white. As West Africans, the Kru were also (erroneously) seen to be more physically adept at working in soaring temperatures, especially in the tropics, even though in the late nineteenth century Europeans had done this work with equal success. In general, West Africans worked in all positions bar officer status, thus enduring inferior prestige, pay and safety than their white 'superiors'. Such racially-based employment practices reinforced the colonial stereotypes which defined the racial and class distinctions between the white, colonial ruling class and the black, colonized working class. At the same time, preferences given to the Kru bolstered their ethnic identity, perpetuating ethnic divisions and competition with those groups that were excluded.

## Ethnicity and intra-class conflict in Freetown

Kru identity became very closely bound up with work, to the extent that the term 'Kru' became an ethnic-occupational identity. Kru came to monopolize stevedore work from Freetown, and were disproportionately recruited as seafarers. They had a tradition of ship work that stretched back to the slave trade – when they acted as navigators, seamen and interpreters on board European slave ships – and, in their native Liberia, many Kru clans monopolized coastal trade with Europeans. They were particularly 'expert' in negotiating the large rock outcrops and dangerous currents that dominate the surf coast of Liberia, and they could paddle their way to the European ships anchored several miles off the coast. This early history bestowed on the Kru a reputation that was difficult to shift, one that was actively encouraged by the group itself in the early nineteenth century.

The Kru from Liberia were encouraged to migrate to the British colony of Freetown (an important deep water port), so that a ready supply of seafaring and stevedoring labour could be recruited for work around the coast. West African labour began to be recruited more systematically with colonial expansion at the end of the nineteenth century, mainly to 'save' white sailors from heat exhaustion and tropical diseases such as malaria, and to supplement white crews that succumbed to the 'white man's grave'. The Kru came to dominate ship labour from Freetown. This suited the British colonial authorities because it meant they had a reliable and 'expert' supply of labour to work the cargoes around the coast and further afield, and it fitted a colonial mentality that believed certain ethnic or tribal groups were 'naturally' good at certain types of work. The Kru themselves not only encouraged such belief, they also actively defended their monopoly. When the time came to open up the labour market to other groups, this inevitably led to 'palaver' manifesting itself along ethnic lines. With the outbreak of war in 1914, ship labour was widely recruited from outside the ranks of the Kru because of the labour shortage. Sierra Leoneans, such as Mende, were employed and worked alongside Kru. After the war, many of those who had contributed to the war effort found themselves thrown out of ship work and unemployed. According to the Colonial Office, these came to constitute a 'great part of the hooligan element in Freetown'. The Kru's desire to reassert their ship-labour monopoly then brought conflict between them and other groups.

The situation in Freetown in 1919 was already tense because of food shortages, high prices and mounting unemployment due to demobilization. Social unrest in the major urban centres broke out, mainly directed against Syrian shopkeepers accused of hoarding food and charging extortionate prices.[22] Competition for employment increased, and disturbances broke out between Kru and Mende labour. It appears that a Kru and a Mende gang went to work on the same ship, and the Kru gang, having arrived first, began taunting the Mende. The disappointed Mende labourers were then said to have begun assaulting Krumen in town, and at around 10.40 am the Kru chief's court was attacked.[23]

Although the local press referred to 'latent hostility between Mendes and Kroos', smouldering discontent among Mende labourers had its roots in the employment situation. Mendes claimed they could work with the same efficiency as Kru and resented the fact that Kru were given most of the work.[24] In an attempt to rectify the situation, the Mende requested that the shipping companies should make arrangements so that they could have the opportunity of working on ships in the harbour whilst allowing Kru to work the ships at sea. But the Kru wanted both harbour and sea work and felt in a strong enough position to demand it. When Mendes were informed they could not have the work, this provoked a riot. The local press reported:

> [an] unprecedented and sanguinary fight ... led to the death of a Creole man and several cases of severe wounding of men and women, and gave rise to serious plundering and pillaging of the general kroo community ... sticks, stones, revolvers and other deadly weapons were made use of, to say nothing of bottles used by some as a means of defence ... stones were freely and blindly used. Many of the houses owned or rented by the kroo were damaged and some kroo were absolutely bereft of their property of which they were plundered, having fled from their homes seeking refuge, some betaking themselves to the bush ... the police were helpless, and it was only with the arrival of soldiers of the West African Regiment with fixed bayonets, that order began to be restored. Soldiers had to be stationed at the Kru Court House, but still disturbances started again the following evening. These were however quelled by soldiers, who continued to occupy the Kru Court House. The disturbances had involved a few individual Creoles who had been part of the gang of Mende labourers. These as well as Mende were said to have been attacked by the kru, for working as ships labourers.[25]

Kru dominance over other ethnic groups, such as Temne and Mende, was bitterly resented, and in 1926 a fight broke out between Kru and members of these other groups. Governor Slater stated that the Temne and Mende had not been given the opportunity to prove themselves 'worthy seamen', and promised that when they could prove this, 'every assistance would be given them by the government, with a view to getting the shipping companies to put them on an equal basis with the kroos.'[26] In the meantime, Temne and Mende seamen were almost totally excluded from seafaring. Part of the reason for this was that both the Royal Navy and the Merchant Navy had a preference for Kru labour. In 1929, a Colonial Office official reported:

> It is a well established fact that kroos are far more satisfactory for work on ship board than any of the other local tribes. At times Mendi and Timne men are engaged by ships, but whenever possi-

ble practically all ships' Masters prefer to take Kroomen [Kru] ...
HM ships when engaging any native seamen in this port, also insist
on their being kroos [Kru]. If there is any remedy, it lies with the
Timini men ... for them to show they are fully equal to or superior
to the Kroos as workers on shipboard.[27]

This statement was made after the Temne Tribal Ruler of Freetown
had appealed for Temne seamen to be recruited. He had argued that
'competent seamen with good testimonials from previous sea jobs'
were being kept out of seafaring and lay idle. Non-Kru responded by
organizing against the Kru and, in 1929, set up the Sierra Leone Native
Seamen's Benevolent Society. Whilst providing benevolent support in
the form of unemployment and distress relief, the society also sought
to damage the Kru's reputation by making what can only be regarded
as slanderous statements regarding the quality of their work and their
behaviour. Kru could not be members of the Society since 'native'
Sierra Leoneans were defined as 'Africans born within the colony of
Sierra Leone and its Protectorate, but ... not ... Liberian Kru subjects
or their children born within the colony of Sierra Leone and its
Protectorate.'[28] Membership was also closed to 'known gamblers,
quarrelsome men or those who had given trouble on board ship', as
well as those who were 'lazy' or had been imprisoned for theft. The
implication was that such weaknesses epitomized the Kru, who should
be replaced by 'honest, hard working native' Sierra Leoneans 'thrown
out of their seagoing livelihood by [Kru] chicanery'.[29]

The Kru's almost complete monopoly over seafaring employment in
Freetown throughout the interwar years began to show signs of fracture in the late 1930s, as both Temne and Mende seamen came to
constitute increasing proportions of sea labour on certain shipping
lines. By 1937, six shipping companies crewed their ships in Freetown:
Elder Dempster, Barber West African Line, Woermann Line, SCOA,
United Africa Company (UAC) and Holland West African Line. Whilst
most of these companies engaged only Kru, UAC had a third of their
vessels engaging only Mende labour, whilst the Holland West African
Line engaged men of Temne ethnicity. Although this represented a
gradual movement towards the greater employment of non-Kru
seamen, the Temne and Mende did not see it in such terms and
continued to make complaints to the Acting Governor. The colonial
authorities chose not to intervene, claiming that choice of labour was
entirely a matter for the firms themselves to determine.[30] The absence
of government intervention in this matter and the preference of ship-

ping companies for Kru seamen ensured that by 1938 the Kru were still dominant, constituting 75 per cent of Freetown's seafaring community.[31]

In 1938, the All Seamen's Union was established with the object of securing better wages and conditions for seamen and labourers, through collective action. Kru seamen were approached and invited to join since they represented the bulk of the seafaring community. However, the Kru chief, speaking on behalf of his followers, and suspicious that the union would force them to share their predominance in seafaring with others, stated they would have nothing to do with the union. He insisted that the Kru had a tribal organization of their own, which was in effect a seamen's union exclusively for Kru. The implication, then, was that the Kru needed the union less than the union needed them. Unfortunately for the union, the refusal of the Kru and a few others to participate meant its membership in that year represented no more than 10 per cent of the seafaring community in Freetown. The fact that Kru seamen did not join the union undermined any potential effectiveness.

During a dispute in 1939 between lightermen and Elder Dempster over low wages, the representative for Elder Dempster arranged for a gang of Krumen to do the work for the price that the lightermen were demanding, 2/- a day.[32] According to the *African Standard*, when the lightermen (Mende and Temne) refused to work until wages were increased, 'policemen were secured to eject them out of the wharf'.[33] The lightermen brought the issue to the union in the hope of avoiding a repetition of similar events that had occurred in 1921 and 1936. But, since the Kru were not in the union and government refused to 'interfere in a trade dispute', the lightermen were powerless. Elder Dempster kept a permanent gang for working lighters, but this only amounted to 12 men (later increased to 18), and these were supplemented by up to 70 casuals. The casuals, who had come out on strike, went back to work after a day and were forced to accept the same terms as before, 1s 3d a day plus a meal. Part of the problem was the casual nature of the work, and in some months these men did not earn sufficient to support themselves. The Commissioner of Police in Freetown recommended a minimum monthly wage for casual labour as a way of solving the matter.[34]

Ethnic identity was used by the Kru to safeguard their interests, perpetuating their monopoly in shipping to the exclusion of others. In common with Hausa migrants in Sabo (southern Nigeria), described by Abner Cohen, they actively strengthened their exclusiveness through the use of myths, symbols and customs, to consolidate their economic position against the rivalry and competition of others.[35] For Cohen, ethnicity in West Africa is a political phenomenon, used in some situations to promote the social and economic interests of the 'in-group' against the 'out-group'. Thus, it has little to do with promoting archaic and conservative cultural expressions, and a lot to do with informal political action. Indeed, in order to thrive, ethnicity has to be constantly recreated and adapted to changing socio-economic conditions; in this sense, it is a dynamic social process that relies on human agency.[36] In the context of colonial West Africa, indirect rule encouraged ethnicity, and, in doing so, strengthened and privileged the interests of some – the Kru and Hausa of Sabo, for example – whilst underprivileging others.

## White labour versus black labour in Liverpool

In Britain, unlike colonial West Africa, notions of ethnicity were lost in relations between black and white workers. Here, racial differences took on a more significant meaning as a demarcator of difference.[37] Racial differences were used by white workers to exclude black workers from trade union organization and from employment, both aboard ship and ashore. For white workers, 'race' was also a way of differentiating themselves from cheap, exploitable black labour. White labour in Liverpool was thus fighting on two fronts – against their white employers, and against black workers, who they saw as competitors.[38]

Similarly, West African seamen in Liverpool – like Kru stevedores in Freetown – were also involved in conflicts both with different sections of labour and with capital. Again, the historical context of this hostility is important. The late nineteenth century saw the growth of scientific racism and ideas on eugenics, and, whilst such ideas had initially been used to differentiate the 'lower orders' from the middle classes, they were quickly adapted to differentiate according to colour.[39] This was a time when Britain had recently expanded its empire and notions of imperial superiority abounded. Racial differences were not only used to distinguish colonial subjects in the empire, but also to underline differences at home between white English and black West Africans. In the realm of work, such differences took on significant meaning, with black labour seen to be undermining the position of white workers. The National Sailors' and Firemen's Union in Britain had campaigned against the use of 'foreign' labour before the First World War. This was mainly aimed at

Asian seamen – Indian and Chinese – because they, like West Africans, were paid lower rates and endured inferior conditions. White British seamen in ports such as Liverpool refused to work alongside West Africans[40] (although at the same time, in 1911, the Union supported a strike of black seamen in Cardiff).[41]

With the outbreak of war in 1914, in order to safeguard existing rates of pay, the seamen's union insisted that 'foreign' seamen be paid the same rates as British seamen. But after the war, hostility towards black seamen increased as the crisis in British world trade began to manifest itself in mounting unemployment and competition for jobs, especially in shipping. The trade unions campaigned for the employment of white British workers before black.[42] In 1919 – the same year as a record level of industrial militancy in Britain[43] – unemployed workers in ports such as Liverpool directed anger and resentment towards West Africans, and in the riots which followed one person was killed.[44] Racist hostility was not confined to the working class; institutionalized racism by the British establishment expressed itself in various ways, providing a broader framework within which general racist hostility could thrive.[45] Thus, in the 1920s the Home Office decided that repatriation of West Africans would offer one solution to the violence and tension that afflicted port cities such as Liverpool. The Seamen's Union joined the campaign for repatriation and ensured they had representatives on the various repatriation committees throughout the country.[46]

In the post-Second World War period, tensions between white British and West African labour persisted. Kru remained outside the major seafaring unions, received lower wages, and could be used as 'black-leg' labour during disputes involving British seafarers. One Kru seaman explained that the shipping companies 'started recruiting seamen in Freetown in the 1950s when the whites [went] on strike'.[47]

## Kru seafarers and industrial action

West African labour was also mobilized to undercut and undermine Kru wages and conditions. Two accounts – one from a British captain, the other from a Sierra Leonean Kru man (who was President of the Seamen's Union there in the early 1990s) – both show how Nigerian labour was used in an effort to undermine Kru industrial action, and both illustrate that on occasions West African seamen were prepared to take strike action. The first describes how Elder Dempster used Nigerian firemen to undermine the Kru monopoly and wages during the interwar years, showing, fortunately for the Kru, that this back-fired. Captain James explained:

> Major Cripps decided to do some economising, we had to take our
> firemen at Lagos ... The idea in taking men from Lagos was to put
> some competition in the labour market with the Kru and keep
> wages low. Only one ship ever tried and that proved fatal. They just
> could not fire these ships ... Almost a week after leaving Lagos the
> ship staggered into Takoradi and lay there ... and it was all over
> and finished with the Lagos boys as firemen. They had to get them
> off before they got the Freetown fellows on board otherwise there
> would have been trouble. The Freetown people were very good
> firemen.[48]

The second account describes a strike for higher wages by firemen in
Freetown during the Second World War, with Elder Dempster turning
to Nigeria for replacements. Mr. Sherman told the author:

> going to England and back for £5!, the people said no, and so they
> get strike during the Second World War of Sierra Leone firemen
> [mainly Kru but also Mende]. We went on strike for 3 months. Was
> a captain called J. J. Smith of Elder Dempster, he said, okay if Sierra
> Leoneans don't want the job, I'm taking my ships to Nigeria – took
> all the ships to Nigeria and start taking Nigerians. This Elder
> Dempster got three sister ships with 21 fires. So these Nigerians
> they can't stand it, they can't fire the ships! From Lagos to
> Takoradi, they don't fit. They have to send to Freetown back. Now
> they get two pounds ten [shillings], bringing the money to seven
> pounds ten a month.[49]

In 1946, the Tribal Administration Rules having legal force in Sierra
Leone stated that any dispute over wages was to be settled through the
Kru Tribal Ruler.[50] He would act as a kind of arbiter between the two
sides and may have averted much strike action thereafter. Whilst
many of the industrial disputes involving Kru tended to involve ships'
labourers rather than seamen, at least two cases – in addition to the
one above – have come to light of articled Kru seamen refusing orders
during the Second World War. The first, in 1942, involved the alleged
refusal of 15 Kru firemen to work in dangerous areas. Apparently,
these men, members of the crew on the SS *Calumet*, had drawn a war-risk bonus, but when the ship was ordered to proceed to the UK and

pass through dangerous waters, the firemen refused to sail. The men were arrested and imprisoned under the Merchant Shipping Act. The second case, also in 1942, involved the refusal of Kru seamen to re-sign articles immediately after finishing 12 months at sea.[51] They reportedly went on strike, and initially the Board of Trade withheld their voyage pay. A former striker explained:

> We strike. What we all strike for? We sign the ship for 12 months, that was 1942 on the hospital ship, Red Cross boat. We sign this for 12 months from Freetown to Gibraltar, Iran and this place [Liverpool]. So when we came, they want we to take a trip again, go east. We say no. They go to Board of Trade for we to sign the ship, we say no, we sign no more article, we finish this 12 months. The company, they say, what you boys want? You want more wages? You want more money? We don't want to cross no ship, we finish ...[52]

In this case, the seamen were not breaking the law and could not be forced to re-sign articles because their contract of service had finished, though the offer of higher wages demonstrated the desperate wartime need for ship's labour.

## Conclusion

The Kru in Freetown successfully monopolized stevedoring and seafar-ing work up until the Second World War to the virtual exclusion of other groups. Labour competition between various groups led to conflict and in some cases physical attack. Such intra-labour competi-tion did not so much indicate the importance of nationality, as that of ethnicity or what is often referred to as 'tribalism', something that was certainly encouraged by colonialism. Thus, within the West African context, British colonialism encouraged economic specializa-tion among different ethnic groups, and specialization was cultivated within certain areas of work. In shipping, for example, Gold Coasters were usually recruited for steward work, whilst Kru dominated engine-room work as firemen and trimmers.[53] Intra-labour conflict was as much a product of the prevailing social, political and economic condi-tions as was worker–employer conflict. Both Freetown and Liverpool during this period were important interlocking trading centres in the wider framework of British colonial activity. Ethnicity and 'race' inter-acted with, and at times subsumed, broader class relations. This could be most clearly seen in the conflicts between various West African groups in Freetown, as well as the intra-class tensions between black and white labour in Liverpool. Yet such tensions have to be placed in the wider context of British capital that encouraged and cultivated divisions between different ethnic groups in West Africa and between black and white workers in Liverpool. Indeed the process of colonization, and the subsequent ideology that emerged, did much to create and maintain ethnic divisions between various groups as a means of political and economic domination. Again, colonial ideology was not confined to those areas that were colonized but found expression in the bigotry and racism that afflicted British society at large. Such ideas were inevitably embraced and gained greater currency in times of economic crisis and competition for employment. Thus 'race' and ethnicity assumed a more prominent position in historically specific social and economic conditions, though such processes have to be placed in the broader context of class society if we are to understand them.

## Notes

1  R.W. Davis, 'Ethnohistorical Studies on the Kru Coast', *Liberian Studies Monograph* Series No. 5 (1976), 1.
2  E. Tonkin, 'Creating Kroomen: Ethnic Diversity, Economic Specialism and Changing Demand', *University of Aberdeen Symposium* (1985), 41.
3  J.M. Sullivan, 'Fishers, Traders and Rebels: The Role of the Kabor/Gbeta in the 1915 Kru Coast (Liberia) Revolt', *University of Aberdeen Symposium* (1985). The term 'Kru' refers to the ethnic group originating from Eastern Liberia, and 'krooboys' denotes stevedoring labour. In Freetown, Kru constituted a substantial proportion of the krooboys, though in Freetown and elsewhere krooboys also included members of other groups.
4  D. Frost, 'Racism, Work and Unemployment: West African Seamen in Liverpool 1880s–1960s', and M. Sherwood, 'Strikes! African Seamen, Elder Dempster and the Government, 1940–42', in D. Frost, ed., *Ethnic Labour and British Imperial Trade: A History of Ethnic Seafarers in the UK* (London, 1995).
5  Tonkin, 'Creating Kroomen'.
6  Coastwise stevedoring labour was casually recruited at various points along the West African coast, supplementing a ship's crew. This often served as an informal apprenticeship for would-be articled seaman. The latter were those who signed an official contract, 'Articles of Agreement', binding them to rules and regulations and a set wage rate. Articled seamen travelled beyond the coast, spending more time at sea than coastwise labour.
7  'A Negro Strike in Sierra Leone', *Illustrated London News*, 10 January 1874.
8  D. Frost, 'The Kru in Freetown and Liverpool: A Study of Maritime Work and Community During the Nineteenth and Twentieth Centuries' (PhD

thesis, University of Liverpool, 1992).
9  Colonial Secretary's Office (CSO) Minute Papers 1904, No. 5291. All CSO Papers and Local Matters Papers are at Public Archives, Fourah Bay College, University of Sierra Leone, Freetown, Sierra Leone.
10  CSO Minute Papers 1905, No. 5291.
11  Articles of Agreement for various Elder Dempster ships 1894–1912. See *Lloyds Register*.
12  CSO Minute Papers 1906, No. 5081.
13  CSO Minute Papers 1906, No. 1128.
14  CSO Minute Papers 1907, No. 2465.
15  *Ibid.*
16  CSO Minute Papers 1906, No. 4038, and 1907, No. 2465.
17  Local Matters Minute Papers 1911, No. 82.
18  *Ibid.* Also, in the case of a labourer being killed on board ship, the expense of burial was left to the deceased friends, and no compensation was awarded for injury on board.
19  *Ibid.*
20  CSO Minute Papers 1906, No. 5974.
21  J. Goble, interviewed by T. Lane, Liverpool, 1980s. Transcript loaned by interviewer. It was also customary for workers to bring home 'gifts' for their family.
22  B.E. Harrell-Bond et al., *Community Leadership and the Transformation of Freetown* (The Hague, 1978), 159.
23  Colonial Office (CO) 267/583, Sierra Leone Despatches, Vol. 14, 1919. CO files consulted at Public Archives, Fourah Bay College.
24  *Sierra Leone Weekly News*, 22 November 1919.
25  *Ibid.*
26  CSO, Z/41/37.
27  CSO Open Policy Files Miscellaneous 1929, Z/33/29.
28  *Ibid.*
29  *Ibid.*
30  CSO, Z/41/37.
31  The Kru continued to battle for increased wages and better conditions, and wages were increased from 1/6 to 2/- per day during the 1930s. Increasingly Mende and Temne labour began to acquire a larger share of stevedoring work, though this was still nominal. Mr Sabo Lewis interviewed by author, Freetown, 1990; Mr Howard Morris interviewed by author, Liverpool, 1988.
32  CSO, Labour 5/39 (confidential), Letter from 'All Seamen's Union' to the Acting Governor, March 1939.
33  *The African Standard*, 10 March 1939.
34  CSO, Labour 5/39 (confidential), Commissioner of Police to Colonial Secretary, March 1939.
35  Hausa migrants in Sabo used the concept of 'custom' to monopolize long-distance trade in kola and cattle between northern and southern Nigeria. Competition with Yoruba groups pushed other Hausa groups together and saw the Hausa strengthening their ethnic exclusiveness through the building of political organizations. A. Cohen, *Custom and Politics in Urban Africa: A Study of Hausa Migrants in Yoruba Towns* (London, 1969), 183–4. Also,

Frost, 'The Kru in Freetown and Liverpool'.

36   Cohen, *ibid.*, partic. 192–3.

37   Of course ethnicity continued to be significant to the groups themselves, but in relationships with whites this had the effect of homogenizing black identity.

38   There was little competition in reality because West Africans were consigned to certain positions on ships sailing to West Africa.

39   See, K. Malik, *The Meaning of Race* (London, 1996).

40   M. Banton, *The Coloured Quarter* (London, 1955), 32; P. Fryer, *Staying Power* (London, 1984), 295.

41   K. Lunn, 'The Seamen's Union and "Foreign" Workers on British and Colonial Shipping, 1890–1939', *Labour History Review* 53 (1988), 21.

42   Banton, *Coloured Quarter*, 33.

43   C. Rosenberg, *1919, Britain on the Brink of Revolution* (London, 1987).

44   CO 323/848. Also, see J. Jenkinson, 'The 1919 Race Riots in Britain: Their Background and Consequences' (PhD thesis, University of Edinburgh, 1987), and N. Evans, 'Across the Universe: Racial Violence and the Post-War Crisis in Imperial Britain, 1919–1925', in Frost, ed., *Ethnic Labour*.

45   To give just one example, during the racist violence of 1919 the police blamed the black community itself for the attacks by white mobs. In addition, the courts failed to prosecute those whites who had instigated the attacks. See Home Office (HO) 45/11017/377969, 1919 (Public Records Office, London).

46   P. Gordon and D. Reilly, 'Guestworkers of the Sea: Racism in British Shipping', *Race and Class* 28:2 (1986–7), 76.

47   They were also used in Liverpool in 1948, and in the 1960s. Messrs. Johnson, Suku and Seekie, interviewed by author, Liverpool, 1989.

48   Captain L. James, interviewed by T. Lane, 1980s.

49   Mr. Sherman, interviewed by author, Freetown, 1990.

50   *Laws of Sierra Leone* Vol. 3, 1946, Tribal Administration (Colony), CAP 244, Sec. 5.

51   See T. Lane, *The Merchant Seamen's War* (Manchester, 1990), 165.

52   Mr. Toby, interviewed by author, Liverpool, 1988.

53   Home Office records contain data collected by Liverpool police in 1919 of unemployed and employed West Africans and West Indians. These show that the majority of West Africans listed were Sierra Leoneans and firemen. See HO 45/1101/377969.

# 8
# Becoming 'Men', Becoming 'Workers': Race, Gender and Workplace Struggle in the Nigerian Coal Industry, 1937–49

*Carolyn A. Brown*

> Miners have always had difficulty in comprehending the simplest of propositions as to the market-regulation of wages, and have clung tenaciously to unscientific notions such as 'justice' and 'fair play'.
>
> E. P. Thompson, 'A Special Case'[1]

> ...we are the people who always got accident in the Mine for this reason the amount of 1/3d ... we are receiving ... is not sufficient for us. Many of us have got wives and children, after receiving our monthly wages is not enough to support ourselves and them.
>
> 'Tub Boys', Iva Valley, 21 August 1937[2]

> The workers ... believe that the approved Underground allowance is not only applicable to European Underground workers, but also to the African workers. If the Colliery Manager allows only the European workers to get their allowances ... then he is showing a grim discrimination in that respect.
>
> Okwudili Ojiyi, General Secretary, Colliery Workers Union, 1947[3]

On 18 November 1949, police fired on a group of miners engaged in a sit-in strike at the Iva Valley mine of the Enugu Government Colliery in south-eastern Nigeria. They killed 22 miners and injured 50. Additional fatalities occurred during demonstrations led by radical nationalists in eastern Nigeria's major cities of Calabar, Aba, Onitsha, Port Harcourt, and Enugu. The shootings riveted the Colonial Office and opened the Labour government to attacks over the pace and nature of political change in Nigeria. The riots involved radical nationalists, the urban working class, the unemployed and disaffected indigenous traders – just the broad-based political alliance that imperial labour reforms sought to prevent. In the context of the Cold War such a combination could create the type of political instability that opened space for 'communist infiltrators'. For the Nigerian nationalist movement, the tragedy temporarily unified the rival groupings, leading to a new coalition that portended to represent the Enugu miners in the investigations to follow.

By exploring a series of strikes we can begin to understand how Africans shaped their workplace and the communities in which they lived; how, even in non-settler colonies, they developed ideas about race; and how a racial awareness became an important part of their personal identities. European 'whiteness', fused with authoritarian systems of industrial management, impugned the men's dignity and sense of social justice and racial parity. In launching industrial struggles, miners not only fought for material improvements, they also challenged the 'African worker', a racist category laced with colonial notions of a static, 'primitive' society. In numerous creative ways, the miners refashioned their lives and reformulated ideas about work, self-respect and masculinity. Fortunately for historians, they also left a richly documented record of their ideas in a series of petitions and letters written by professional writers, and in the minutes of their meetings with management. In these documents they express their thoughts about the conditions under which they lived and worked, their own economic importance, and their pride in arduous labour – attitudes characteristic of coal miners throughout the world.

Many of the men, especially the hewers, came to see themselves as part of an international community of mine workers, citizens of 'the country of coal'.[4] Radio reports on British and American miners and interactions with expatriate staff, most of whom came from Britain's northern coalfields, encouraged Nigerian miners to appropriate European models in developing their own ideas about what they deserved as workers and as men. They began to argue that, because of their low wages, they could not fulfil their role as breadwinner, nor protect their families from the indignities of overcrowded and unsuitable housing. During the war, they utilized new reformist labour legislation to engage in a discourse on their rights as working men, subjects of the Crown and loyal supporters of the imperial war effort, and they astutely manipulated tensions within the state on social and labour policy. Legislation that attempted to structure industrial unrest – by legalizing trade unions, prescribing dispute procedures and mandating various forms of consultation – failed to deter the men from pressing issues that reflected their sense of dignity as men.

In an era when the Atlantic Charter and attacks against fascism had discredited racial systems of authority, racist work practices became difficult to defend. Moreover, postwar general strikes throughout Africa – in Lagos, Dakar, Zanzibar and Mombasa – emphasized the urgency of further social reform and the necessity for acceptable procedures to channel worker protest. The environment of political change, emanating from the Colonial Office, gradually tricked down to the local level of the colliery, shaking the racial protocol of the workplace. The average expatriate 'boss' experienced the shift in state policy as a betrayal. Assaults on workers, insulting forms of address and dismissive attitudes towards workers' complaints – all acceptable in the past – could no longer be justified. In 1947, the colliery manager even directed that the word 'boy' should not be used, either in addressing the men or as a job title.

Suddenly abuses that were hidden in the darkness of the mines were brought into full public view as workers took their 'bosses' to court and the nationalist press reported it for all to see. Enugu, now a city of 30,000, was the home of the 'New African' – those politically educated young men who were disenchanted with conservative rural leaders, supported a vibrant and radical press, and debated colonialism in the palm-wine bars, 'hotels' and urban 'tribal' associations.[5] Their concerns resonated with the coal miners' experience of racism, and the latter carried the new sentiments into the villages surrounding Enugu. In November 1949, imagining connections between miners and radical nationalists, the state brutally crushed a miners' sit-in strike, thereby closing a chapter in Nigerian labour history. It was a chapter in which workers had succeeding in appropriating the state's labour reforms to articulate their demands for 'entitlements' to a living wage, safe and decent working conditions, and respectful treatment by expatriate bosses.

## Work and 'race'

Two mines were in operation during this period – Iva Valley and Obwetti – and both used the pillar and stall system of extraction, still widespread today. This encouraged a series of values that became important for the development of the miners' self identity. Special labour gangs – rail men, timber drawers and others – built the main road or adit into the coal outcrop on the side of the hill. Branching off from the adit – like ribs from a spine – were secondary roads or side entries, which were mutually parallel and extended some distance into the seam. The area between two side entries, a panel, was managed as a distinct unit of the mine. At regular intervals along the entries, each of a group of miners would open a heading into the coal face, and these headings were the miners' workplace.

Headings were between three and six feet high, depending on the seam. In thin seams the men worked kneeling or prone, and with four foot seams they stood spread-eagled, with their backs touching the roof. First, the miner sheared the seam with two parallel vertical cuts, thereby defining the coal face to be worked. Then, lying prone, he undercut the coal about two feet from the wet floor, making a cavity three to five feet deep. According to James Alo, who began mining in 1916, 'in some sections of the mine, water reaches one as far as the chest'. He explained that, although 'special labourers' drew the water outside the mine, 'hewers stay inside the water and do their job', adding: 'When they came out from the mine their body would look like that of a lizard.'[6] This was the most dangerous and demanding phase of extraction because the miner worked under a shelf of coal, with only wedges of wood supporting the overhang. Candles provided the only light, and one worker recalled: 'whenever [the candle] goes off ... because the mine is very, very dark ... you have to find your way by feeling blindly along the walls or along the rail line to next person's position to light up your candle.'[7] Coal was dislodged by driving wedges or pneumatic picks between the coal face and the roof, or by using explosives. Finally, the miner loaded his coal into a tub, to which he attached his tally disk, so that he was credited with the output. From the end of the First World War, when the influenza pandemic created a labour shortage, miners brought their own work teams to extract the coal. Management neither knew, nor cared to know, the numbers of men working in a team, because they were all paid by a tonnage rate attributed to one miner 'recognized' on the tally sheet.[8]

The driving of headings is known as 'development', and it divided the panel into pillars 50 feet by 80 feet. When a whole area had been developed, the pillars could be extracted, a process called 'robbery'. In the course of robbery, timber men shored up the roof with timber, and when this was completed the timber was withdrawn, allowing the roof to cave in. Robbery was particularly dangerous, and the men who performed it had a very strong sense of the importance and danger inherent in their job. Development and robbery could occur at right angles with the coal cleavage, 'on bord', or parallel with the cleavage, 'on end'. Working at a face that was 'on end' was easier, because the coal came off in sheets with the line of main cleavage. Workers should be moved between various workfaces, but Enugu's corrupt 'native' and European supervisors used workface assignments to punish or reward the men.[9] Complaints about unjust assignments flooded the manager's office during the war.

The fragmentation of tasks in the Enugu mines followed the Derbyshire system used in the northern coal fields of Durham – the home of the colliery's first manager – and in Northumberland.[10] All tasks preliminary to the actual coal getting were performed by specialized workers. To William Leck – the first and, until 1943, the only manager – this fractionalized division of labour seemed appropriate for 'his' 'African worker', whom he considered incapable of handling more than a single task. None the less, the Derbyshire system made each category of workers aware of the importance of their task to the total operation of the mine. Recognition of the expertise and intuitive knowledge which was required encouraged a personal pride among the mine workers that fuelled their demands during the war.

Coal mining had long been associated with the concept of 'race'. As Anne McKlintock has noted, from the 1840s when mining capitalists tried to bring British coal miners under factory-like discipline, their fierce independence and protest culture became evidence that they were a 'race' apart, 'outcasts, historically abandoned, isolated and primitive'.[11] For men like Leck, the idea of miners as a 'backward race' must have been especially salient, since the Enugu miners were, or at least seemed, so very different from himself. Colonial masculinity and white authority were articulated in an industrial discourse that reflected the family, a social institution in which hierarchy was enshrined. Thus 'pick *boys*' (hewers) undercut coal and loaded the tubs; 'tub *boys*' hooked the tubs to the central haulage system in the main roads; tracks were laid by the 'rail *boys*'; 'timber *boys*' reinforced the roof with timber; and 'boss *boys*' supervised individual groups of each category in a given coal district.[12] A retired tub man recalled: 'Everything, boy, boy! Only the Europeans were called overman and foreman.'[13]

When men first entered the mine they not only experienced socialization into the world of wage labour, but also into a racialized system of authority in colonial society. Indeed, in the non-settler colonies of

West Africa the workplace was one of the few places where African men had direct contact with Europeans. Both 'European' and 'African' were signified through a host of practices, inbred assumptions, privileges and abuses. These were ritualized in arbitrary and 'emasculating' physical violence. Beatings, extortion and random assault were enshrined in mine culture, and defended as necessary to force the 'lazy', 'irresponsible' 'African worker' to behave as a 'worker'. White managers, often from the British working class, exercised this power with relish on men considered to be of a subordinate race. During my interviews in Enugu, retired coal miners frequently mentioned one particular ritual. All expatriate underground foremen and overmen were transported daily to work from their residences, high on a hill, in a hammock. The mine workers, who walked several miles to work, resented this flagrant demonstration of their own subordination.

Management felt that the 'African worker' did not deserve the standards of workplace safety won by British miners, and they reproduced conditions that were a hundred years behind those in England. The workers had no protective clothing – they worked barefoot, wearing only a loincloth – but managers accepted high accident levels, maimings and serious injuries as 'normal', attributing them to the 'primitiveness' of the men. Additionally, since the mines had none of the coal dust, black damp and fire damp that made anthracite and bituminous mining so hazardous, management failed to develop an adequate system of ventilation.[14] It assumed that Africans were acclimatized to oxygen deficiency, humidity levels of 80–100 per cent saturation and temperatures of 85–90 degrees. It was not until after the war that scientific testing revealed what work behaviour indicated all along, that African tolerance of heat and humidity did not differ significantly from that of Europeans. The average hewer lost ten pounds in weight per shift.[15] Miners were physiologically unable to work efficiently under these conditions, and they developed a tradition – which resembled the 'marras' of the Durham coal field[16] – where, with two miners occupying one site, one worked while the other rested, fanning himself in the main airways to recover from the heat. Management, so enamoured with their imaginary 'African worker', assumed that lack of will, rather than physical inability, created both this behaviour and also absentee rates which approached 20 per cent.[17]

Industrial discipline merged with the philosophy of 'indirect rule', which shaped the colonial state. Industrial 'indirect rule' – like its broader societal cousin – was consistent with the colonialists' construction of rural Africa as 'tradition-bound' and 'stable', with an 'organic harmony' rooted in 'ancient social structures'.[18] For colonial officials, just as autocratic chiefs ruling compliant villagers were a necessary a protection against the 'detribalized', so too were corrupt 'boss boys' a necessity to insure industrial order. European supervisors abdicated power to these 'boss boys', who 'understood' the 'native' and could – because they were often related to the authoritarian colonial chiefs – use 'traditional' methods to control labour. 'Boss boys' determined who worked,[19] and they demanded bribes for jobs and good work sites, as well as for currying favour with European supervisors. Some even dismissed their work crews before pay day, and then drew their wages.[20] Similarly, interpreters demanded bribes lest they falsify management commands and/or mistranslate instructions.[21] The state tacitly protected these abusers by denying Africans the right to contest their treatment in the courts. Thus, until the war, workers' experiences were shrouded in the obscurity of the mine, invisible to a disinterested general management and to the political authorities.

Despite the despotic nature of the colliery, workers still had considerable power in the regional and national economy and in the mine workplace. Theirs was the only coal mine in West Africa, giving them a strategic power far exceeding their numbers – 2,500–7,000 in this period.[22] Although Enugu coal was uncompetitive internationally, it was used more widely during English coal strikes, which reinforced the workers' awareness of their regional importance.[23] Additionally, workers had some control over when, for how long and with what intensity they would work. The dispersal of work sites and the small number of 'boss boys' made supervision difficult. European managers even had difficulty insuring that men, once appearing at the face, would, in fact, remain throughout a full shift. Even as late as 1947, European managers complained that men often left the coal face without notice, not to return for several days.[24] Moreover, workers were empowered by the sub-bituminous character of the coal and the problems with mechanization. The coal was difficult to store without decomposing, making consumers vulnerable to work stoppages, and the mine roof was so unstable that coal cutting machines could not be used. Thus, there was space for Africans to shape the workplace and construct an identity that challenged the colonial conception of 'African worker'.

## Mine 'boys' as socially mature village 'men'

All the mine workers were Igbo, one of Nigeria's three largest ethnic groups. For locals from the Agbaja region, where there were severe land shortages, mine work replaced slavery and migration to farms outside the area.[25] For other locals from the fertile Nkanu region, mining was a job of last resort, where 'a man might as well be buried alive'.[26] In addition, there were the 'foreign' Igbo from Onitsha – a large market town on the banks of the Niger River – whose contacts with British officials and missionaries began in the mid-nineteenth century. They, and men from the Owerri palm belt, gradually dominated clerical and skilled surface jobs.

Deprecating colonial job titles contrasted with prestigious rural 'titles', which miners bought with their wages. Village improvement, a very important feature of the colonial period, was accelerated by their earnings, which financed the construction of schools, churches and village halls, and homes with zinc roofs, a sign of 'progress'. Mine workers also acquired commodities that symbolized 'modernity'. These varied from imported motor cars, for the richest, to bicycles and certain types of western clothing, for the average labourer. Village councillors were eager to place their men in colliery posts, and the colliers themselves were reluctant to terminate their connection with the village, where polygynous households were established and their manliness was culturally validated. In some villages mine workers were also watchdogs on autocratic chiefs. One Agbaja miner commented: 'The miners were most modern and power[ful] ... they were always after democracy ... they don't allow the chief ... to harass his people, and [they] always succeeded in opposing him.'[27]

A powerful man was expected to dispense patronage and largesse to his neighbours and family. Miners adapted two dynamic norms of Igbo 'manliness' – self-improvement and an obligation to uplift the village – to the European ideology of progress. Having wealth and helping one's own family was not enough to earn status and prestige. A man had to help others to 'get up', to demonstrate social responsibility. Thus the miners financed new buildings, educated their own and other village children, and helped others to secure jobs in the colliery. Most used their income in 'traditional' *and* 'modern' ways. For instance, one Agbaja worker married six wives, bought membership in the Ozo title society, and paid for his children's education. He recalled:

The development of [the] coal industry did a lot to my village. But for coal industry civilization would have not reached us as early as it had reached us. The coal industry initiated me into Ozo title. Now I am Ozo Samuel N. Onoh. I was able to train up my children, build good houses. We contributed money and build schools and churches.[28]

Most men lived a reasonable distance form work and commuted daily or weekly. They crafted a syncretic model of 'responsible' worker which diverged significantly from the 'disciplined' industrial man. Agbaja and Nkanu men absented themselves from the mines to plant and harvest crops, and to fulfil family and community obligations – funerals, marriages, festivals, and so on – thereby forcing the industry to acknowledge the priorities they gave to their social commitments. The British interpreted this spirit of rural-based independence as confirmation of the irrationality, laziness and inherent moral inferiority of African workers. Racism blinded them to the similarity of Nigerian miners' patterns of integrating mining and agricultural work, with the behaviour characteristic of early coal miners in their own country.[29] Mine work was integrated into the life cycle of Agbaja and Nkanu men. For young men, money from mine jobs was used for bridewealth payment. Older men used mining to finance rural social rituals that enhanced personal status or to become titled men, as noted above. One miner cited these obligations as an incentive for entering the mines.

I joined the mine when I felt like. In those days what normally happened was that whenever the villages wanted to celebrate certain feasts, people will rush to the mine to get money. (That is to work for sometime) and get money for their feast. When you must been you retire home to celebrate the feast with the money you got from mining work. When the money finished you go back again to another money.[30]

By the late 1930s officials acknowledged that the coal miners began to 'act' like industrial men. They formed associations that met and discussed grievances, they negotiated with management, and they developed and articulated a vision of industrial life that incorporated many of the standards of mine safety and home life that they had heard existed in Europe and the Americas. Informing these actions was a gendered consciousness evolving from the same type of masculine work culture that coal miners had in Britain. The harsh and dangerous underground conditions stimulated a strong solidarity among the men. Like the independent miners of England and Scotland, Enugu's hewers were proud, self-improving men whose manliness was expressed in their command over their craft, their dispensation of mine jobs within their work group, and their use of wages to establish networks of patronage and secure symbols of Igbo male prestige. No matter how they were infantilized by the depredations of the workplace, once in their communities and the work camps of Enugu they were respected, influential men to their friends and neighbours. Thus, the 'real' men who mined Nigeria's coal held a constellation of peasant values, which included an historically constructed and culturally defined concept of masculinity. This influenced their workplace traditions.

The hewer's independent self-identity was encouraged by a number of workplace traditions and 'the aggressive celebration of physical strength' that encouraged the masculine ethos of coal mining. He was the only worker whose wages were based on piece rates, and this reinforced his sense of skill; the practice of contracting work groups of 'helper' hewers and tub men meant that only his name was on the payroll, and all the team's output was attributed to him; and, because of the high worker to supervisor ratio he functioned with little direct supervision, and therefore had considerable control over the labour process. As in Britain, the hewers took particular pride in their skills, strength and independence, and these values often shaped a social hierarchy within mining communities that coincided with ranking within production.[31]

## Colonial reforms, 'labour love' and resistance

In the late 1930s, colliery protest took a more sophisticated form, with workers appropriating a gendered discourse about their entitlement to a living wage, suitable for dignified men who were responsible for their wives and children. The men held self-help meetings (*Nzuko Ifunyana*) which drew on a rural, male political tradition of consultation. Colliery *Nzuko* imitated the more general 'meetings' that evolved into urban associations founded by clerks and skilled workers during the First World War. Urban *Nzuko* acculturated recent immigrants and raised money for development of the home village.[32] Colliery workers adapted the *Nzuko* form to discuss 'food shortages, token cheating, bribery, and corruption in the securing and retaining of jobs and in the allocation of work'.[33] Colliery *Nzuko ifunanya* were structured by job category, with each class of men holding their own meeting under a president and secretary;[34] they were secret, often using oaths to insure solidarity and deter informants, and could be violent.[35] By the 1930s, management begrudgingly recognized their usefulness and met them regularly to discuss the men's complaints. Leaders were men of 'energy, personality and slight extra knowledge of affairs', who were selected by the 'ordinary unsophisticated local men', allegedly because they could produce concrete gains.[36] After being quiet during the depression, they launched a series of strikes that reshaped the industry.

The British government was shaken by labour uprisings and popular insurrections in the West Indies in 1934/5 and 1937/8 and on the Zambian Copper Belt in 1935. As Peter Weiler has noted, colonial workers had 'the potential to threaten British rule because of their strategic position in the colonial economy, their potential support for political movements, and their militancy'.[37] Between 1937 and 1942, Britain engaged in a two-pronged reform: supporting improvements in the living and working conditions of colonial workers and their families, while deflecting working-class discontent through new legal and bureaucratic structures and selective repression.[38] However, initiatives taken in London were not embraced by the Nigerian government or the colliery management until after a wave of post-Depression strikes. These occurred just as Governor Bourdillion was deflecting pressure from W.G.A. Ormsby-Gore, the Colonial Secretary, to establish a labour department, appoint labour inspectors and become more involved in securing better social conditions for African workers. Ormsby-Gore, angered that the Nigerian government had failed to apply enlightened labour practices, noted that he 'should find great difficulty in defending the Nigerian Government from the criticisms which would inevitably be provoked'.[39]

The first of the strikes occurred in March 1937 when the 'pick boys' downed tools to demand a wage increase. William Bulkeley, the senior government official responsible for both the colliery and the Nigerian Railway, came immediately to the colliery. Shocked by the danger and poor conditions of underground work, he ordered a comprehensive review of the colliery, uncovering mismanagement, corruption and extortion. The labour registry listed over 4,000 names for the colliery's 2,600 positions, and camp conditions were insanitary and over-crowded.[40]

Given the potential for an industrial dispute to trigger broader unrest, the colliery was required to take greater control over its camps and embark upon a process of social engineering. A colliery labour master and staff welfare officer were commissioned to report on the camps and workplace; redundant workers were dismissed and hundreds were evicted. However, in late 1938, following a request from the men, management introduced 'rostering', rotating the work on a daily basis. This allowed the management to determine the composition of the work group, and it converted the adjacent villages into a pool of labourers who were required to show themselves for work when required. Whenever the manager needed more workers he did not need to recruit them anew, but could simply add to the daily roster. This was not what the men had intended, and they soon found it more difficult to integrate mine work with farming. The state also sought to reduce the control the men had over the conduct of industrial disputes. For consultative purposes, the management replaced the secretive *Nzuko*, which operated outside its control with appointed Representative Councils. But *Nzuko* members became leaders of these councils, and they transformed them from advisory boards into bargaining units, leading many workers to assume that the state legitimized the *Nzuko*. Moreover, council members challenged the influence that village leaders held over their men. The racialized system of authority crumbled as the men challenged racist practices in the mines.

From 1937 to 1938, when they were disbanded, the councils exploited the legislative initiatives on labour conditions and dispute management, hiring a Lagos lawyer to represent them in negotiations. In their first meeting they presented seventeen demands, which, together, constituted a comprehensive critique of colliery policy. They called for standardization of management procedures to eliminate arbitrary and corrupt practices by European and African bosses; advancement in pay within designated scales; written notice of all disciplinary actions, and their review by the council; and workmen's compensation. Noting that many men had worked for twenty years, they also asked for gratuities at retirement. They also demanded overtime pay for holidays and Sundays. In addition to requests for generalized wage increases for various categories of labour, they asked for free protective footwear for 'pick boys'.[41] The council demands were a workers' blueprint for colliery reform, which the workers would spend the next ten years trying to achieve. In the short term, Bulkeley restored a 1d per day cut, made in the Depression, and unknowingly restructured the labour process by changing the wage system. He granted the hewers a daily rate, in addition to the customary piece rate, effectively releasing them from dependence on tonnage.[42] This reduced the role of the hewer's piece rates as the incentive for productivity among all categories of workers at a time when European supervisors were in short supply.

Four months after the demands had been presented, the Nigerian government had still not responded, although the men had fulfilled their commitment to return to work pending a response. When no decision was announced the Representative Councils contracted professional letter writers to compose petitions stating their demands.[43] Despite their clumsy and self-deprecating language, the petitions express a discourse about work and family life that reveals a moral universe through which the workers conceptualized their lives. Each occupational group emphasized the importance of their work for the safe and economic operation of the mines, and the danger and skill inherent in their work, and they complained of the difficulty that they had in being male providers.[44]

Housing was a special concern. The men were humiliated by the poor living facilities available for their families. Housing created differential access to daily posts and indicated varied strategies and commitments. In this respect the workforce fell into three categories. One third, predominately 'foreign' Igbos, had always been permanent residents in the 'native' areas of Enugu township and the labour camps. A quarter of the remaining two-thirds, largely 'locals', lodged in the labour camps but left their wives and children in the adjacent villages, to which they returned every weekend. The remainder lived in the villages and walked from 5 to 14 miles daily to work.[45] In 1938, some 1,600 of the over 2,400 men living in the Iva Camps, Coal Camp and Alfred's Camp (an unofficial camp) were from Agbaja and Nkanu, presumably composing the weekend commuter category.[46]

The colliery camps were rent-free and offered an important alternative to high-cost rentals in Enugu. But the camps were built in the style of range-type housing, which the International Labour Organization and the British government had declared inimical to family life. These consisted of a row of rooms 12 feet by 12 feet by 10 feet separated by partial partitions and topped with corrugated roofs. They were insufferably hot during the day, and rooms housed on average 5.5 people.[47] The overcrowding violated Igbo marital norms and the men considered them to be demeaning and immoral. They attacked them on these grounds, and because they exposed their families to unhealthy, substandard conditions, which were beneath their status as working men. Being at the top of the hierarchy in production the 'pick boys' felt morally compromised by the conditions. They were especially outraged at having to board an additional miner or another family in the same room as their own family.[48]

Conditions were extremely unpleasant for polygynous families, exemplifying how a rural symbol of masculine status clashed with the spatial constraints of urban living. Some rooms housed an employee, three to four wives, seven to ten children, and one or two servants.[49] Additional overcrowding resulted from the domestic arrangements of 'local' men, who left their wives in the village and brought young male relatives to cook, clean and perform other domestic chores. Although several men shared one 'boy servant', many 'big men' had several. There was a practical rationale for miners having domestic servants – the burden of cooking after work and the need to protect property. But these arrangements also reflected male ideologies about status, age and prestige.[50] For instance, mature men did not expect to cook, and 'pick boys' enjoyed having 'small boys' carry their tools to work every day.[51]

In their petitions the special labour men noted the risks they encountered when laying rails. Although management considered rail and timber jobs to be unskilled, the men recognized the intuitive knowledge that enabled them, for instance, to recognize a hazardous roof ('where a crackling noise is heard'). They explained that the hard and dangerous work they 'laboriously' undertook was 'not for the stead of avarice but for the *labour-love*'.[52] Echoing the traditions of British miners, the men framed their case for higher wages and improved housing on the morality and justice of their cause, and never on the condition of the coal market. Management recognized that the arguments were rooted in the dignity of their work, the uniqueness of their skill and the consciousness of themselves as a cultural and economic elite. According to a 1938 report: 'long-service labourers have gradually come to regard themselves and the "coal people" generally as "different" from the other inhabitants of the township and entitled to all kinds of special privileges and consideration.'[53]

## The Second World War, reorganization and conflict

The slow pace of colliery reform was overtaken by the exigencies of the Second World War. In Enugu, as in other African cities, inflation raged; indeed, Nigeria's cost of living increasing by 75 per cent between 1939 and 1942. To prevent an explosion of unrest – which, given a shortage of British personnel in the colonies, would have been difficult to manage – the state accelerated the pace of labour reform. From 1939, African trade unions were legalized, but only on condition that they were registered, and registration could be withdrawn at the discretion of Nigeria's registrar of trade unions. Although the option of violent repression was occasionally exercised and was always latent, the state preferred to prevent unrest by channelling worker activism into a maze of bureaucratic innovations.[54] In addition, three other significant reforms were adopted at Enugu. First, in order to stabilize the workforce by reconstructing family life, there was new housing and intervention by social welfare experts. Although these changes recognized that workers were 'industrial men', the rationale behind them was also based on the British notion that a 'respectable' working class required male-headed, nuclear families. Secondly, the state attempted to reduce the workers' autonomy by deepening managerial power over the labour market and restructuring the labour process. Thirdly, they attempted to channel workplace disputes through industrial relations machinery.

At Enugu, the manager was ill-disposed towards independent African trade unions, still smarting from the Representative Councils' ability to circumvent him by presenting their grievances directly to his superiors in Lagos. He encouraged 'trusted' workers to form unions, and in 1940 clerical workers and 'native' staff founded two bodies, the Colliery Surface Improvement Union (CSIU) and the underground Colliery Workers' Union (CWU). Both regarded the labourers with contempt. The clerks felt that, as literates and leaders in the improvement associations, they should run the industry's workers' organizations. Similarly, the 'boss boys', feeling humiliated by the Representative Councils, resolved to seize command of the new government-endorsed unions. Predictably, neither group had the support or trust of the workers, but there were endless feuds, with men tricked into either following or breaking strikes. Then, however, three significant events transformed the colliery's industrial relations.

First, the Colonial Office initiated an ambitious welfare and housing programme that aimed to reconstruct the African family and create a differentiated working class. In 1942, with funding provided by the Colonial Welfare and Development Act, it began a £104,000 housing project. Two-room cottages – each with a veranda, electric lights and a small garden – were built on plots 40 feet × 60 feet. There were wide roads, open spaces, bathrooms, social halls and chlorinated water. This was an adaptation of an English mining village – not the rowdy village that had fostered workers' unrest, but an idyllic, pastoral mining village. This was the 'garden city' model and the Udi Siding Camp was even called Garden City. The estates were intended as a demonstration of the perceived superiority of European systems of organizing living space, and it was assumed that once miners had seen the beautiful, modern new buildings, they would modify their own construction in the villages. But the response was quite the opposite. Mineworkers had already developed their own modern homes, with zinc roofs and piped water. Initially, people boycotted the project and the houses stood empty. Later, the men protested in the press that the social welfare officers were 'harassing' their wives. Many of the urbanized men were polygynous and insisted on having adequate housing for their families and, often, for servants as well. Authorities found that it was easier to build new structures than to reshape family life according to Western norms.[55]

The second event was a request, made in September 1943, by the Combined Production and Resource Board in London, to increase Nigerian coal output by some 250,000 tons. This was to compensate for coal shortages resulting from worker unrest and manpower dislocation in Britain.[56] Responsibility for expanding production fell on a new, 25 year-old manager, Roy Bracegirdle, who replaced Leck in 1943. This was a formidable challenge for a new manager and Bracegirdle approached it with zeal. He hired new workers and added another shift but made technical decisions that reduced the hewers' output per man shift from 3 tons in 1940/1 to 2 tons in 1945/6.[57] The percentage of hewers within the workforce declined from 21 per cent in 1940/1 to 14 per cent in 1946.[58] Most new workers were placed on robbery work – the quickest way of increasing output – with development work deferred until absolutely necessary. Eventually, however, the larger workforce exceeded 'the demands of development and got out of proportion with the strict needs of the circumstances'.[59] But workers and not management would be blamed for the consequent decline in output.

Thirdly, the CWU came under new and more effective leadership, when Okwudili Isaiah Ojiyi, a management trainee and former school teacher, became the union's general secretary. Ojiyi was recruited by a group of disenchanted underground workers disgusted with the officials of the two unions who sowed confusion in the workers' movement. Beginning as a temporary clerk in 1938, he was initially embraced by management as a brilliant, promising, young African member of staff. However, his career as a candidate for a new Junior

Technical Staff position was cut short when he refused to be sufficiently obedient to European supervisors. A flamboyant articulate
worker with radical nationalist sympathies, he relished opportunities
to confront European staff who he felt were arrogantly ignorant.
Unlike many other African staff, who saw their posts as opportunities
for personal advancement, he used his training in Nigerian labour law
to develop demands that fully exploited the legal parameters set forth
by the state. His contempt for the racial culture of the mines and his
arrogance towards his European superiors made him a natural hero of
the workers. While the CSIU floundered in disarray Ojiyi strengthened
the CWU by building support among the underground labourers. A
'foreigner' from Onitsha, he rejected clan-based policies and targeted
the Agbaja hewers and other underground workers as his
constituency.

By the end of 1943, he was the union's general secretary. Ojiyi's
political sympathies led him to frame the workers' struggle in the
rhetoric of radical nationalism. This encouraged workers to relate the
intolerable conditions in which they worked to their political status as
colonial subjects. These linkages were even more obvious to workers
in a state enterprise such as the colliery. Ojiyi clarified the political
contradictions in his presentation of the colliery workers' demands.
He used allegations of racial discrimination to galvanize support,
appropriating an anti-racist nationalist discourse to highlight industrial complaints. A key assumption in his ideology was the expectation
that those in authority – the state – had a responsibility for the social
development of their employees. While it is difficult to determine the
involvement of individual miners in the nationalist movement, Ojiyi
certainly utilized issues raised by nationalists to enhance the union's
demands. In his confrontations with the state and the new colliery
management he often startled them with his knowledge of pertinent
trade union ordinances and his awareness of the gains of the national
trade union movement. Further, like a true nationalist rebelling
against the racial practices of colonial society, he failed to observe the
protocol of colonial deference to his European superiors, whether in
the industry or the state at large.[60]

From August 1944 until the end of the war, the union was locked in
wave of disputes that began when it tabled a memorandum demanding a seven-hour working day, workmen's compensation and an
underground allowance. Reflecting the industrial health standards of
metropolitan and Nigerian labour codes, the memorandum enumer-
ated a series of industrial illnesses attributed to underground

conditions. Although the demands were a reasonable request for a colonial application of standards found in England, the colliery manager did not feel that African workers deserved these conditions. Also, like many local officials, he preferred older approaches to industrial relations, rather than the innovations being promoted by the Colonial Office. He forced a confrontation, rejecting the workers' demands and recommending that all hewers, tub men and special labour be placed on piece wages, which he claimed would give the wage increases the workers desired.[61] He made two proposals. The first grouped the men into syndicates of 60 men – 30 hewers and 30 tub men – with an aggregate wage divided equally between them. Tub men were to fill rather than push tubs, a further fragmentation of the hewers' skill. The second option used the same workgroups, but with piece rates based on individual work.[62]

The unions rejected both options, and the dispute went to arbitration under the Nigerian Defence Regulations (1941). This, like Britain's Essential Work (Coal Mining Industry) Order of 1941, prohibited strikes in strategic industries and mandated compulsory arbitration in trade disputes.[63] The syndicate system was endorsed in the form of the Long Award, which eliminated the daily rate of the Bulkeley Award. Wages were totally dependent on output, with all members of a syndicate pressurized to discipline slow workers. The award eroded hewer autonomy and appeared to reinstitute a contractor system, with membership determined by the management, not the hewers.[64] For those independent hewers who had been 'helpers' under the old system, the proposal revived memories of exploitation. For the manager, by contrast, the system promised more productivity with less supervision, and he decided to conduct a trial exercise before full implementation of the award in March 1945. When a sharp drop in output indicated the men's continuing opposition, he then demanded that all 1,800 underground workers sign the award as a condition for employment.[65] Only 117 men, mostly headmen, complied and he declared that all others had resigned. Having instituted what was in effect a lockout – also illegal under the Defence Regulations – the manager moved to recruit new workers from the 'foreigner' Igbo area of Owerri Province.[66]

By this stage, the manager had revoked the CWU's recognition, arguing that it had failed to convince the workers to accept the award. Nevertheless, Ojiyi contested the dismissals as a violation of the law prohibiting lockouts. When the manager eventually allowed individual pay, many workers agreed to return to work. However, they were far from defeated. They brought the struggle right into the workplace, challenging the authority structure in the mines. The miners sabotaged production, claiming that 'the coal was hard or they were waiting on the tub-boys' while the tub boys 'stated that they were waiting on the coal'.[67] In a further complication, disgruntled clerical and 'native' staff plotted to remove Ojiyi from the leadership. By the time of the Nigerian General Strike, in the summer of 1945, the colliery was in such disarray that its workers did not participate.

Having disbanded the union, management and the state tried to impose alternative representative bodies which failed to undermine workers' solidarity with their union. They boycotted an election arranged by a representative of the British Trades Union Congress (BTUC), serving as a labour adviser to the Department of Labour, and they ignored rural clan councils and urban 'tribal' unions that attempted to represent them. From the standpoint of industrial discipline, the industry was ungovernable.

In November 1947, to underscore demands first raised in 1943, Ojiyi launched what he called a *ca'canny*, a Durham term for a 'go slow'.[68] In the nationalist press he queried whether the underground allowances recently granted to European bosses would be extended to African workers. This caused considerable embarrassment at the Colonial Office, and when the manager began dismissals it intervened by requiring conciliation meetings. Conciliation produced an historic agreement which incorporated many of the principles of postwar labour reform. It ended racial discrimination in pay, conceded many amenities and awarded £100,000 in back wages. But, the money was linked to production requirements, establishing minimal output levels for hewers and tub men. The agreement also attempted to break the material conditions of solidarity by introducing an extensive grading system that segmented the workforce. The militant hewers were given an artisan classification, which strengthened their consciousness of themselves as the central producers in the mines.

This partial victory for the workers, however, became the occasion for another attempt by the state to increase its intervention into production. During the negotiations, a BTUC representative, Robert Curry of the National Union of Mine Workers, reorganized the CWU. Officially, he was introducing a branch structure like that used in Britain; more significantly, he was trying to create bureaucratic tiers to separate Ojiyi from the militant rank and file. The previous CWU had a unitary structure in which leaders called mass meetings and dispensed patronage among the rank and file. It reflected Igbo styles of leadership and the consultative tradition. Leaders had reciprocal responsibilities, and the more powerful dispensed gifts to the community in exchange for their support. Ojiyi followed this model. He dispensed tins of snuff when visiting the mines – which was interpreted as a sign of good leadership – and the men would then strike when he wanted.[69]

The hewers' response to the union's restructuring demonstrated the problems of applying industrial practices cross-culturally. According to Igbo organizational principles, Curry had created autonomous unions, not branches linked to a central secretariat. The five sectional branches that represented surface workers, hewers, mechanics and fitters, underground workers (general) and clerical staff, became, in the eyes of the men themselves, five separate unions. While this diffused the executive's powers, it institutionalized the hewers' autonomy by creating an organizational structure, the hewers' executive, to plan and lead their protest. The hewers believed that they were exempt from negotiations conducted by the union executive. Similarly, the clerical and supervisory staff, the main centre of union opposition, also had an institutional structure from which to conspire against Ojiyi's influence. The union's recognition had been restored, but it had unwittingly been transformed into a more turbulent organization.

The consequences of this structural transformation were exhibited in the events of 1949. At that time, the union executive negotiated with management over grievances remaining from the 1947 award. Central to this discussion was an allegation, apparently encouraged by union dissidents, that the hewers were owed additional arrears for a period in which 'rostering' was practised in violation of the June 1946 labour legislation. The details cannot concern us here. Suffice it to say that the claims were sufficiently plausible to send the manager and Chief Commissioner scurrying to Lagos for interpretations of the ordinance. The tragedy occurred, however, when the hewers, assuming that they were owed additional arrears, began a sit in. They had little reason to expect the state to respond violently to yet another sit-in, but some state officials felt that the political context had shifted dangerously. The nationalist movement had developed roots in the urban working class and, while its moderate wing was negotiating with the state, the radical Zikist Movement, appeared with considerable strength in Enugu. Fearing that mine explosives would fall into the hands of political radicals, the state decided that they should be removed. Troops sent to retrieve the explosives were confronted by shouting miners, and panicked. Even here, race played a role. The British officer in charge, describing the scene, noted: 'the place was black with them.' Fifty miners were injured and 22 were killed.[70]

## Conclusion

The Iva Valley Shooting of November 1949 was the tragic culmination of a period of continuous labour unrest in the colliery and of state attempts to differentiate and control the colonial working class. African workers struggled to be seen as industrial men, rather than as 'African workers', an 'imagined' category constructed from racist assumptions, imperial arrogance and administrative ineptitude. Over the decades they had woven waged work into their social lives – in the villages as well as in town – and they had developed their own approach to work and to conceptions of what was 'just'. This was a critical period in colonial labour history. The state had chosen to recognize in the Enugu miners 'an opponent whom they thought they could understand',[71] and it had moved to control them using mechanisms familiar to the British working class. But in this instance, as in many others, European knowledge was not superior to studied attention to local custom and approaches to work.

The earlier conception of 'African worker' as 'intrinsically different' had outlived its utility in the face of worker activism.[72] However, there was no such thing as a generic 'industrial man'. Class and masculinity are both located in space and time, influenced by the cultural context of the society involved. The complex ways in which Enugu miners merged industrial labour with village socio-economic priorities underscores the erroneous superficiality of linear notions of 'proletarianization' in African labour history. Similarly, the failure of Curry's union reorganization underscored the importance of understanding work and organizational culture. It is, after all, of critical importance for labour to be understood from the perspective of the worker.

## Notes

1  E. P. Thompson, 'A Special Case', in *Writing by Candlelight* (London, 1980), 66.
2  NIGCOAL 2/1/94, 'Petition from Southern Native Location, Enugu Township, to the Colliery Manager, Iva Valley Coal Mine, Enugu, 21 August 1937'. NIGCOAL papers are held at the Nigerian National Archives, Enugu.

3 Nigerian Coal Corporation Files, New No. P. 1/3, 'Memorandum of Agreement – 1947', 10 November 1947.

4 D. Frank, 'The Country of Coal: A Review Essay', *Labour/Le Travail* 21 (1988), 234.

5 'Hotels' were feeding sheds where women prepared meals for urban workers and others. Enugu was founded when the mines were opened in 1915.

6 Interview with James Alo, 6 July 1975. Another informant mentioned that the water in the mines also served as a toilet, and human waste floated throughout the mine workings. Interview with B. U. Anyasado, Owerri Town, 23 July 1975.

7 Interview with Anyasado. He added: 'Whenever there was much heat inside the mines the candle light goes [out] as soon as it is lighted.'

8 Powell Duffryn Technical Services, 'First Report to the Under-Secretary of State for the Colonies, on the Government Colliery, Enugu, The Characteristics of the Coal Produced and the Investigation into the Other Coal and Lignite Resources' (mimeograph, London, 1948), D-19. This section draws on my forthcoming book, C. A. Brown, *'We Were All Slaves': African Miners, Culture and Resistance at the Enugu Government Colliery, 1914–1950* (Portsmouth NH, forthcoming). A typical work group included one rail man, eight tub men, eight hewers and two timber men.

9 I.C.F. Statham, ed., *Coal Mining Practice* vol. 1 (London, 1958), 265. For a discussion of this corruption, see C. A. Brown, 'A History of the Development of Workers' Consciousness of the Coal Miners at Enugu Government Colliery, Nigeria, 1914–1950' (PhD dissertation, Columbia University, 1985).

10 For a good discussion of the system of work in these fields, see M.J. Daunton, 'Down the Pit: Work in the Great Northern and South Wales Coal Fields, 1870–1914', *Economic History Review* 34:4 (1981).

11 A. McClintock, *Imperial Leather: Race, Gender and Sexuality in the Colonial Context* (London, 1995), 115.

12 This discussion of coal mining is based on Powell Duffryn, 'First Report', D-19.

13 Interview with Eze Ozogwu, Amankwo-Ngwo, 2 June 1975.

14 Powell Duffryn, 'First Report', Section D, Part IV. Blackdamp is air in which oxygen has been displaced by carbon dioxide and firedamp is methane gas, which is highly explosive and prone to spontaneous combustion. D. Douglass, 'Pit Talk in Country Durham', in R. Samuel, ed., *Miners, Quarrymen and Saltworkers* (London, 1977), 321.

15 W.S.S. Ladell, 'Some Physiological Observations on West African Coal Miners', *British Journal of Industrial Medicine* 5:16 (1948), 16–20.

16 'Marras' are two hewers who work the same coalface, either during the same shift or on alternate shifts. They share the pay which they receive for their combined output, and develop personal friendships that extend beyond the workplace. See Douglass, 'Pit Talk', 227–8.

17 See A. Akpala, 'African Labour Productivity – A Reappraisal', *Africa Quarterly*, 12:3 (1972), 246.

18 F. Cooper, 'From Free Labour to Family Allowances: Labour and African Society in Colonial Discourse', *American Ethnologist* 16: 4 (1989), 751.

19  C. H. Croasdale, 'Report on Labour at the Enugu Government Colliery' (mimeograph, Enugu, 1938), 25. This report was destroyed during the Nigerian Civil War and I thank Dr. Hair of Liverpool University for sending me a xerox of his copy.
20  Interview with Chief Thomas Ozobu, Imezi Owa, Udi, 21 June 1975.
21  One informant noted: 'If you didn't bribe them they'd advise the European that you were unsuited for your position and should be replaced with another person who did pay bribes.' Interview with Anyasado.
22  Powell Duffryn, 'First Report', Section G and D-26.
23  *Ibid.*, D-185.
24  See C.A. Brown, 'A History of the Development of Workers' Consciousness' and *'We Were All Slaves'*, forthcoming.
25  For a discussion of the importance of slavery in this region, even into the twentieth century, see, C.A. Brown 'Testing the Boundaries of Marginality: 20th Century Slavery and Emancipation Struggles in Nkanu, Northern Igboland 1920–1928', *Journal of African History* 37, (1996). In an interview, one mineworker responded to a question about the impact of coal mining by saying: 'People did not have to sell others into slavery.' Interview with Thomas Noisike, Owa Imezi, Udi, July 1975. Also, G.I. Jones, 'Igbo Land Tenure', *Africa* 19 (1949).
26  P.E.H. Hair, 'Enugu: A West African Industrial Town' (mimeograph, Nigerian National Archives, Enugu, n.d.), 10.
27  Interview with Augustin Ude, Umuaga, Udi, 5 August 1975. Ude began work at the colliery as a messenger in 1919, aged ten, and in 1922 he became an interpreter. His name was raised many times in my interviews as a perpetrator of extortion and bribery.
28  Interview with Samuel N. Onoh, Ngwo-Etiti, Nigeria, 9 August 1975. Onoh began work in 1915 as a tub boy, but eventually, after the Second World War, became an underground foreman. Ozo is the highest rank of the title society. Title societies were ranked organizations that men or women joined by paying an increasing amount of fees. Those in the upper echelons have sacred characteristics and gain political influence in the village.
29  For discussion of the rural base of coal mining in England, see R. Colls, *The Pitmen of the Northern Coalfield: Work, Culture and Protest, 1790–1850* (Manchester, 1987).
30  Interview with Alo, retired rail and tub boy.
31  Colls, *The Pitmen of the Northern Coalfield*, 12.
32  *Nzuko* is a generic term meaning any type of meeting. The urban 'tribal' unions were also characterized as *Nzuko*.
33  Croasdale, *'Report'*, 29.
34  The only study that explicitly mentions the *Nzuko ifunanya* is Croasdale, 'Report'.
35  Interview with Anyasado.
36  Croasdale, 'Report', 29–30.
37  P. Weiler, 'Forming Responsible Trade Unions: The Colonial Office, Colonial Labour and the Trades Union Congress', *Radical History Review* 28–29 (1984), 370.
38  Weiler, 'Forming Responsible Trade Unions', 371.

39  CO (Colonial Office) 583/216, Ormsby-Gore to Bourdillion, 13 May 1937. CO files are held at the Public Record Office, London.

40  This account of the strikes is based on C. A. Brown *'We Were All Slaves'*. CO 583/216, 'Report of Acting Colliery Manager to Colonial Administration, 8 June 1937'.

41  NIGCOAL 2/1/94, 'Representation and Deputations from Surface/ Underground Colliery Staffs', 9 November 1937.

42  CO 583/216, Bourdillion to Ormsby-Gore, 3 April 1937.

43  Professional letter writers were somewhat like para-legals, having some knowledge of the law, and they were a critical element in the multifaceted strategies of urban colonial workers.

44  For the whole series, see NIGCOAL 2/1/94, Colliery Department to Colliery Manager, Enugu, 30 August 1937.

45  Hair, 'Enugu', 71.

46  Croasdale, 'Report', Appendix A.

47  C.O. 583/263/30544, Colonial Office Press Section, 11 May 1943, 'Model Villages for African Miners'.

48  NIGCOAL 2/1/94, Letter from Colliery Department, Iva Valley to the General Manager, Railway, Lagos, 12 July 1937 and to Colliery Manager.

49  This information followed a survey of the camps during the period of labour force stabilization in 1939. CO 583/237, Bourdillon to MacDonald, 30 August 1939.

50  For an interesting treatment of these themes, see L. A. Lindsay, 'Shunting among Masculine Ideals: The Nigerian Railway Men in the Colonial Era' (African Studies Association Annual General Meeting, Orlando, 1995).

51  Croasdale, 'Report', 23.

52  Colliery Department to Colliery Manager.

53  Croasdale, 'Report', 40–1.

54  For a discussion of this period see Cooper, *Decolonization and African Society: The Labor Question in French and British Africa* (Cambridge, 1996) 58–65, 141; Weiler, 'Forming Responsible Trade Unions', 370–2.

55  CO 583/263/30544, 'Model Villages for African Miners'.

56  B. Supple, *The History of the British Coal Industry, 1913–1946: The Political Economy in Decline* vol. 4 (Oxford, 1987), 558. There is an extensive literature on the 'garden city' movement and its application to the colonies. On England, see B.I. Coleman *The Idea of the City in Nineteenth City England*, (London, 1973), 197–8. For a colonial introduction, see A. King, *Urbanism, Colonialism and the World-Economy: Cultural and Spatial Foundations of the World Urban System*, ( New York, 1991).

57  Powell Duffryn, 'First Report', D-18.

58  *Ibid*. The 1947 Powell Duffryn study considered the ratio of productive to non-productive face workers to be an important contributing factor in a 30 per cent reduction in overall productivity.

59  *Ibid.*, 18.

60  This account is based on the personnel files of Isiah Ojiyi. Nigerian Coal Corporation Files, P.2/1/1, CS from ?B., 14 July 1938.

61  Agwu Akpala, 'Background of the Enugu Colliery Shooting Incident of 1949', *Journal of the Historical Society of Nigeria*, 3 (1965), 352.

62  Great Britain, *Report of the Commission of Enquiry into the Disorders in the*

*Eastern Provinces of Nigeria* (London, 1950), 18; NIGCOAL 2/1/182, 'Long Award, General Correspondence Re'.

63  Supple, *History of the British Coal Industry*, 551; *Report of the Commission of Enquiry*, 18.

64  *Report of the Commission of Enquiry*, 18. For complete documentation see NIGCOAL 2/1/182, 'Long Award, General Correspondence Re'.

65  Long Award – General Correspondence Re.'; Testimony of P. H. Cook, *Proceedings* vol. 1, 14.

66  'Coal Miners Tender Wholesale Resignation', *Nigerian Eastern Mail*, 7 April 1945.

67  NIGCOAL 2/1/182, Patton in Obwetti Mine to Bracegirdle, 3 May 1945.

68  Douglass, 'Pit Talk', 311.

69  Interview with Agwu Akpala, London, 14 February 1975. The following account is based on '*We Were All Slaves*', forthcoming.

70  For the Zikist movement see E. Iweribor, *Radical Politics in Nigeria, 1945–50: The Significance of the Zikist Movement,* (Zariam, 1966) This description is from '*We Were All Slaves*', forthcoming.

71  F. Cooper, 'Work, Class and Empire: an African Historians' Retrospective on E.P. Thompson', *Social History* 20:2 (1995), 140.

72  *Ibid.*

# 9
## 'Did Not Come to Work on Monday': the East London Waterfront in Comparative Perspective, *c.*1930–63

*Gary Minkley*

This chapter is about labour struggles on the docks of East London, a South African port. In a fundamental sense, the docks in colonial cities like East London focused the question of the form and nature of black wage labour. The dichotomies between free and coerced labour were first played out around a set of tensions between labour supply and labour militancy. In the process there was a shift in the broader understandings of race and class. It is also about these tensions cast in a wider frame. The port occupied a particular nodal space in colonial societies. This is true of Mombasa, Lourenço Marques and Durban – which are briefly considered – as well as East London. The 'riverport' of East London was an 'artery' in which power was concentrated and through which it flowed, although in many respects it was also representative of the period's urban colonial economy. At the same time, the twentieth-century African (and colonial) waterfront was an ambiguous place.[1]

   Like other colonial ports, East London's docks always seemed to be on the edge of transition; inhabiting spaces that faced, at a distance, the looming power of industrialization and the homogenization of work, but also spaces of work that drew on and shaped the urban structure with different labour forms and conceptions of time. East London was very much a dense transfer point of colonial power, reflecting and condensing the tensions of colonialism in a capitalist context, while forcing the recognition of the incompleteness of capitalist transformation.[2] The chapter attempts to explore aspects of this tension or ambiguity in relation to issues of labour supply and labour militancy on the city's waterfront, relating these to the 'labour question' in other similar settings.

# 1

East London was certainly no Mombasa, Lourenço Marques or Durban. Its port, considerably smaller in size, handling capacity and labour requirements, was much more the centre of a regional, settler-dominated, agricultural economy. Wool and maize, the main products of this hinterland, were the port's principal exports, while its chief imports were clothing and textiles, foodstuffs and grain, metals and machinery, and petroleum. It was, and remains, South Africa's smallest commercial port, but it was still 'a port of some significance'.[3] Major infrastructural developments increased its handling capacity in the decade after 1927, and subsequent mechanization and other forms of capitalization – particularly grain elevators and new handling capacity introduced in the late 1940s and 1950s – enhanced its relative importance among South African ports.

However, in common with the other three cities, East London's black labour force was concentrated in the docks (and railways). In 1930 nearly 2,000 of its approximately 5,000 industrial workers found employment there. And, in keeping with these other cases, this waterfront labour force was primarily 'casual'. It was employed by the Cape Eastern System of South African Railways and Harbours (SAR&H), and by private stevedoring, petroleum and handling companies. By 1930, SAR&H employed 511 'regular' workers on the docks and railways, together with around 700 daily 'casual workers', sometimes described as 'togt' labour. The largest stevedoring firm, the East London Stevedoring Company (ELSC), had a pool of 200 'daily casuals', while the other two major companies – Newman, Watson and Newman, and Dreary and Company – employed 200 'casuals' between them. In addition, the Union Castle Shipping Company employed around 80 workers and the Oil Companies had 240 daily workers. Although the total size of the waterfront workforce varied – particularly during the Second World War, when numbers slumped – its distribution between the various employers remained fairly constant, at least until the late 1940s.[4]

As elsewhere, dock work was irregular and flexible in terms of labour time, so demand was variable. Daily hiring was also determined by 'casuals offering in crews' or gangs operating in wider stevedore and shorehandling pools. Despite attempts in the 1910s to register 'casual workers', using a registration office and badges, and despite its continued nominal existence through the 1920s, work was invariably organized through informal 'homeboy gang' networks, each headed by an 'induna' (a term which seems to have circulated through South African ports, at least in official terminology).[5]

Wages were low and also relatively static, declining in real terms against the cost of living. In 1903, wages were 3/6d per day, in 1911 they were between 2/6d and 4/-, in 1926 approximately 4/-, and by 1930 between 3/6d and 4/4d per day. By the 1940s, they averaged between 3/6d and 5/- per day. Work patterns varied. During the Depression, 'casual boys' worked four or five days a month, in the late 1930s three or four days a week, during the Second World War 'hardly at all', and after the Second World War 'some crews worked whole weeks, including overtime Sundays'. During 'planting season' day labour became a real problem at the harbour – right into the 1930s 'there would be no boys in sight' and 'none offering'.[6] Right into the 1950s, dock work remained patterned by the uneven energy of gang-centred labour.[7] Wage and labour-time disputes marked much of the visible moments of labour conflict in the docks, with minute details of rates, quotas and work rules the key causes of conflict, as in Mombasa or Durban.[8]

In addition to organizing the work, indunas arranged accommodation for the 'casual gangs' in the locations of East London. These workers were housed in 'squalid slums' of largely self-built, packing-case rooms, rather than in barracks or compounds, as was usual for African workers. Policed and patrolled by the local authorities and urban registration queues, dependent on 'homeboy' and dock-gang networks, immersed in the insecurity of 'native city' and living in squalid accommodation, the 'hard-pressed' relationships between dock work, labour time, security, wages and the ability to be 'men of tomorrow' were negotiated, disputed and assessed. These processes occurred in relation to rural life within a city context, but also in relation to consumption, needs and desires in the city, and to work.[9]

In one respect, tensions between the supply of casual labour, the docks as a key urban space within the colonial city and the development of more stable worker identities has a familiar trajectory. Casual dock workers struck work, organized themselves and supported workers in other sectors, and they did this on practically every significant occasion in East London's history up until the 1960s. In 1930, they were instrumental in one of the few city-wide strikes that South Africa has witnessed, and in 1946, they initiated the city's longest and largest strike for 15 years. In the latter case, they were joined by SAR&H day workers, who were sacked for refusing to scab. The strike – which centred on low wages – was sustained by shouts of 'Don't offload the ships!', and by meetings, marches and negotiations.[10]

David Hemson's observations, made in relation to Durban – and, to some extent, Fred Cooper's in relation to Mombasa – seem appropriate here. There were diffuse links with, on different occasions, the Industrial and Commercial Workers' Union (ICU), local organizers of the Communist Party (CPSA) and the Council of Non-European Trade Unions, and location and dock worker gatherings, but, as in Durban, organization and activity appear to have relied much more on 'underground networks', or to have been built on a bedrock of informal organization and strike activity. Notwithstanding the long and distinctive record of militant action, much of this culture remained hidden.

East London's first recorded black workers' strike occurred in 1903, and involved the 'dockboys'. They demanded and secured an increase in their wages from 3/- to 3/6d per day.[11] Seven years later, in September 1911, there were a series of harbour disputes, starting from a wharf workers' stoppage in support of a demand for an all-round increase of 6d on their wage of 2/6d per day. Lighter, yard and baggage-room workers – who were more highly skilled and received higher wages – did not take part,[12] but the action did spread to municipal workers, to unskilled railway workshop workers, to the railway goods shed 'daily boys', and finally to other commercial sector workers in the city. These were the first strikes by black workers to spread outside of the docks. On 22 September, in order to maintain a 6d differential over the wharf workers, the stevedore workers demanded an extra 1/- on their 3/- to 4/- per day wages. The strikes, having returned to the riverport, ended with a 'lighter boys' stoppage for higher wages, which were set at 4/- per completed trip.[13]

Just after the First World War – when the cost of living, including the cost of housing, was rising dramatically – there were a range of protests and demands for general wage increases. In 1918, demands for a general 1/- a day increase attracted over 2,000 people to mass meetings, and a 6d per day rise was negotiated with the Chamber of Commerce and the City Council.[14] In early 1920, a similar process saw the emergence of the East London Native Employees' Association (ELNEA), which attempted to develop what it called 'trade union principles of operation'. Although, by 1921, dock workers formed a central core of its claimed membership of 2,000–4,000, the union largely functioned as an additional pressure group for a location elite.[15] Direct strike action was left to the dock workers. In September 1921, separate from the ELNEA, 300 casual stevedore workers and the railway goods shed workers engaged in a strike over the 'working of 20 minutes extra per day at the same wages'.[16]

Influenced by the presence of first the ICU, and then the Independent ICU (IICU), the 1930 strike began as a dock and railway strike for increased wages. The 'harbour strike' began on the 16 January with a 'grey sky and a miserable drizzle'. It involved about 450 SAR&H workers, including 326 'casual workers', the wharf, slipway, harbour engineer's, stores and goods yard workers, and approximately 400 of the casual stevedoring and oil company workers. Over the next few days there was an increase in the number of striking casual and SAR&H workers. From 20 January, the strike became general across the city, incorporating about 500 commercial sector workers, 560 factory workers, 280 building workers, 310 municipal workers and around 1,000 domestic workers. Although the stoppage officially ended, without success, on 27 January, between 500 and 1,000 workers, largely composed of 'stevedore boys', casual workers and 'domestic servants', remained on strike for a number of months. Many of them, though, 'didn't have jobs to come back to because they have been filled by unemployed, or strikers anxious to get back to work, and lastly by Europeans'.[17]

This group of workers constituted itself as a 'rank and file committee', and according to one report: 'there appears to be a more or less continuous gathering of natives on the football ground, and it is stated that the atmosphere is cloudy with impending trouble. Scrub women and casual labourers, at work during the day, join the gathering in the evenings and appear to support the non-workers.' The spillover from the strike continued for the rest of the year, as the IICU was pushed into 'novel and distinctive local and traditional idiom[s]' incorporating location and rural contexts and constituencies. Lloyd, the Location Superintendent, saw the strike as having 'roused the native mind to such a pitch as was never previously witnessed by myself, in fact to such an extent that I expected rioting to commence at any moment.' Despite this rhetoric, and although the strike was seen to have its core support amongst casual dock workers, there was little official or employer reaction. It was dismissed as the work of agitators, and, more broadly, the colonial port remained securely within official designations of casualism.[18] Dock work in East London was not restructured – as it was in Lourenço Marques – following the spate of labour conflicts that culminated in the 1930 general strike.

As has already been suggested, the next significant moment of black worker strike action occurred in 1946, and it was followed by others in 1947, 1951 and 1952. 'Stevedore boys' and casual dock workers were again to the fore, and the strikes, almost predictably, raised issues of wages and of labour time, including overtime, weekend work and night labour.[19] This time around, employers and officials noted with alarm that casual dock workers drew on unknown networks. '[I]t was well planned and cleverly executed', they argued, and it was, they added, outside the ambit of visible organization. The strike was smaller than in 1930, but worry, fear and concern were much more apparent; products perhaps of the colonial conjuncture as much as of the events themselves. Meetings, reports, enquiries and investigations about organization clogged the work of officials and employers.[20] Part of this was the desperate scurry for 'agitators' and leaders. Samson, No. 3568, Shortie, No. 1990, Jackson, No. 3908, Freddie, No. 4304, and Jack, No 4603 – the actual leaders of the strike – were not regarded as eligible candidates.[21] The ICU, Clements Kadalie, its former leader, the CPSA, and three officials from the mainly white Trades and Labour Council (Selby, Muller and Behr), all claimed some involvement and influence, even promising general strikes, but in practice there impact was minimal.[22] The Railway and Harbour Staff Association had been completely unable to organize landing and shipping workers, and was clearly without any say. Thus, it was difficult to pin the unrest on any specific individuals or organization.

Explanations turned to the city, to the locations and to the workplace. 'Casualism', which had already been placed under the spotlight by a Wage Board investigation in the early 1940s, was thought to be culpable, and the problem was traced back to its apparent source – the port.[23] The response by Tindell of the ELSC was blunt and to the point: 'What we need ... [he said] is a factory port – without it we are in deep trouble in this town.' He later elaborated: 'labour is not as good as it used to be ... it is very unreliable, full of malingering and unsufficiency [sic] ... you have to employ more than is actually necessary and you get more of the won't-works. Native labour is therefore not cheap. A higher wage will satisfy no existing casual Union. They need to be thrown out of action and new Natives made out of the stuffing.'[24]

With almost the same urgency and elaboration as in Mombasa – and officials in East London looked to Mombasa, and to Durban and Cape Town, rather than to Johannesburg – the 1946 strike hastened a series of local investigations, commissions and reports on migrant labour, on conditions in the locations, and on dock work.[25] The subsequent 1952 'riots' confirmed all of the worst fears. The 'unruly', the unknown mob and the dangerous mass, incorporating the *tsotsi* (i.e. criminal) youth, were posing a threat to the city. The 'responsible and well sought after native' was thus losing 'a great deal of sympathy which he would otherwise have got'.[26]

However, more importantly here, the day after the 'riots' there 'was a shortage of togt workers at the docks',[27] and this absence from work was officially interpreted as one of sympathy and support for the 'riots'. This followed a series of disputes in 1951 and 1952. These were over rates of pay, overtime work, registration, conditions of service (with dismissal if a worker was absent for more than six continuous days), and attempts to transform the induna's into '*basebenzi* boys' (i.e. foremen).[28] Officials and employers rapidly drew the two processes of labour action and 'riots' together, and affirmed connections between togt labour, casualism, what was called 'casual unionism', and the dangerous mass in the city.

## 2

This was not altogether unsurprising. Running beneath these largely visible forms of labour organisation, there was a less obvious, though cumulative layer of conflicts over when, under what conditions and how labour should be supplied. By the late 1940s, these 'everyday' and longer-term disputes had tended to cement a series of common-sense connections between the docks, the city and the locations. These contests over labour supply linked with conflicting systems of belief, and with the development of new expressions and languages of racial and class identity. In every case the city edged closer to providing an explanation of its problems. Three examples will help to illustrate this layering; each highlighting, in some degree, the special significance of Monday.

On Monday, 20 January 1930, when the 'native workers' of East London declared a general strike, an important aspect of this layer emerged. The day before, there had been a series of meetings, during which Mgadi, one of the strike leaders, is said to have argued:

Some of you do not realise that we are at war. At 6 am yesterday there were 2325 employees of the Railways and Harbours on strike. Hertzog [the Prime Minister] and his goddam Government must realise that they are dealing with a new Native race ... we will not fight them with sticks. Our way of fighting on this occasion is going to be to remain at home and let them do their own dirty

work ... Now that we ask for money he sends police ... those who
go to work tomorrow will be traitors, who must know they are near
their graves. We do not mean that we will kill you, but you will die
by supernatural powers. Those of you who do go to work don't
come back to the Location to sleep, and don't blame us if you die
on the way to the Location.[29]

After the strike, 'Monday' and 'harbour work' appear to have shifted
their meaning. The Port Captain reflected in the later 1930s that, 'as a
consequence of the recent strike my boys no longer consider Mondays
to be a working day ... they demand overtime for Monday work ...
otherwise they will not work at all.' Over the same period the general
strike became inscribed as the general harbour strike, with harbour
workers as 'strike boys'.[30] Workers, apparently, began to call Monday
*'isiphelo'* – the death of one's hopes (*isiphelo sethemba lakho*) – which
marked, for a time, a space to avoid.[31]

Seven years later, in June 1937, many of the same dock workers –
stevedores, 'gangway boys' and 'berthing boys' – refused to work on
Mondays. In a weekend disagreement between shorehandling and
stevedoring workers and the harbour officials over productivity, the
harbour berthing master had likened casual workers to *'umhlambi
girls'* (i.e. washerwomen). The following Monday 'about 200 native
servants arrived at the docks', claiming they were coming to offload
the ships because their 'men had stayed at home to do the washing'.
Although the women were refused entry to the riverport and did not
return to the docks, no 'casual natives' turned up for work for three
successive Mondays; 'work started each week on the Tuesday'.
Grudgingly the berthing master, 'under order' and in the presence of
the Port Captain, finally 'apologized to the boys'. Work, it was
recorded, 'resumed in its normal pattern, starting on Monday the
following week'.[32]

On a Monday morning in August 1943, the Medical Officer of
Health (MOH), an army doctor and two nurses, accompanied by a
group of soldiers and an interpreter, arrived on the docks as part of a
drive to inoculate key workers. In the months prior to this visit there
had been a growing 'fear' of a 'TB epidemic', identified as originating
from the docks and found chiefly among casual dock workers (that is,
among those regarded as ill-disciplined, volatile, migrant and suscep-
tible). The workers refused, *en masse* to be examined and treated, and
they 'walked out of the port'. The MOH later quizzically explained
that this was, as he understood it, because the 'boys' believed that

after the injection, 'they would die and wake up again in the desert war'. After a number of failed attempts over the next month and half, involving different personnel, and various attempts to negotiate arrangements, the MOH received a letter from the Port Authorities asking him to desist from any further port visits. 'There is a rumour doing the rounds that you are lying in wait here at the beginning of each week ... that you will take their blood and they will die and then when they awake ... [you will have] turn[ed] them into white zombies for King George's army (I ask you?). The upshot is that we have no boys here at work every week.'[33]

As we have seen, there were also other moments when the accepted timing of work was contested, and in the 1930s, 1940s and 1950s harbour officials repeatedly grumbled about this. For the workers, 'won't work on Mondays' became a refrain that included a range of differences (and desires) about incomplete expectations, acceptances and understandings of dock work. As they struck work, failed to appear, organized their own systems of time management and productivity, and challenged who could and would 'master the situation' on the docks, they demonstrated that this was part of the necessary trouble associated with worker identity. All of this had a further effect. Increasingly within official circles a shift emerged towards considering a transition from casualism to permanence in dock work, and away from 'native boys' towards togt workers. In parallel with this, attention increasingly turned towards the need for stabilizing the city, as well as the workplace.

This discursive shift from 'native boys' to 'togt workers', which occurred in the 1940s, was significant, and reflected new discourses about the 'classness' of African labour. The 1950s entailed a further shift. Dock workers were differentiated between a 'regular class' and 'intermittent togts', and the one systematically replaced the other.[34] By 1958, dock work had become patterned between weekly paid and monthly paid workers, co-ordinated through, respectively, regular SAR&H contracts and the East London Labour Supply Company (ELLSC). The ELLSC operated outside of, but in association with, the local labour bureau, and dock work became tied to stable work and a stable existence in the locations.[35] Reliable, responsible and regular dock workers rapidly 'earned' themselves 'sex ten' qualifications. That is, under the Urban Areas Act, which was applied to East London after 1952, they qualified as 'Section Ten' workers, with a right to reside in the city, eventually on a permanent basis. 'Sex ten' or 'East London is full' was seen to remove 'the little freedoms in choice of work', replacing these with the need to 'marry' an employer and 'stick to the job or be chased out'. In effect, this was the 'law that compels a man to remain in his job for at least ten years'.[36] The parallel between East London and Durban is interesting here, although in East London it was much more the 'riots', rather than – as Hemson suggests for Durban – dock workers' struggles, that led to local implementation of the Urban Areas Act.

As in Mombasa – or, more ambiguously, as in Durban – urban space, locality and 'community' were not necessarily 'stabilized' at this point. Alongside official lines of management and control – exemplified in the police raid, the registration queue and the curfew, and in the magistrates court and 'Loyiti' (the Location Manager's office)[37] – struggles, conflicts and the politics of difference were ongoing. Various lines of 'instability' can be identified among Africans – between town and country, between different categories of workers, between 'Red' and 'School', along lines of age, gender and status, and on the basis of residence, permanence, permission and removal. Yet, for employers and local officials the lesson, as in Mombasa, was clear: 'the classness of the working class was rooted in the stability of its attachment to the city, and residence was as important as workplace in creating that attachment'.[38] The power of 'Loyiti' had to become the power of class.

However incomplete it was in practice, the principle of changing dock work and creating a permanent class of dock workers was as clearly delineated in East London as in Mombasa. To transform and stabilize dock work was to transform casual labour, and thus to begin to stabilize, urbanize and regularize the city. 'Tomorrow's men' would only be 'useful citizens' – reasonable, responsible, law-abiding, loyal – if they were accepted as a 'new [working class] race' in the city. This would enable council officials to attend to their first duty – that is, 'protect the European community' and its welfare[39] – while at the same time resolving the 'native question' (stability of labour was the answer).

Not all agreed with this new vision of rule and workplace organization. Various employers, council and state officials, local political organizations and welfare groups, all had their say. Competing agendas for using power, and competing strategies for maintaining control, were articulated and engaged. Many argued not for the 'voice of reason', but for intensified exclusion, backed by a growing cadre of Native Affairs Department bureaucrats and more vigorous, white settler nationalism. Translated onto the docks this implied white foremen, random agitator identification (to question was to challenge and thus to 'agitate'), and the language of removal and the *sjambok*.[40] In the changing context of dock work the 1950s, the language of 'Kaffir' and 'kaffir boy' prevailed. The workplace stereotypes of colonial racism – of the African worker as lazy, unreliable, cheeky and stupid – is present in practically every statement recorded and archived from this period.[41] Class was being pushed back into an earlier discourse of race, and – in the era of a developing official discourse of apartheid or 'separate development' – this was accompanied by new imaginings of tribe.

Young white foremen, often with dreams of war in their head, went into the East London waterfront sure and confident of their superiority. There, often unable to manage the transitions in class identity expected from above, they resorted to a repertoire of racist imagery and behaviour that was as much about manliness as about envy and fear. Black workers, so-called 'casual won't works' in the public discourse of the late 1940s and early 1950s, were all the things they shouldn't have been: hard-working, strong, tireless and disciplined, organized and 'treating each other properly on the job'.[42] In consequent conflicts over supervision, a line of exclusion emerged that was far clearer and 'cleaner' than it had been before.[43] Recalling the 1950s, one ex-foremen remembered:

> I want to say it was the Dutchmen [Afrikaners] but it was all of us there. You had to join in, it was like a club, the 'foremen's gang', and if you wanted to belong you had to klap [hit] and to treat the kaffirs like rubbish. That's when they got lazy and thick [stupid]; they did what we called them … they became kaffirs then, and it wasn't so bad …[44]

The making of a 'factory port' was carried through with a moral superiority and 'naturalized' cultural difference that justified new forms and different intensities of racial violence. Nevertheless it was transformed mainly within visions of permanence, stability and 'universality' of class, where the expectations were of weekly and then monthly work, of differentiated labour registration and rates and hours of work, and of labour discipline. Work on the docks became part of the bureaucratic power of *'Layini idokisi'* (the dock office).[45] Such expectations confronted the difficulties of the port and of work, but the reality by the early 1960s was of a monthly, better paid, more stable, and – as in Mombasa and Durban – more distinctive and differentiated dock labour force.[46]

Social memory suggests how it became part of a more regular grammar. To quote one dock worker: 'the white basebenzi [foremen] were pleased to suck our blood out until there was nothing left ... they called me Samson one day and Jim the next ... all that mattered was being on the job, every day, every day; on time, on time; and then kick and shout and run until you are finished ... the days of freedom were over then ... that was not for a man – work was dead.'[47] As reflected in 'supervisor reports', daily routine was not only more authoritarian, it classified and surveilled dock workers as differentiated racial subjects in newly established ways.[48] Recently appointed white foremen drew on the nourishing intensities of colonialism's violences, including those of settler nationalism, to instil racial modes of self-surveillance onto a changing workforce. As in Lourenço Marques and other colonial ports, dock workers began increasingly to 'work as required', hold onto jobs, avoid confrontations, and work 'out of sight'.[49] Tensions, conflict and ambiguity marked these processes as they had others, and the docks remained an unsettled place of contestation. More significantly, though, the 'informal' expressions of dock worker organization and the troubles of dock-worker identity shifted locality and shifted focus as dock workers themselves took the waterfront into the city once more.

In Mombasa, restructuring included – and was partially shaped by – the development of formal trade unionism, which became an integral part of creating a distinctive and differentiated working class. In contrast, East London's port workers were hesitant in adopting this route. Disillusion with Kadalie, remembered as a thief, and with formal organizations, remembered as full of big words and empty promises, had something to do with this. Also, as Cooper shows, union and class developments in Mombasa were directly connected to national mobilizations around decolonization, and in this respect South Africa was rather different. In Durban, according to Hemson, the labour repression and apartheid control that accompanied port restructuring in the 1950s and 1960s forced dock worker organization back into its long-established 'underground' networks. These informal networks were able to survive longer than more formal methods of organization, and they continued to be capable of sustaining social action, as reflected in the 1969 dock workers' strike.[50] Again, this was not the case amongst dock workers in East London. The informal networks were decisively broken on the docks in the 1950s and early 1960s from above, but also significantly from below.[51] As the state and employers resolved the questions of labour supply on the docks, the lens of dock worker struggles shifted in form and in content. In particular, new and different networks were built and transplanted from the docks into the city's locations.

The dock workers, caught between new identities about class and the anatomies of 1950s racial violence in the workplace, and faced with an increasingly stabilized and permanent future in the locations, set about remaking the place and the space of older urban solidarities – in the locations and through gender and 'tradition'.[52] As the spatial terrain on which black dock workers defined their identity shifted (and as the status of the docks as an arterial point of power declined), so the sense of class as stable, urban and modern began to disappear. The men 'ruled' the locations in the early 1960s, and dock workers were 'everywhere with their sticks' in the name of tradition – of being Xhosa.[53]

## 3

Mombasa, Lourenço Marques, Durban, East London – a route south marked by similarity and by difference. As part of the conclusion, I want to disembark at each port in turn.

Mombasa was the key colonial port in East Africa. In his pathbreaking study, Cooper shows that between 1934 and 1947 a series of strikes, in which the docks were central, thrust upon officials the fact that workers were social beings, and not just a quantity of labour power – not just an 'urban mass' of casual workers. Among officials and employers, two general strikes provoked a crisis of ideas, though they came to see the problem as an 'unexpected, unwanted, but very real presence of an African urban working class that had come to the city'.[54] Their diagnosis, as Cooper argues, 'pointed to the importance of casual labor to the most vital and vulnerable of Mombasa's industries, dockwork'.[55] It was here, on the African waterfront, that 'the Kenya Government discovered the dangers and complexities of the existence of an African working population'.[56]

The relationship of dockers to other workers in Mombasa – and the relationship of dock work to the totality of workers' economic lives – was thus of central importance. The port defined and localized the meanings of, and about, the African working class, both in the city and in the colony. The port was responsible for a labour situation that facilitated and depended upon an irregular, unknown and 'unstable' 'anonymous mass'. In the 1940s, the emergence of notions of 'dangerous urban working classes' was located or read through the 'casualism' of dock work and the incomprehensible movements and solidarities of dock workers. And, in the 1940s and 1950s, the reforms and transformations of class were shaped, and patterned by, advocacy for a stable, respectable and permanent urban working class, that was located on the docks.

This complex and contested reconstruction of dock work meant that a differentiated, distinctive and fragmented working class was stabilized more widely in the city's workplaces. At the same time, developments and transformations at the port, and in the trade union organization of dock workers, helped frame a different vision – at least in the workplace – and particularly in the docks. Cooper argues: 'while it had been the workers who "initiated" these changes ... it was the state who read the struggles in the image of casual labour and began to "reshape" Mombasa into another vision, a universal image of modernity, rational industrial organization, and planned urbanism.'[57] With postwar reforms, and with formal and bureaucratized union structures and organization, dock workers became a group set apart from the rest of Mombasa. At independence, they were 'the best paid African manual workers in Kenya'.[58] In reshaping dock work – in creating a compact, efficient and stable corps of urban workers – the colonial state believed that it could not only control the city, but also recast the relationship of city and country, isolating the former from the seemingly atavistic currents of rural Africa. But, Cooper concludes, 'better able to impose that image on the workplace than on the city as a whole, it was unable to reconcile the new vision of society with its own continuing problems and practices of political control.'[59] The ambiguities and struggles for the stabilization of the city and for political control remained unresolved.

In part, East London experienced a similar trajectory. However, in the riverport, change depended rather more on the cumulative effects of trouble associated with worker identity, and on informal networks and dramas of labour militancy, than it did on large moments of formal strike activity. In place of the universal image of modernity, rational industrial organization and planned urbanism, that guided Mombasa, the new vision of apartheid channelled a different path for dock workers in East London. They were not 'tamed' with material rewards but ruthlessly constrained in the strictures of tradition.

In East London, the result looked markedly similar to what had happened further down the coast in Lourenço Marques, the port of a regional economy dominated by Witwatersrand gold mining, and the capital of a Portuguese colony. Here, in the docks and in the city, a highly coercive system, with racist and arbitrary sanctions, aimed to encourage a 'scrapping, marginalized working class' which 'trapped' the majority of dock workers 'in the struggles of the working poor'.[60] Basic adulthood, security and human dignity were effectively denied. As a result, there were markedly few labour confrontations at the port and rail complex between 1933 and 1962, and isolated moments of protest were unable to force change, as in Mombasa. In both East London and Lourenço Marques, the difference between 'workers' and 'natives' remained as a fundamental distinction, carrying its own coding of authority and respect. The 'port–rail complex' of Lourenço Marques was integral to a system which continued to privilege social relations based on colonial definitions of race over class relations.[61] Local discourses of class that did emerge failed to find expression in unions, in stabilized industrial relations, or 'universal' parameters of the working class differentiated and fragmented from the dangerous classes. In apartheid East London, as in Lourenço Marques in an earlier period, it was more through violations of the body, race, dignity, and tradition that the docks and the city articulated meanings 'about class'.[62]

Hemson shows that during the 1940s and 1950s a comparatively 'free' form of labour – migrant and casual workers, paid on a daily basis and housed in labour barracks (or compounds) – was 'transformed into contract labour under a strict labour regime'.[63] He makes a number of other important points in relation to labour supply and labour militancy in Durban. The first is that despite a range of rural connections and the casual togt nature of dock work, dock workers were, certainly by the 1940s, a core component of the Durban working class. Secondly, in this context, they developed, mobilized and sustained a range of 'informal' networks of organization, association and expression that enabled them to act coherently and effectively as workers. Thirdly, these networks were both militant and challenging – radical in maintaining their own independence, though diluted and fragmented in association with other more formal political and trade union organizations.

In the late 1940s and early 1950s, the state and employers responded by restructuring dock work, taking control of labour circulation and restricting and directing labour supply into a more permanent labour force. Through the 1950s, struggles intensified these processes. In 1958 and 1959, the control of dock labour was centralized in one institution (the Labour Supply Company); 'gang' labour was eliminated; supervision of dock work was restructured, turning indunas into company sergeant-majors; differential wage rates and weekly paid 'permanent' work were entrenched; labour-time was intensified; dismissal – the sanction of the sack – put in place; and togt labour ended. Dock labour was thereby 'stabilized'.[64]

More generally, Hemson has argued persuasively – though he has not, I think, been taken seriously enough by South African scholars – that, in order to understand class struggles in Durban (and by extension other port cities in South Africa), one needs to understand dock workers. As with port cities further up the coast, the docks 'defined' the power of the city, and dock workers spelt out the power of labour struggles. He goes further, arguing: '[t]he struggles of the dock workers had a significant effect on the development of administrative measures to deal with labour leadership, on the argument on how to reconcile a smooth-flowing labour supply with tightened influx control, and on the intra-working class relationships between Indian and African workers. The process of laying down minimum wages for unskilled labour was initiated, controls were introduced to contain and direct the flood of workers from the reserves, [and] influx control was implemented for the first time.'[65] In essence, for Hemson, the flow is in one direction: what is learnt on the docks provides the subsequent basis for apartheid, stability and control in the city. Class determines racial policies, and practices, arising from the labour supply company, act a model for apartheid employment.

In East London, while there are important similarities around attempts to stabilize labour and regulate its supply, there are also important differences. Here change needs to be understood within the wider context of empire in the 1940s and within the uneven parameters of apartheid in the 1950s and 1960s. The nature of struggles around labour supply in East London was significantly shaped by being a port on the margins of the Witwatersrand. As a result the material and imaginary landscapes and structures of power in East London were constituted and envisaged more sharply by the broader history and geography of colonial inheritances and imperial presents. In the 1930s, a general strike was effectively isolated. In 1946 – the year of a massive strike by African mine workers on the Rand and of unrest elsewhere in Africa, and indeed the world – a much smaller dock strike prompted the reordering of dock work and the search for a stable and permanent working class. In the 1950s, in a period when the 1952 riots were dramatically likened to Mau Mau, and rural social unrest was seen to be entering the city, this approach floundered. 'Casualism', displaced from the docks, was increasingly being read as an essentially rural phenomenon in the towns – more specifically, in the locations, 'where town and tribe can be said to remain at unusually close quarters.'[66] Now, the casual mass (of youth), 'must be beaten and removed', and in the name of age, maturity, authority, and tradition, dock workers could hold power.

The spatiality of power shifted in the city. The workplace would not stabilize the city and neither would thorough control of urban space, as attempted through local state legislation and intervention in the 1950s. The location was, quite simply, understood as too rural and out of place: mass, tribalistic, backward-looking and dangerously colonial, in a European and modern setting.[67] It would need to be removed, and labour supply controlled through 'bantu self-government' located at the bordering Ciskeian 'commuter city' of Mdantsane. Apartheid, finally, found its way into one of the margins of colonial South Africa.

By 1963 'Monday' was no longer in dispute – it was a working day on the East London docks. In the same year, stevedores climbed into homeland buses in Mdantsane for the first two to three hour journey to the docks. The buses were as full on a Monday as they were on a Friday. The 'new Native race' of workers, invoked in the 1930 strike to face 'Hertzog and his goddam Government', would have seemed a long way off for this class of fellow working travellers. Strike dreams of tomorrow, though, in the disturbed sleep of travel, were not so easily displaced or forcibly removed.

## Notes

1  See also, F. Cooper, *On the African Waterfront: Urban Disorder and the Transformation of Work in Colonial Mombasa* (New Haven and London, 1987); J. Penvenne, *African Workers and Colonial Racism: Mozambican Strategies and Struggles in Lourenço Marques, 1877–1962*, (Portsmouth, London and Johannesburg, 1995).

2  F. Cooper, 'Conflict and Connection: Rethinking Colonial African History', *American Historical Review* 99 (1994), 1532.

3  H. Smith, 'Transport', in D. H. Houghton, ed., *Economic Development in a Plural Society: Studies in the Border Region of the Cape Province* (Cape Town, 1960), 157–77.

4  CA (Cape Archives), LIE, File 17; SAR&H, 20/3/6 – 8/E, and 20/3/14 – Wharfs; BCI (Border Chamber of Industries), File ELSC, Docks and Stevedores.

5  CA, 3/ELN, Box 938; BCI, *ibid.*, including Report to President of BCI from Port Superintendent, 30 June 1937.

6  SAR&H, CSE, File 16 – Labour, and Files 24–37, Reports and Correspondence/Work/Native Boys; BCI, *ibid.*

7  Cooper, *On the African Waterfront*, 175.

8   *Ibid.*, 174. See also SAR&H, CSE, 37, Work Stoppages, Reports from Harbour Personnel, 1932–1953; BCI, File ELSC, Docks and Stevedores, Report on Port Labour, 21 April 1947.

9   See G. Minkley, 'Border Dialogues, Race, Class and Space in the Industrialization of East London, c1902–1963' (PhD thesis, University of Cape Town, 1995).

10  *Daily Dispatch*, 17 May to 11 June 1946. For a more detailed discussion of this strike see G. Minkley, 'Class and Culture in the Workplace: East London, Industrialisation and the Conflict over Work, 1945–1957', *Journal of Southern African Studies* 18 (1992), 739–60.

11  SANAC Evidence, vol. 2, 835, 836; H. H. Smith, 'The Development of Labour Organization in East London, 1900–1948' (MEcon thesis, Rhodes University, 1949), 147–51.

12  Smith, *ibid.*, 147–51; *Daily Dispatch*, September 1911.

13  Smith, *ibid.*; *Daily Dispatch, ibid.*

14  Smith, *ibid.*, 151–7; *Daily Dispatch*, August–September 1918.

15  Smith, *ibid.*; *Daily Dispatch*, 10 January 1920; CA, 3/ELN, Box 374, Letters from ELNEA to Resident Magistrate, 14 February 1920, January 1921, 26 October 1921.

16  CA, 3/ELN, Box 374; 1/ELN, CID Reports, 20 November 1922.

17  CA, 1/ELN, Files 86 and 87, CID Reports; Divisional Inspector of Labour, LIE, File 17, Reports on Strike, 1930. See W. Beinart and C. Bundy, 'The Union, the Nation and the Talking Crow', in W. Beinart and C. Bundy, *Hidden Struggles in Rural South Africa* (Johannesburg, 1987); and G. Minkley, 'To Keep in Your Hearts' (BA thesis, University of Cape Town, 1985).

18  CA, 3/ELN, Box 113, Evidence of Location Superintendent, 1 May 1933, and Box 3, Letter, bearing MOH stamp, 27 February 1930.

19  CA, LIE, File 1/13/3, Department of Labour, Departmental Annual Reports, 1951 and 1952, East London Inspectorate.

20  Reflected in LIE, SAR&H and BCI files from this period.

21  CA, LIE, File 1/13/3, Report on Dispute in Stevedoring Trade, East London, June 1946.

22  CA, LIE, File 1/13/3, Report on Dispute in Stevedoring Trade, East London, June 1946, see also *Daily Dispatch*, May–June 1946; and BCI, ELSC File, Report dated 12 July 1946.

23  CA, LIE, File 6, Wage Board Investigation, correspondence and Report, 1940/1.

24  BCI, ELSC File, 12 July 1946.

25  CA, 3/ELN, Boxes 938, 1240, contain the details and the Reports. In particular, detailed correspondence is contained in these files, with reports, advice and personal correspondence between officials in Mombasa, Durban, East London and Cape Town. Within this correspondence the similarities and comparative importance of the ports is explicitly drawn, and directly comes to frame policy interventions in East London.

26  A. Mager and G. Minkley, 'Reaping the Whirlwind: the 1952 Riots in East London', in P. Bonner et al., eds., *Apartheid's Genesis* (Johannesburg, 1993).

27  *Daily Dispatch*, 11 November 1952.

28  BCI, ELSC Files; CA, LIE, 1/13/3.

29 CA 3/ELN, File 86/7. This file contains a series of police reports on ICU meetings between 1922 and 1933. These date from 20 January 1930.
30 SAR&H CES (Cape Eastern System), Correspondence Files 15 and 19.
31 SAR&H CES, File 16 and Report, 12 December 1931.
32 SAR&H CES, File 15, 'Report on Disturbances', August 1937.
33 CA, 1/ELN, File 96, Health, File 46, War Measures, and Correspondence between MOH and Port Superintendent, December 1943.
34 SAR&H, CSE, Files 33–7; BCI, ELSC Files, Docks and Stevedores, 1951–62.
35 SAR&H, CSE, Files 33–7; BCI, ELSC Files, Docks and Stevedores, 1951–62.
36 P. Mayer and I. Mayer, *Townsmen or Tribesmen* (Cape Town, 1961), 59.
37 The name was derived from Lloyds Building, named after the first Location Superintendent, and in Xhosa eyes it was the 'seat of all effective power in East London'. See, *ibid.*, 52.
38 Cooper, *On the African Waterfront*, 176.
39 CA, 3/ELN, Boxes 1240, 938; 10/11/52. Notes on Informal Meetings.
40 BCI, ELSC Files, Docks and Stevedores, and particularly File: Investigations, 1951–1959 which contains details of effectively racist assaults with alarming frequency and intensity. A *sjambok* is a kind of whip, popular in South Africa.
41 *Ibid.* See also, SAR&H Files, 33–7; CA, LIE, Files 1/13/3.
42 Interviews, V. L., East London, December 1991 and December 1996.
43 For a wider discussion on race, see F. Cooper and A. Stoler, 'Between Metropole and Colony: Rethinking a Research Agenda', in F. Cooper and A. Stoler, eds., *Tensions of Empire: Colonial Cultures in a Bourgeois World* (California, 1997), especially 4–11.
44 Interviews, J.L. and other ex-dock foremen, East London, January 1992 and January 1997.
45 Interview, C.S., East London, January 1997.
46 BCI, ELSC Files; SAR&H, Files 33–7.
47 Interview, S.M., December 1992.
48 BCI, ELSC Files, Reports and Investigations, 1951–59.
49 BCI, ELSC Files, Reports and Investigations, 1951–59, East London Stevedore Company Correspondence; SAR&H, File 34, Harbour Reports: Dock Workers, 1953–7.
50 D. Hemson, 'Dock Workers, Labour Circulation, and Class Struggles in Durban, 1940–59', *Journal of Southern African Studies* 4 (1977), especially 123.
51 In Lourenço Marques, Penvenne implies that the restructuring of dock work took place after the 1960s.
52 See Mayer and Mayer, *Townsmen or Tribesmen*, 83–9. See also BCI, SAEL File, Disturbances, 1958, and CA, 1/ELN, Files 66, 75, 94, 95.
53 Interview, D.R, East London, January 1997; BCI, ELSC File, Disturbances, 1958.
54 Cooper, *On the African Waterfront*, 7.
55 *Ibid.*, 2; 3.
56 *Ibid.*, 247.
57 *Ibid.*, 12.
58 *Ibid.*, 246.
59 *Ibid.*, 12.

60  Penvenne, *African Workers and Colonial Racism*, 155.
61  *Ibid.*, 5.
62  *Ibid.*, 103–16.
63  Hemson, 'Dock Workers', 89.
64  *Ibid.*, 115–22.
65  *Ibid.*, 90.
66  Mayer and Mayer, *Townsmen or Tribesmen*, xv.
67  Cooper, *On the African Waterfront*, 185–6, for a comparative context.

# 10
# Back to Work: Categories, Boundaries and Connections in the Study of Labour

*Frederick Cooper*

The task I was given at the conference on 'Racializing Class, Classifying Race' – to summarize the conference papers and discussions – was an impossible one.[1] This was not just because the papers were so numerous – 46 in all – and the discussions so wide-ranging, but also because the contents of these contributions were so rich. Many of the papers represented microhistory at its best – they asked questions of wide interest, but insisted that they can only be answered by looking at the historical context of each situation, at the specificities of production and the complexities of culture, and at the institutional structures which could permit people to carve out a niche for themselves in a capitalist system or could allow them to fall victim to the more powerful. Even the more general papers argued for fine-grained analysis. The groundedness of these papers – including those published in this volume – is particularly welcome now. One reads these days too many attempts to read 'the female body' off a magazine advertisement, to locate 'the colonial subject' in a text by Kipling, to find 'governmentality' in a marriage law, or to embody 'resistance' in a passage from Fanon. In these conference papers, coal miners dig coal, dock workers carry loads, domestic workers clean floors. To talk seriously about how whiteness or masculine respectability was constructed should not be to assume people spent all day thinking about who they were; they had other things to do. Fresh and thoughtful analysis has emerged from confronting representations with the nitty-gritty of labour. It is not clear that the recent laments about labour history losing its drive or creativity are valid or that the 'post' in William Sewell's call for a 'postmaterialist rhetoric' for labour history actually tell us where we want to go.[2]

It is, however, valid to observe that the labour history of twenty years ago often assumed a universal narrative, when most labour historians were actually writing about white males in industrial jobs. It is now widely recognized that class, race and gender need to be seen in relation to one another. The problem is what to make of that realization. The papers at the Oxford Conference and in this book provide an answer, or rather as many as 46 answers. For to a significant extent, if it is true that social life can only be analysed in terms of the intersection of these variables, and if those variables themselves are not natural givens but the product of history, then the processes that one wants to analyse are necessarily specific. We could leave it at that, relish the insights we have had into a variety of places we knew nothing about a few days ago, and celebrate the end of metanarratives and grand theory. But the world we live in is far from a kaleidoscopic array of cultures gyrating to their own rhythms. Capitalism may be less than the juggernaut its apologists or its most damning critics claim it to be, but it is present throughout the globe, not simply in the abstract but in institutions that people encounter in their daily lives. The forms that labour relations took in Nigerian coal mines, British docks or Louisiana sugar estates emerged from quite specific struggles, but in each instance, capitalists were linked to other capitalists, not just via markets in commodities and credit, but in terms of interlocking knowledge systems, which both opened their eyes to ways of controlling work and workers, and closed their imaginations to ideas that might emerge from the work place itself.

Whatever one says about grand theory, and however much one wants to avoid the reductionism of capital logic or world systems theory, one cannot escape asking questions about interconnections across space and long-term developments over time – about the kinds of questions Marx suggested long ago. And sensitivity to the specific contexts of processes of resistance and adaptation should not make us reduce the story to the confrontation of global capitalism with local resistance, for liberation movements have in their own ways been as global as capitalism.

The strength of these papers is how they deal with particularity without losing focus on conceptual questions. Their weakness is really the weakness of history generally: the difficulty of writing in an empirically rigorous and precisely focused way about processes that are not spatially located, about connections. Our papers, with only a couple of exceptions, do more to juxtapose case studies from Africa, Great Britain and North America than to link them. Our discussions brought out many valuable comparisons, but we are much further from being able to do global history or a history of connections. In some of the more general and theoretical papers – as well as in the local studies – I sense that many scholars are chafing at some of the concepts that have only recently come into vogue. I share this unease. My comments will be devoted in the first place to discussing the theoretical implications of the papers, and secondly to looking at the question of how one can study the questions these raise in a way that puts more emphasis on global connections.

It would be nice to declare some questions settled. The interlocking importance of race, class and gender may be one such issue. Whether one can go beyond noting this – perhaps adding ethnicity, nationality or another dimension to the list – is less clear. Disputes over which of the three is most important seem, blessedly, to have passed. Two schemas are most in vogue, implicitly or explicitly. The first we might call the cube model, and the second the constructivist argument.

The cube model causes us to focus on gender, race and class in relation to each other. If one saw, for starters, each dimension of the Big Three as binary (e.g. male vs. female, white vs. black, bourgeois vs. proletarian), then we have three dimensions with two positions each, giving rise to a model of society as a cube divided into eight compartments. One could add values along each dimension, introducing a middle class or more numerous or refined race/gender categories, but that would expand the model to 16 or more boxes without fundamentally changing it. Or one could go to four dimensions, but that requires a better geometrical imagination than I possess. In any case, each compartment then becomes the collectivity in question.

The white male worker ceases to be the paradigmatic figure for working class history, but only one compartment. One can write, say, about the black female worker, not only emphasizing the specificity of the category but also pointing to conflicts and interactions along each dimension. One can ask how male workers, capitalists and women developed overlapping or conflicting interests in production and reproduction without reducing everything to an unrooted concept like 'patriarchy'. One can look at the fleeting alliances and feuds of black and white dock workers in southern US ports, without either assuming a norm of 'worker solidarity' or a norm of 'racism'. The model is useful politically – a reminder of the importance of making connections if one is to get beyond one of eight boxes or 16 boxes and that liberation in one sense does not necessarily mean liberation in another.

The danger, obviously, is that each of the compartments is treated as a block. Some conference papers pointed out this danger explicitly – noting for example the contradictory tendencies and tensions among people labelled 'the Irish' or 'the Germans' – but others found the 'group' so analytically useful a unit that they left its groupness largely unexamined.

The constructivist argument comes in here, and I will turn to that in a moment. First, a couple of points about the relationship of our three central categories. We tend to assume – certainly the cube model does this – that they are comparable. Even if we say that all are important, it does not follow that they operate in the same way. We sometimes refer to class identity, gender identity, racial identity, ethnic identity or national identity, but in seeing them as variants of a common phenomenon we may be assuming something quite misleading. We don't have a theory of identity formation that takes into account all these phenomenon. I am not convinced we want this sort of theory.

Indeed to invoke 'race' as a category in, say, the history of the United States is already to flatten a history: a history of forced migration, of slavery, of the openings of emancipation and citizenship and the subsequent closures, of Jim Crow and the reinscription of race, of the possibilities and failures of the Civil Rights era. It is this history that gives the experience of *being* African American its power and its poignancy. But if the label 'race' already flattens this experience, to refer to 'racial identity' is to flatten it further, and the implied or explicit conflation of race with gender – experienced historically in its own ways, with particular pains and possibilities – is to deflate the significance of difference, not to recognize it.

Class is sometimes seen as a relationship that is then cross-cut – some might say contaminated – by race, gender or ethnicity. Several papers showed that racially exclusive practices by unions were not simply imposed from above, but fostered by trade unions and by workers who acquired a stake in seeing themselves as white. One presenter hoped to see the day when workers would look beyond race to where their interests 'really' lay. But is 'cross-cut' the right word and are there real interests independent of a scheme by which they are perceived? If E.P. Thompson is right, class processes have their origin in artisanal culture, and William Sewell has made an even stronger case for France about the continuing strength of *compagnage*, centring around the preservation of particular trades as capital tried to devalue all of them.[3] Class struggle, in these times, was very largely about *not* being made into a class, about avoiding becoming generic sellers of labour power but retaining a bounded, culturally rooted sense of difference and particularity. Being a carpenter was a way of life, and entry into that social category was often hereditary and always carefully controlled, and admission was ratified by elaborate rituals. Carpenters defending their trade were not only talking about class, they were also engaged in a process akin to ethnicization: inventing a body of like-speaking men, with their ritualized solidarity, and their patriarchal conception of their women and their role in reproducing the ethnos.

Class does not spring directly from relations of production, but emerges from a *history* of production relations.[4] It does not help to describe a 'universal' system of class relations against the 'particularism' of race, ethnicity, or gender. It is more constructive to begin by asking how different forms of particularist solidarity emerge, and how distinctions are created, marked, narrated and used. This is not to say that history can only be studied at the microlevel, but rather to argue for a complex engagement with the history of capitalism.

Such a history cannot be confined to places of work, but at the same time gender and racial exclusions cannot be seen as simply external to the class process. If in some contexts white male workers, protecting a vulnerable set of work practices, drew the cloak of maleness and whiteness closer around them, in other contexts the rich and the powerful fostered racist and masculinist ideologies in efforts to attract support across class lines.[5] The exclusion-making elaborations of work culture worked hand in hand with discourses about the place of different social categories in politics. Worker mobilization in turn reflected the constraints and possibilities of racial ideologies. Several conference papers documented the vicious circle of certain trade unions in the late nineteenth and twentieth centuries, whose leaders thought that they might gain a point by appealing to racial categories shared with employers or state officials. But any gains so won would deepen the culture of racism.

Other papers point to ways out of this circle, focusing on the different kind of workplace created by the advance of industrial capitalism. Although the transition from an artisanal struggle against being a class to the industrial struggle of workers as a class was never fully analysed by Thompson, even a partial effort at turning workers into the generic sellers of labour power would create the *potential* of a workplace in which all sorts of people were present, their particularities of little concern to capitalists. Labour organizers then had the possibility of taking the polyglot workplace as it was, and working with people of

different appearances and histories. Several papers document a learn-
ing experience, where racially inclusive and exclusive strategies were
both tried; others show the influence of international trade unionism,
or the role of state institutions like the Fair Employment Practices
Commission, or shifting labour markets (as in the entry of women or
blacks into factory labour during wars). All this created possibilities to
pry open cracks in precisely those ideologies that had seemed to
cement racial or gender ideologies to the defence of the jobs of established workers.

   Politics is about forging connections, about finding conceptions
that resonate across differences. Resonances can amplify ugliness, as
when trade union exclusivity interacts with elite racial or gender prejudice, or they can widen solidarities. Workplace changes, for example,
cannot explain by themselves the opening up of racial questions in
the US after the Second World War, but the expansion of heterogeneous work sites in industry, the growth of inter-racial unions, and
the institutional support of the New Deal government – as well as the
effects of the war itself – changed the relationship of racial politics to
the daily lives of large numbers of working people. In Africa, in
roughly the same era, the reality of concentrations of workers in key
places also forced changes in the discourse of race and class among
colonial officials and trade unionists. Colonial regimes which had
tried before the 1940s to insist that African workers could only be
thought of in tribal or racial terms – and surely not in terms of class –
shifted their control strategies after the war to erase race in favour of
class. Trade unions used this opening to make claims.[6]

   Is the constructivist argument an answer to the inability of the
multidimensional model to grasp the dynamics of racial, class, and
gender ideologies and practices? The question is whether it actually
makes the break with essentialized conceptions of race, gender and
class as it purports to. It is easy to agree that the basic categories into
which people group themselves are not 'objectively' determined by
biology or economic processes, but are constructed and shaped by
people in their interactions with each other and therefore contested,
contingent, contradictory and multiple. We are none the less left, in
today's scholarship, with class, race and gender. If historians really
mean to be constructivists, there should be as many discarded 'identities' as there are the ones that are currently in the forefront of political
and social debate. The problem with constructivism is that it is often
done backwards: scholars show how 'women' or 'African Americans'
or 'whites' were constructed over time, but we knew that was how the

story was going to end before we began and we do not see the constructions that were discarded along the way.

The second problem is how to assign individuals to the categories that one can show emerged from the conflicting discourses and imaginings that shaped collective self-conceptions. What does one do with the individuals who don't quite fit or with the sheer fact of diversity, intermarriage, cultural interaction and cultural innovation? Not only could yesterday's Bavarian migrant to America become today's German, but the process could go in other ways: Irish Americans could look towards a generalized sense of Catholic respectability, towards a generalized working-class urban culture, towards making Irishness into good business and effective political mobilization, or towards aspirations to be both middle-class and ethnic, and therefore not too ethnic. People are often accused of passing or assimilating if they fall foul of the currently correct line, just as they might be accused of separatism if they go too far in another direction. The accusation of rejecting one's culture, however, presumes that the culture is one's own; to refer to passing is to assume that one really is something else. But how does one know which of many available historical constructions produced an individual, unless one has already classified that person?[7]

Cultural difference is protean. It does not stand still. To turn cultural difference into cultural identity is to make another kind of statement. The constructivist logic is soft: people build whatever identities they build, if not exactly as they would have liked. But the same word is used to designate something very hard: identity politics is all about convincing people that one dimension of their lives matters and others do not. The root word has a literal meaning – 'same as' – which specialists forget at the peril of divorcing themselves from ordinary speech, and it is in those terms that the concept of identity does political work. Nobody actually *has* an identity; identity does not refer to who we *are*. It refers to a project, and as such to an impossibility, for we are necessarily many things. How we get from the soft to the hard is nowhere clear. Is there something about a particular soft claim that makes it amenable to being hardened? Isn't that to say that identity is foundational after all? Claiming that identities are multiple and shifting only displaces the problem, for it mixes up soft and hard and doesn't help us sort them out from each other.[8]

The assimilation of identity talk to talk of difference makes things more difficult. What people think and do depends very much on the possibilities of a particular conjuncture, on opportunities they may or may not take, on histories that converge and diverge. But those complicated and messy histories map very poorly onto the categories of identity. Normatively as well, we might be better able to debate in what contexts and in what manner cultural difference can be addressed in a political system if we were not bound to the assumption that certain 'groups' correspond one-to-one to certain 'cultures'.[9]

On the left, identity politics has been criticized for burying the project of universal social justice under a host of projects of particular groups, and it has been defended because its evocation of particularity enhances the worth of human beings as they are, rather than as an abstract and monotonal humanity.[10] But this version of the debate gets wrong something that is very important. The old Marxist distinction between a class in itself and a class for itself assumes that one can first define a bounded category objectively, then analyse whether it is conscious of that fact or has been bewitched into false consciousness – rather the way identitarians talk about people losing 'their' culture. There is an implicit model of how classes form and act here: from production to cognition to action. There is a double hole in this logic: a cognitive psychology question of how one goes from structure to thought, and a problem of how one gets from cognition to agency. The teleology which jumps over this hole misses the much more complex ways in which action both establishes and blurs borders; it ignores how contingent class definition can be; it looks away from the process by which class action is constantly affected by other sorts of affiliations, by strategic alliances, by the victories and frustrations of struggles. Perhaps it is because so many Marxists in the 1960s and 1970s thought of class as an 'identity' that they later found it so easy to substitute ethnicity, nationality, race, or gender for class, and say what they had said before.

There is an important corollary to this discussion. Adam Przeworsky has argued that class struggle is only sometimes a struggle between classes; often it is a struggle about class.[11] One can make the same argument about race. When W.E.B. Du Bois argued in 1900 that the 'problem of the Twentieth Century is the problem of the color line', he was using exactly the right word.[12] The resurgent racism of the United States set out a stark division between two races, reducing to irrelevance differences among African Americans and eliminating the possibility of political interaction across the line. Colonial conquest in Africa also had a powerful polarizing tendency, and regimes spent a lot of effort preventing their own people from going native or having relationships that blurred the colour line, while limiting how much education or Christianity would change the status of an African.

African Americans and Africans often fought back in precisely these terms – so that a school teacher who maintained certain standards of decorum, who successfully distinguished herself from a domestic servant, was making a certain point about herself, but also about the very categories of race and class. She was accepting that American middle-class conventions were relevant to her, while insisting that that showed people of her race were capable of advancing in class terms. White working-class respectability, for Irish or Jewish Americans, could have a related meaning, as did the activities of 'improvement associations' among Nigerian workers, or churches and civic organizations in South African cities. Respectability is a class concept, one which builds on behavioural differences between top and bottom while asserting the possibility of movement in between. Cultural adaptation may partially imply that the weak act as if the way of life of the powerful is a model, but cultural adaptation and synthesis may subtly change what that way of life is. People thus experience race and ethnicity in dynamic and complex ways, not simply as boundary-drawing. Close analysis in conference papers of how individuals and collectivities sought respectability or cultural redefinition reveals how much these processes involve careful thinking about strategy, drawing on people's ability to locate themselves in complex social and political constellations and assess their possibilities in terms of historically rooted patterns. The papers also reveal the high personal costs paid in the quest for respectability and the high political costs paid collectively when assertions of citizenship depended on class criteria that only some African Americans could meet.[13]

At the same time, the public claim to civil rights, to political rights, to equal treatment, rejected the colour line altogether. It took long and bitter struggles, but the colour line is not, at the century's end, what it was at the beginning. An uncrossable divide no longer preserves professional training, respectable working class jobs, or elite status for whites only, either within a country like the United States or in international organizations. But questions about race are very much with us, as much as in Du Bois's time. White Americans can glorify Colin Powell, accept that a black lawyer may sit at the next table in a fancy restaurant, and at the same time condemn the culture of the urban ghetto as the cultural backwardness of African Americans; newspapers can represent Africa as the land of tribes, famines and peculiar customs, and not blink at the fact that the UN is headed by someone whose skin is the same colour as that of a Hutu refugee. Racialized imagery has survived the blurring of the colour line, and access to education or status has not come to mean equal access or the irrelevance of race in daily life.

Yet, for all the evidence of the impermanence and ambiguity of boundaries, the language of ethnic groups or racial groups is still very prevalent. Perhaps we think too much about groups and not enough about networks. When people ask 'to whom am I connected?' scholars are likely to assume that they mean to ask 'who am I?', forgetting that the second question – laden with Eurocentric notions of individualism – does not make the same assumptions as the first. We can easily acknowledge the constructed nature of collective labelling, but then write as if we were dealing with bounded groups. This does not mean that sharply bounded groups are not important – a lot of people have died in the name of bounding the category of Serb from the intermarriages and cultural interactions that have over centuries overlapped the categories of Croatian, Serbian and Muslim. Workers have in many contexts thought of themselves as 'German workers' or as 'white workers'.[14] But we will not understand when boundedness matters if we assume that groups are necessarily our unit of analysis.

We might not even ask about the great variety of social networks that people have constructed, such as West African Muslim brotherhoods, which build tight webs of affiliation based on loyalty to particular religious leaders, which act as trading diasporas across thousands of kilometres in Africa and connect to the brotherhoods' outposts as far away as New York and Paris, and which act as welfare societies and political organizations in several countries. They are not ethnically bounded or spatially confined, and while their members are Africans and Muslims, they make no effort to embrace Africans or Muslims as categories.[15] One could speak in a similar way about the Chinese diaspora in East and Southeast Asia which does not act at all as a group, involves no rhetoric of groupness, but in which cultural specificity is one element of forging close networks, capable of transmitting information and capital around vast economic spaces, and capable of holding their own in business with multinational corporations. Conference papers about Irish migrants reveal Irish ethnic networking linked to a broader pattern of establishing political clienteles, in which Irish followers helped patrons integrate into an American middle class. Diasporas are not just affinity spread out, but interface spread out.

So, if the idea of social or historical constructions gets us away from some of the box-like and static qualities of the three (or multi-) dimensional model, the constructivist model itself can be made more useful by making sure that our time runs forward. A constructivist historical account sensitive to diverse elements of the human experience will take us onto pathways that history did not take, into forms of human affiliation whose moments came and went.

Lest one think that I am saying that such processes produce warm and fuzzy connectedness or happy hybridities, I will conclude this section by mentioning one of recent history's worst instances of violence against people who were 'different', the Rwandan genocide of 1994. There are myths, Rwandan as much as western, of clear physical distinction between Hutu and Tutsi. But there are reports from the midst of the slaughter that gangs of Hutu thugs had to ask people for their identification cards, which since the days of the Belgian colony classified people by ethnicity, to see if they were Tutsi (absence of an ID then becoming a sign of being Tutsi). When children were being murdered, it was not the blood tie – as westerners often perceive ethnicity – that counted, but a genealogical one consistent with patrilineal kinship systems of the region (the child of a Tutsi father and a Hutu mother might be killed, the child of a Tutsi mother and a Hutu father spared). Rwanda turns out to be a place of nearly complete linguistic homogeneity, little cultural difference and religious distinctions (Catholic versus Protestant) that do not line up with the violence. Difference *per se* turns out to have little to do with this – a 'worst case' – and difference-making turns out to be a complicated process.

A theory of difference is not going to tell us much about Rwanda. A specific history will – and it is important that analysts not leave such events unexplained, for that is tantamount to ascribing them to the peculiar ways of Africans. Rwanda began centuries ago as a conquest state, with a political distinction between victors and losers and significant, if far from categorical, differences in access to resources between the conquering royals and the conquered commoners; it was, however, the language and religious practice of the 'losers' to which the victors had to assimilate, and distinctions were mitigated by considerable intermarriage and by category shifting though the acquisition of patronage or wealth. A colonial state which tried to turn these differences into ethnic divisions – marked by the ID cards – came next, and the willingness of postcolonial officials to turn the colonial ethnic categories into systems of patronage went further, and the genocide – following years of systematic hatemongering by clients of top government officials – came in the context of a clash of rival elites in a situation of economic stringency. This is only the outline of an explanation; the point here is that a prior conception of 'ethnic group' would be a hindrance to analysis rather than a help, and the extent of cultural difference is a poor predictor of the seriousness of conflict.[16] Each kind of marker of human difference, obvious or subtle, creates potential for polarization and distinction, but also for linkage and common ground; it might be a basis on which people seek or are forced into assimilation, but also a point around which a nuanced articulation of differences and commonalities takes place.

In writing about the categories of difference, I have been trying to open up analysis, to emphasize that one can achieve a deeper understanding by starting out with notions of linkages rather than groups, and seeing the development of group boundaries, separation, and conflict as part of a range of possible outcomes. Now I will shut down some of that space. We should not simply talk about commonality and difference in the abstract, but rather consider them at a moment of history. Fashions to the contrary, we are telling a single story of global dimensions, but it is an immensely complicated and contradictory story, a story which we should not tell as it has long been told but which we should not shy away from telling either.

There is a lot of talk these days of being in the era of globalization. Most such claims are off by about 500 years. The most dramatic break in linking the world via movement of commodities, goods and human beings came in the sixteenth and seventeenth century. We need to tell a story about conquest, enslavement and capitalist development – of the African slave trade and colonization movements extending from South America to South East Asia. We can tell this story by starting with a slave in Jamaica. Such a person would have been sold from African to African – in exchange for European commodities – before being shipped on a European ship financed from Liverpool sailing to the Caribbean where he or she would be bought by an English colonist and fed dried fish imported from North America while growing sugar on land from which the indigenous population had been eliminated. The sugar would keep the English working class awake so that it could process cotton grown by slaves in Alabama, on land stolen from Native Americans, living in the shadow of the big house filled with commodities from Europe, Asia and the American North. This kind of commodity chain was pioneered in the era of the slave trade, and the industrialization of work was pioneered in the sugar estates. If there is such a thing as globalization, this was it, and in telling the story one sees race and class being made together.[17]

The articulation of race to the development of capitalism can be traced over several phases. Enslavement itself was not new in either Europe or Africa, but the unprecedented scale of the Atlantic slave trade, its vast spatial dimension, the density of interaction which it inspired, and the magnitude of the wealth involved linked this enslavement process to the racial distinction between African and European. In its first phase, racialized enslavement was one of a variety of systems of subordination, hierarchy, conquest and exploitation. Second, in the era of the American and French Revolutions, the possibility that a discourse of freedom and citizenship might apply to slaves generated a certain degree of enthusiasm among Parisian ideologues, hope in the West Indies, and grave concern among advocates of a self-governing citizenry who also owned slaves; their ability to expand their political movement beyond narrow bounds depended on their being able to draw a racial distinction, sharper than ever, between the potential citizen and the slave or the slave's descendants.

Third, the enormous expansion of wage labour in England raised further questions about the meanings of freedom. Capitalist development rested fundamentally on primitive accumulation, on the forceful removal of people from the means of production. It was this class violence that made possible the illusion of a self-functioning market in labour as well as other commodities. By the late eighteenth century, British ideologues, worried about the legitimacy of a system that dissolved custom, community and patrician power into market relations, were articulating a distinction between the legitimacy of free labour by contrasting it to slave. What is striking about anti-slavery ideology is that, as Thomas Holt has shown, a moment of racial openness appeared in the heart of political economy. Colony and metropole, Africans and Europeans, were brought together into debates over economic and moral laws. Although the anti-slavery movement drew on diverse currents, its triumph in the political realm came when British rulers accepted that slaves of African origin, freed from the tyranny of slavery, might at least prove to be diligent workers, fitting as well into evolving British models of family and gender roles.[18]

This leads to the fourth phase of this articulation process. Slaves did not follow the script. Ex-slave societies were rent by tensions over the incomplete extent of primitive accumulation. Ex-slaves did not necessarily accept that freedom should leave them landless, and they struggled to obtain *de facto* access to small plots and for a chance to market some of their crops. They fought their masters over the precise terms of access. Poor whites – their own sense of security and community threatened by both the claims of ex-slaves and the extension of market relations – saw themselves at risk and at times sought desperately to find a basis for commonality with rich planters. Violence and the myth of black laziness were basic to these conflicts, and where they were the most convoluted – in the southern United States – they were characterized by excess, as a wide range of relationships and linkages among whites were rendered uncertain by the struggle over land, labour and participation in community affairs. In any case, the idea of black inferiority – as a worker – was reinscribed into American and European ideology in the age of capital.

One could go on from here; these articulations between class and race took varied form in English, French, Spanish and Portuguese colonies, in diverse economic, social and political situations. It is the power of this history – and the compelling effects it has on the perceptions and aspirations of people who have lived it – that one risks losing beneath bland and static terminology about difference and identity. One might stress instead the specific ways in which people formed connections – formed affiliations and alliances in struggles against oppression – and drew boundaries in the course of their complex intersection with capitalist development.

Let me move to a more theoretical discussion of capitalism and class. The working class in Marxist theory is not a category that refers to all times and places. The worker becomes a meaningful social category only when labour power becomes a commodity, that is when a class of people without access to the means of production is created. Before then, people have various relations to the production process, which may or may not be comparable. Capitalism created the *possibility* of a pure worker, detached from context. Such a worker became imaginable, not just to Marx but to an anti-slavery ideologue or to someone trying to organize social movements. That does not mean the abstract worker existed in any concrete situation.

Capital, as Marx pointed out, took human labour as it found it – and that meant it came with different complexions, in the form of men and women, young and old, of people who came to the labour market with different beliefs, affiliations, and antagonisms.[19] The early operatives of textile factories in England or New England were young unmarried women; miners in Africa were young unmarried men, with quite different relations to the cycles of reproduction and to authority in their respective households. Scholars of different regions of the world are for the most part agreed that a too determinant a view of global capitalism obscures the conflicts and adaptations that have shaped world economic history.[20] But one cannot escape the juggernaut either: to assume that people discursively define their worlds is to give up on explaining how the world has come to be what it is. Labour history has in the last few decades shown its greatest possibilities by looking at women and men who work in dynamic fashion, constrained by the power of capital but seizing possibilities as they rose within and against that system, constrained by their own histories of gender or race relations, yet building on a variety of solidarities to adapt to or challenge capital.[21] In the process, they also defined and redefined gender and race.

What we have here is a creative tension between capitalism in the abstract, with its logic of class definition, and capitalism in all its historical complexity.[22] That capitalists had the cleverness to exploit divisions in the working population and the blindness to measure skill as a gender or racial attribute are basic parts of the story. Even in England itself, the crucial early phases of industrialization depended not simply on generic labour power extracted from the victims of primitive accumulation, but on obtaining labour for varying periods of time from young unmarried women and from regional inequalities and oppression (particularly in relation to Ireland). The national labour market slowly became increasingly integrated and the barriers the local elites and communities put up around the integrity of parishes were eroded.

In Africa, on the other hand, capitalists stood little chance of depriving the population as a whole of access to land even if they wished to do so. Struggles over primitive accumulation were tenacious, even in South Africa where the institutions available to the state and capital were by far the strongest. Africans in many ways deepened their own attachments to their soil, their relations with each other, and their ways of producing and distributing commodities in defence against the encroachments of capital and the colonial state. Over the course of history, Africans paid a high price for their partial success in refusing to be reduced to labour power. The reinscription by colonial regimes, especially in the 1920s, of Africa as the continent of tribes was to a significant extent a reaction to the fact that their quest to detach labour power from its social roots had failed. The strategies of African workers which so frustrated colonial states depended not simply on their sense of 'community', but on mobility and the broadening of affiliations; geographic and cultural flexibility was more useful than boundedness and fixity. The colonial regimes sought to turn a flexible landscape into a series of iron cages known as tribes. In so doing, they gave particular power to male elders – who were doing their best to manipulate colonial officials' need for their cooperation – in keeping tabs on women, young women in particular.[23] These transformed gender relations were also intrinsic to the spatial system in which viable, but hemmed-in, African agricultural zones were linked via oscillatory migration to wage labour areas.

If Africans who worked were denied the name of worker, African Americans were forced into the category of subservient labour power even when they were trying to claim rights to land and to control of family labour. The ambiguity manifested itself – and landlords with modernizing pretensions may have been the worst – in terror orchestrated from above and shared in by lower-class whites whose position was itself precarious. Whereas production and reproduction in Africa were played out in continual movement across spatial divides, in the nineteenth-century South planters tried to pin down African Americans (via debt contracts and Klan violence). The Great Migration of the twentieth century, plus movements to southern cities, eventually changed the significance of space and mobility in the United States.[24]

All this is to put the questions of difference and of labour power into the same framework, to stress dynamic interaction and to make clear that capitalists and states were not remaking the world as they would have liked. The contradictions of race and class – and above all attempts to represent Africans and African Americans as marginal, as underclasses, as exceptions, as people to be written out of society – are as much rooted in the frustrations of power as in its successful exercise.

It is tempting to see capitalism or colonialism as a global force encountering resistances which are locally rooted. Liberation movements have been global too, and their relationship to capitalism something that could not necessarily be controlled from above. The anti-slavery movement may have helped a British elite articulate a seemingly universalistic morality, but West Indian slaves could seize part of the message and ignore or reject the rest. Even before then, the Haitian Revolution had echoed several variants of the rhetoric of the French Revolution from mulatto property owners, who claimed their rights against racial exclusions, and from slaves, whose inspiration came as much from African religious solidarities as the rights of man, and who fought the entire plantation system. Elsewhere, not only did ex-slaves participate in certain key moments of anti-slavery mobilization, but rumours about impending reforms found their way into

Caribbean islands and stimulated actions which in turn forced the hands of antislavery fence-sitters. This process would be repeated in Africa at the century's end, when colonial powers found that African slaves took their anti-slavery policies far more seriously than they did. There, too, ex-slaves took advantage of the openings provided by worldwide top-down ideology, but did not fall into the wage labour mould that had been made for them.[25]

One finds echoes of this process in anti-colonial and anti-apartheid movements and in the multidimensional involvement of different African American organizations and liberal whites in the Civil Rights Movement. Anti-colonial and anti-apartheid movements were truly border crossing, and both sprang from movements that developed within Africa itself; the European left, on its own, would have debated until the end of time whether colonization was reactionary or a step toward global socialism. But once they gathered steam, anti-colonial and then anti-apartheid movements were able to *convince* certain people, across lines of race, nationality, and ideology, that colonialism and apartheid were wrong.

The articulation of locally rooted protest with transoceanic movements was a powerful one. Its transformative power lay in the way it moved in and out of political concepts that European politics identified itself with. Europeans' own image of Africa – the unfathomable, dangerous, dark continent – made officials, worried about their burdens, all the more willing to grasp at signs that Africans really wanted to build societies modelled after their already 'developed' brethren. The trouble with this dual imagery was that, as in the case of slave emancipation, it retained negative imagery of racial distinction at the same time that it held out the hope of racial assimilation.

I have argued elsewhere that such considerations played themselves out in the field of labour in Africa: a labour movement was able to combine street-level militance with arguments – made in colonial capitals and in organizations like the International Labour Organization (ILO), the United Nations (UN), the World Federation of Trade Unions, or even the International Confederation of Free Trade Unions – that African workers were like any other worker and should be treated as such. At one level, colonial officials wanted to believe this, for their fantasy of postwar development depended on reimagining Africans as 'modern'. By the late 1940s, Britain and France and African labour movements were trying to 'classify' the African worker, the one to better control him, the latter to demand a decent standard of living. The rhetoric of race and tribe was explicitly rejected in

French and British discourse about Africa. It was quite the opposite in South Africa in the same years, even if the reality of workers' lives was not so diametrically opposed. Tribe and race were reified and class systematically denied, until the system began to unravel in the 1970s. Neither system could control the process of transition within the dialectics of race, class, and nationality. In colonial Africa in the 1970s and South Africa in the 1990s, the fiction of difference fell to the fiction of equivalence, and with that white elites could not even convince themselves that they had any business to keep governing.[26]

Let me conclude by stressing the political implications of my argument for an analysis of difference that stresses linkages, networks, affiliations, and sees group boundaries as only one possible outcome. The Euro-American left has tended to like its capitalists very capitalist, its workers very proletarian, its colonizers very imperialist, its patriarchs very sexist; its anticolonialists very authentic. The implicit theory I alluded to earlier has shaped much analysis of politics: first, people get themselves an identity, as a proletariat, as an oppressed race or nationality; *then*, they act on the basis of this identity. The victories that have done most to gain a measure of emancipation have rarely followed such lines. Categories have been defined and exploded in the process of struggle, of forging connections and locating enemies. Movements against slavery, colonialism and apartheid have combined locally specific mobilizations with debates across oceans that have redefined the sorts of politics that were or were not imaginable. Let me only cite the most recent case – anti-apartheid. It involved the principled case for non-racial democracy made by the African National Congress (ANC) for decades, an unusually powerful and politically conscious labour movement, a series of local struggles over rural chiefs, youth violence in cities, Pan-Africanist and Black Consciousness organizations, church groups within South Africa and around the world, student mobilizations in North America, the refusal of union dockers to unload South African ships, women's anti-pass demonstrations and organizations in South Africa, and UN and ILO declarations of principles. The overthrow of apartheid was not, in fact, a definition of a 'we' against a 'them' – and the tensions among different ways of opposing apartheid were very real and even deadly. The multidimensional opposition in the end undermined the South African upper and middle classes' own yearning to see themselves as part of a truly global bourgeoisie, even as it shook their sense of being able to bring order to their daily lives.

Edifices as seemingly powerful as colonial empires have themselves proven to be rent with contradictions and divisions, and their collapse has resulted much more from prying apart such openings – sending elements of the dominant powers in search of new coalitions and new visions – than from a Fanonist inversion of the entire structure.

There was nothing 'pure' or 'authentic' about anti-colonial movements or about the South African revolution, and if one can criticize the ANC government for deviating from practices that, say, a rigorous class analysis would prescribe, such criticisms should be done in relation to specific constraints and opportunities, not an abstract sense of what a 'real' class struggle entails. This struggle drew on the ways in which anti-slavery and anti-colonial struggles had previously redefined the meanings of liberal democracy, of citizenship, of rights. Arguments which see these kinds of constructs as controlling ideologies of an all-encompassing Western modernity, miss the fact that what these constructs signified was shifted fundamentally because particular people were deploying them, and because those people reinterpreted their meanings. Politics has rarely been about purity, and when it has – the Chinese Cultural Revolution – it has taken the form of devising purge categories to define deviants from the one true path. When the politics of difference has become the politics of purity, it too has led to frightful processes of cleansing to make our messy realities confirm to the image.

The alternatives in visioning connections are not as stark as a choice between bland universality and parochial communities. But to live with varied forms of affiliation and differentiation is to accept that one must live with tension, with surrendering a measure of individuality without finding fulfilling cohesion.[27]

At the same time, we cannot forget that politics redefines exclusions as well. As in the days of anti-slavery movements, aspirations to the universal condition of freedom contain a potential for human liberation, but also the danger that the possibility of advance and uplift become conditions for the reinscription of racial distinction. Emancipation – first in the West Indies, later in Africa – was turned by many of its exponents into a test of the behaviour of ex-slaves. And by choosing to live their lives in their own ways, ex-slaves failed the test; they became racial exceptions to the rule of optimizing free markets. Their failure as a race set the stage for further inscriptions of racial distinction and for the elaboration – as with the colonizations of the late nineteenth century or with formal segregation in the era of Jim Crow – of institutions to enforce colour lines and a knowledge apparatus that normalized such practices.

Let us leap ahead one century. Colonialism is consigned to the past. It is not unusual, thinking globally, to see people of African descent in any position of the political and class ladder: as head of state, as civil servant, as educated professional, as media star. But the racialized 'other' is still around – as an 'underclass' in England or the United States, as a tribalized, famine-prone, African. Asians are no longer 'coolies' – they may be business leaders or models of mobility into scientific and professional fields – unless they have been classified as superstitious and caste-ridden or as 'boat people', and hence as an immigration problem. The movements against slavery, colonialism and apartheid have changed history, and they did so, in Du Bois's words, across 'Asia and Africa, in America and the islands of the sea'.[28] The meaning of race at the century's end is not what it was at the century's beginning: the exclusion of an entire race from economic and political life is no longer at issue in the United States, in Britain, in Africa, or in international organizations. But the racialization of difference appears in new forms; the meaning of gender is inscribed and reinscribed in a variety of ways; the exclusions of class still manifest themselves; and hatreds have been fostered based on all sorts of distinctions. And throughout this century, people have found – as they will continue to find – new possibilities for forging networks, for deepening affiliations, for putting together alliances, for broadening the bases of understanding, sharing and common struggle.

## Notes

1  This chapter is a somewhat revised version of remarks made at the concluding session of the conference on 'Racializing Class, Classifying Race'. I have clarified arguments – some of them ad libbed at the Oxford conference – and developed a few points, but I have tried to keep the flavour of the text intact, so as to give a sense of where, in my view, the most important debates were located. I have added references where directly related to my argument, but have not tried to do justice to the rich literatures on topics touched upon in the following pages. I am grateful to Alf Lüdtke and Jane Burbank for critical readings of an earlier draft.

2  W. Sewell, Jr, 'Toward a Post-materialist Rhetoric for Labor History', in L.R. Berlanstein, ed., *Rethinking Labor History: Essays on Discourse and Class Analysis* (Urbana, Ill., 1993), 15–38. Sewell's critique of reductionist materialism is persuasive; less convincing is the 'post' rhetoric.

3  E.P. Thompson, *The Making of the English Working Class* (New York, 1963); W.H. Sewell, Jr, *Work and Revolution in France: The Language of Labor from the Old Regime to 1948* (Cambridge, 1980).

4  Or as Margaret Somers puts it, class is 'narrativized' – a common relation to the labour process remains a social category, not a solidarity, unless it is

constructed as such. At the same time, one must remember that it is work which is being narrativized; the narratives do not spring out of thin air or free-floating discourses. See Somers, 'Narrativity, Narrative Identity, and Social Action: Rethinking English Working Class Formation', *Social Science History* 16 (1992), 591–630.

5  See Edmund Morgan's now classic study of how the planter elite of Virginia, seeking to line up followers in its struggles against the British, sharpened distinctions between white servants and black slaves, mobilizing the former while pressing the latter into a sharply demarcated racial box. *American Slavery, American Freedom: The Ordeal of Colonial Virginia* (New York, 1975).

6  Unravelling the relationship of colonial authority, workplace organization, labour movements, and anti-colonial political mobilization has been at the core of my own research, and – to put it simply – the most important finding has been the shifting and ambiguous relationship of categories often assumed to be either inherently opposed or naturally congruent. F. Cooper, *Decolonization and African Society: The Labor Question in French and British Africa* (Cambridge, 1996).

7  This argument borrows from W.B. Michaels, 'Race into Culture: A Critical Genealogy of Cultural Identity', in K.A. Appiah and H.L. Gates, Jr, eds., *Identities* (Chicago, 1995), 32–62.

8  Stuart Hall wrestles with these problems, for he is eager to espouse a soft, constructivist version of identity, but he is all too well aware that he is going against a use common in political discourse: 'Moreover, they [identities] emerge within the play of specific modalities of power, and thus are more the product of the marking of difference and exclusion, than they are the sign of an identical, naturally-constituted unity – an "identity" in its traditional meaning (that is, an all-inclusive sameness, seamless, without internal differentiation).' At one point, Hall flirts with using the word 'identification' to emphasize process over fixedness, but he remains too attached to the concept of identity to make the break, and in trying to complicate this word he deprives himself of using it as do ordinary people, not to mention the ideologues of particularism, in relation to the all-too-real phenomena of political mobilization around visions of identity built on 'an all-inclusive sameness'. 'Introduction: Who Needs "Identity"?' in S. Hall and P. du Gay, *Questions of Cultural Identity* (London, 1996), 2, 4.

9  The most glaring problem with some of the most thoughtful arguments for why groups and cultures – not just individuals – should be represented politically is that they presume that the boundaries of the group are givens. Rarely is it asked how group boundaries are determined and whether members have or might want an exit option. See for example W. Kymlicka, *Multicultural Citizenship: A Liberal Theory of Minority Rights* (Oxford, 1995).

10  For an example of the attack, see T. Gittlin, *Twilight of Our Common Dream: Why America is Wracked by Culture Wars* (New York, 1995), and for the defence R.D.G. Kelley, *Yo' Mama's Disfunktional! Fighting the Culture Wars in Urban America* (Boston, 1997). Kelley makes good sport of Gittlin's 'neo-enlightenment' universalism, but his own argument is just as 'enlightened'. He insists that a politics which focuses on the conditions,

values and aspirations of particular social groups represents a 'radical humanism,' for such claims implicitly – often explicitly – reinforce the humanity of other groups. Kelley (111–12, 122–4) persuasively argues that leftists who reject identity politics in the name of a 'pure, simple, color- and gender-blind class struggle' diminish the human beings in whose name they speak by denying the affiliations and self-conceptions with which people regard themselves. But beneath this defence of particularism lies a universalism which enables Kelley to distinguish between 'identity' claims that legitimize other similar claims – as from black feminists – from those which do not – white supremacists. In the end, Kelley's humanism rests on universalistic and enlightenment grounds, and his appeal is for a broader sense of affiliation and connection, one which rejects both insularity and the homogenizing of difference.

11  A. Przeworsky, 'Proletariat into a Class: The Process of Class Formation from Karl Kautsky's *The Class Struggle* to Recent Controversies', *Politics and Society* 7 (1977), 343–401.

12  W.E.B. Du Bois, *The Souls of Black Folk* (New York, 1961; orig. 1903).

13  K. K. Gaines, *Uplifting the Race: Black Leadership, Politics, and Culture in the Twentieth Century* (Chapel Hill, NC, 1996).

14  A. Lüdtke, 'Polymorphous Synchrony: German Industrial Workers and the Politics of Everyday Life,' *International Review of Social History* 38 (1993), 39–84.

15  For one study of the Mouride diaspora, see S. L. Malcomson, 'West of Eden', *Transition* 71 (1996), 24–43.

16  A good beginning for an historical analysis is G. Prunier, *Rwanda Crisis: History of a Genocide* (New York, 1995).

17  S. Mintz, *Sweetness and Power: The Place of Sugar in Modern History* (New York, 1985); D. Tomich, *Slavery in the Circuit of Sugar: Martinique and the World Economy 1830–1848* (Baltimore, 1990), and the pioneering work of E. Williams, *Capitalism and Slavery* (Chapel Hill, NC, 1944).

18  C.L.R. James, *The Black Jacobins: Toussaint L'Ouverture and the San Domingo Revolution*, 2nd edn (New York, 1963); R. Blackburn, *The Overthrow of Colonial Slavery, 1776–1848* (London, 1988); D.B. Davis, *The Problem of Slavery in the Age of Revolution* (Ithaca, NY, 1975); T.C. Holt, *The Problem of Freedom: Race, Labor, and Politics in Jamaica and Britain, 1832–1938* (Baltimore, 1992); P. Scully, *Liberating the Family? Gender and British Slave Emancipation in the Rural Western Cape, South Africa, 1823–1853* (Portsmouth, NH, 1997); F. Cooper, T. Holt, and R. Scott, *Beyond Slavery: Explorations of Race, Labor, and Citizenship*, forthcoming.

19  Marx wrote that the capitalist 'must begin by taking the labour-power as he finds it in the market, and consequently he must be satisfied with the kind of labour which arose in a period when there were as yet no capitalists.' *Capital*, vol. 1, trans. by B. Fowkes (New York, 1977), 291. He was not himself interested in the fact that such labour-power came in the form of people who looked differently or spoke different languages, but he did recognize that the capitalist production process was shaped by something that could not be reduced to the logic of capital itself. Workers came from somewhere.

20  F. Cooper et al., *Confronting Historical Paradigms: Peasants, Labor, and the*

*Capitalist World System in Africa and Latin America* (Madison, Wisc., 1993).

21 L. L. Downs, *Manufacturing Inequality: The Construction of a Gender Stratified Workforce in the French and British Metalworking Industries, 1914–1935* (Ithaca, NY, 1995); L. Frader and S. O. Rose, eds., *Gender and Class in Modern Europe* (Ithaca, NY, 1996); T. Liu, *The Weaver's Knot: The Contradictions of Class Struggle and Family Solidarity in Western France, 1750–1914* (Ithaca, NY, 1994); S. Rose, *Limited Livelihoods: Gender and Class in Nineteenth Century England* (Berkeley, 1992).

22 D. Chakrabarty, 'Marx after Marxism: History, Subalternity and Difference', *Meanjin* 52 (1993), 421–34. Chakrabarty and other historians from the 'Subaltern Studies Group' have been critical of Marxist arguments which impose conceptions of labour rooted in Europe on workers in India and which explicitly or implicitly accuse such workers of a 'lack' of something which their western counterparts allegedly possess – class consciousness for instance. Subaltern Studies has in turn been accused of reviving visions of a true 'Hindu' – or perhaps a true 'community' or a true 'subaltern' – in contradistinction to the true worker. See, for example, R. Chandavarkar, '"The Making of the Working Class": E.P. Thompson and Indian History', *History Workshop Journal* 43 (1997), 177–98.

23 M. Chanock, *Law, Custom and Social Order: The Colonial Experience in Malawi and Zambia* (Cambridge, 1985); L. Vail, ed., *The Creation of Tribalism in Southern Africa* (Berkeley, 1989).

24 B. Fields, *Slavery and Freedom on the Middle Ground: Maryland during the Nineteenth Century* (New Haven, 1985); J. Saville, *The Work of Reconstruction: From Slave to Wage Laborer in South Carolina, 1860–1870* (Cambridge, 1994); N.I. Painter, *Exodusters: Black Migration to Kansas after Reconstruction* (New York, 1976); J. Grossman, *Land of Hope: Chicago, Black Southerners and the Great Migration* (Chicago, 1989).

25 Holt, *Problem of Slavery*; M.R. Trouillot, *The Silences of the Past* (Boston, 1995); Blackburn, *Overthrow*; S. Miers and R. Roberts, eds., *The End of Slavery in Africa* (Madison, Wisc., 1990); F. Cooper, *From Slaves to Squatters: Plantation Labor and Agriculture in Zanzibar and Coastal Kenya, 1895–1925* (New Haven, Conn., 1980).

26 Cooper, *Decolonization and African Society*; I. Evans, *Bureaucracy and Race: Native Administration in South Africa* (Berkeley, 1997).

27 Aimé Césaire put it this way: 'There are two ways to lose oneself: by a walled segregation in the particular or by a dilution in the universal'. *Lettre à Maurice Thorez* (Paris, 1956), 15.

28 DuBois, *The Souls of Black Folk*, 23.

# Index

Abrams, Mrs Laura, 34–5
Africa
  changes in discourse of race
    and class, 218
  general strikes, 170
  tribal construction, 227–8, 230
  tribal custom, 155, 163
  *see also* Nigeria; Sierra Leone;
    South Africa
African American women
  in Bell System literature, 61,
    62–3, 66
  as telephone operators, 72–3,
    75, 80n, 83n, 84n, 85–6nn
  and white women's identity,
    57
African Americans
  claim to land rights, 228
  as longshoremen, 95–6
  not excluded from goldfields,
    41–2
  reaction to Italian invasion of
    Ethiopia, 18–19
  urbanization of, 22, 228
African National Congress
  (ANC), 230–1
African workers
  class difference among, 202
  classification of, 229–30
  racial awareness, 169, 184, 188
Afrikaner nationalism, 7
All Seamen's Union, 160
Allen, Theodore, 88
American Civil War, 10
American Federation of Labor
  (AFL), 6, 16, 19

American Revolution, 3
Anderson, Benedict, 11
Anderson, E.J., 67
Angola, 10
anti-apartheid movement, 230
anti-colonial movements, 21,
  229, 230
Anti-Nazi League, 148n
anti-racist organizations, 134,
  148n, 230
Arab community, South Shields,
  108–9
Arizona, 38–9
  Clifton-Morenci, 32–3, 34–5,
    36–7, 46
  copper mining in, 32, 36–7,
    44–9
  gold mining, 40–3, 53–4nn
Arnesen, Eric, 16
artisanal culture, 216–17
Asian workers (UK), strikes by,
  135–7, 139–40, 141–3
assimilation, 112, 118
  role of, 87, 88, 219
Associated Union of Foundry
  Workers (AUFW), 135–6
Association of Professional,
  Executive and Computer
  Staff (APEX), 142
Australia, trade unions, 28n
automobile industry, in US, 17

Bakhtin, Mikhail, 12
Baku Congress of the Peoples of
  the East, 20
Bandung Conference (1955), 21

Banton, Michael, 110
Barnes, Charles, 94
Barrett, James, 88
Bell System
  boy operators, 60–1
  concept of family, 64, 65–6
  discrimination complaints
      against, 71, 75, 83n, 84n,
      85n
  employee benefit plans, 63–4,
      81n
  employment of black women,
      72–3, 75, 83n, 84n,
      85–6nn
  hiring and selection process,
      61–3, 80–1nn
  paternalism of, 76
  and technological change,
      73–4, 76, 86nn
  white exclusivity, 59, 61–3,
      71–2, 76
Bethell, F.H., 61, 62, 64, 65
black radical analysis, 123–6
black workers
  East London docks strike, 196
  self-organization strategy, 14,
      125, 134–7
  stereotypes of inadequacies of,
      26n, 203, 226
  and trade unions in US,
      16–17
  *see also* African Americans;
      white workers
blackface shows (Bell System),
      66–7, 82n
Bodnar, John, 88
Boggs, R.H., 68
Bogle, Paul, 11
Bolick, Lavie, 74
Bonnett, Alastair, 117
Bose, Sugata, 9–10

Boydston, Jean, 9
Bracegirdle, Roy, 183
British and African Steam
      Navigation Company, 154
British Hotels and Restaurants
      Association, 123
British identity, 115–16
  and whiteness, 116–18
British Transport Commission,
      123
Brown, David, Kru Tribal Ruler,
      153, 154
Browne, J. Ross, 44–5
Bryan, William Jennings, 6
Buckman, Joe, 107, 109
Bulkeley, William, 178, 179
Burgess, Ernest W., 24n
Butler, Elizabeth Beardley, 63

California, Gold Rush, 39, 41,
      42, 54n
Campaign Against Racial
      Discrimination (CARD), 134
Cananea (Mexico), 'American
      town', 45
capitalism, 22–3
  and class, 226–8
  development of, 10, 225
  US corporate, 44–5, 46, 48–50
Caribbean *see* West Indies
Carty, John J., 60
casual labour, 11
  East London ('togt'), 194–5,
      197, 198–9, 200–2
  Freetown, 160, 165n
  *see also* peasant proprietorship
Catholic Church
  and London Irish dockers, 91,
      92
  in US, 17, 18, 29n, 84n
Chamberlain, Joseph, 7

Chicago, packinghouse industry, 18
Chinese Americans, 19
  excluded from goldfields, 40, 41, 53n
Chinese immigrants, 3, 7
Chinese Seamen's Union, 108
citizenship
  concept of, 225
  and entitlement, 115
  in US, 39, 54n
civil rights
  and equal opportunity programmes, 73
  in US, 21–2, 229
class
  among New York longshoremen, 99
  aspirations of, 59, 60, 62, 63, 77n, 221
  and capitalism, 226–8
  and definitions of white, 37, 79n
  immigrants', 123
  influence in London docks, 91, 92–3, 99–100
  power of, 202, 218, 230
  and racial definition of Mexicans, 36–7
  racialized nature of, 14–15, 232
  *see also* working class
class conflict, 127
  in 1970s, 125, 138–9
  between ethnic groups, 157–60
class consciousness, 128, 204–5
  and racism, 14–15, 132
  sectional, 130, 134, 143
  shift to corporate, 138–9, 144
class formation, 216–17, 220
class relations, 128, 217
  and race, 202, 207

Clifton-Morenci (Arizona), 32–3, 34–5, 36–7, 46, 56n
Cohen, Lizabeth, 18, 88
COHSE, racism in, 133
Cold War, 21
collective bargaining, 127, 129
Colliery Surface Improvement Union (CSIU) (Nigeria), 182, 184
Colliery Workers' Union (Nigeria), 182, 184–7
colonial governments
  perception of Nigerian workers, 176
  Sierra Leone, 159–60, 163
Colonial Welfare and Development Act (1942), 182
colonialism
  and ethnicity, 161, 164–5, 223–4
  and racist polarization, 220–1
  and tribal construct, 227–8
colonies
  of exploitation, 4
  independence, 21
  productive, 4
  settler, 34, 51–2n
'colour line' (Du Bois's), 5, 220–2
Coloured Seamen's Union, 108
Communication Workers of America, 83n
Communist Party of South Africa, 196
community networks, 108
comparative method, value of, 89–90, 99–100
Coneygre Foundry, strike, 135
Congo, Belgian, 10
Congress of Industrial

Organizations (CIO), 16–17, 19
1946 convention, 20–1
'culture of unity', 18
Conrad, Joseph, 4
Conservative Party (UK), 25n, 128–9, 131
constructivism, 216–19, 233n
convict labour, use of, 10
Cooper, Evelyn N., 71
Cooper, F., 205–6
copper mining, in Arizona, 32, 36–7, 44–9
Corridan, John, 97
cotton production, Africa, 10
Council of Non-European Trade Unions (South Africa), 196
Courtauld Ltd, strike, 135
Crouch, C., 128
cube model of inteconnection, 215–16
cultural adaptation, 221
cultural difference, 131, 219–20
culture, popular, 12–13
Curry, Robert, 186–7

Davies, Sam, 91
Delaware and Atlantic Telephone and Telegraph Company, 61
diasporas, 222
DiFazio, Leonard and Sebastian, 98
difference
and formation of ethnicity, 223–4
and identity, 219–20
and labour power, 228
division of labour, social, 47
dock workers
East London, 194–5, 205–8

familial relationships among, 90, 95, 102–3n
Irish (New York City), 87, 94–9, 100
Irish (Wapping, London), 87–8, 90–4, 99–100
Kru stevedores (Sierra Leone), 151–6, 163–4
Liverpool, 150
trade unions, 92, 95, 96, 97–8
*see also* seamen
Donovan Commission (1968), 138
Donovan, John, 91
Dreary & Co, 194
Du Bois, W.E.B., 5, 12, 220
Dubow, Saul, 6
Durban (South Africa), 193, 202, 204, 207–8

East London Native Employees' Association, 196–7
East London (South Africa), 193, 194
compared with other ports, 205–8
East London Stevedoring Company (ELSC), 194, 198
Elder Dempster shipping company, 153, 154, 155, 159, 160, 162–3
empire
legacy of, 109–10, 114
*see also* imperialism
employee organizations
Bell System, 65
*see also* trade unions
employers
and East London docks, 198–9
mine management, 174, 178–81, 182–3, 187

*employers continued*
  strategies towards unions, 127, 130
Enugu, Nigeria, 170
  miners' housing, 180–1
Equal Rights Committee (TUC), 141
Ethiopia, Italian invasion of, 18–19
ethnic history, and labour history, 106–9, 118
ethnic identity
  among East London dock workers, 205
  and assimilation, 87, 88
  Kru use of, 156–61
  in New York, 94–5, 100
ethnicity
  in colonial West Africa, 161, 164–5
  Mexican, 34, 52n, 55–6n
  and race, 43
  systematic formation of, 223–4
  transformation of, 89
European Volunteer Workers, 113, 117–18

familial relationships
  among dockers, 90, 95, 102–3n
  and kinship recruitment, 152
Fanon, Frantz, 11
Fielding, Steven, 91
First World War, 161–2
Fishman, Bill, 107
Fitzpatrick, David, 89, 92
Foner, Eric, 9
Foreign Miners' Tax (California), 42, 54n
Free Yemeni Movement, 108
Freetown (Sierra Leone), 150, 151, 157–60

French Revolution, 225, 228
Frey, Sylvia, 3

Gaelic League, 92
Gaines, Kevin, 12
gangsters, New York, 97
gender
  meanings of, 232
  *see also* masculinity; 'white lady'; women
Gerstle, Gary, 88
Gilroy, Paul, 89, 105, 123
globalization, 2, 228
  and early trade expansion, 224
gold mining, US, racial exclusion in, 39–43, 53–4nn
government, attempts to curb trade union activity, 137–40, 144
Grantham, Roy, 142
Gray, Barbara S., 74
Great Britain
  and colonial labour uprisings, 178
  colonial policies, 6–8, 11, 170, 182–3
  colonialism, 51–2n
  and legacy of empire, 110
  racist imagery in, 130–1
  welfare state development, 6, 8, 128–9
Great Depression, effects of, 15–16, 22
Green, T.H., 7
Griffiths, Peter, 131
groups, and networks, 222
Grunwick Film Processing Laboratories strike (1976-8), 141–3, 144

Haiti, 3, 9, 228

Hanshaw, Patrick,
  autobiography, 87, 91–2,
  93–4
Harlem Employment Agency,67
Harlem riot (1935), 19
Harwood, John, 110
Hausa people (Nigeria), 160,
  166n
Hemson, David, 202, 204, 207–8
Hickman, Mary, 109–10
hierarchy
  in coal mines, 172–3
  in racial relations, 46, 118
  racialized labour, 115–16, 172
Higginbotham, Evelyn Brooks,
  12
Higginson, John, 10
Hill, Herbert, 14
Hobsbawm, Eric, 89
Holland West African Line, 159
Holmes, Colin, 107
Holt, Thomas, 5, 9
housing
  East London dockers, 195
  for Nigerian miners, 180–1,
    182–3
  and residence qualification
    (South Africa), 201–2
Howe, Darcus, 123, 125
Hunt, Edward, 112
Hunter, Tera, 13
Husband, Charles, 110

identity
  British/alien distinctions,
    115–16
  can be discarded, 89, 100
  constructivist, 233n
  defined by locality, 93–4, 95,
    99–100
  and difference, 219–20

occupation-defined, 156, 169,
  170–4, 176–7, 206
self-definition, 87, 99, 219
*see also* ethnic identity;
  gender; national identity;
  whiteness
identity formation, 216
identity politics, 219–20, 230,
  234n
Igbo ethnic group (Nigeria),
  175–6, 180–1, 190n
immigrants
  and ethnic identity, 88
  as threat to employment, 113,
    132, 143
immigration, and formation of
  stereotypes, 112
Imperial Typewriters, strike
  (1973), 139–40
imperialism
  and internationalism, 13–22
  legacy of empire, 109–10, 114
  Second International and, 4–5
independence movements, 11,
  21
Independent Industrial and
  Commercial Workers' Union
  (IICU), 197
India
  capitalist development, 10
  coal mining, 11
  independence movement, 11
Indian immigrants, 122–3
Indian Seamen's Union, 108
Indian Workers Association
  (IWA), 136
Industrial and Commercial
  Workers' Union (ICU)
  (South Africa), 196
Industrial Relations Act (1971),
  138

industriousness, as American, 55n
interconnections, 214–15, 222–3
International Federation of Free Trade Unions, 229
International Labour Organization (ILO), 229
International Longshoremen's Association (ILA), 95, 96, 97–8
International Socialists, 140
internationalism
  of ideology, 228–9, 230
  and imperialism, 13–22
  role of trade unions, 218
Investigation of the Telephone Companies (1910) (US), 62
Irish
  dock workers (London), 87–8, 90–4, 99–100
  dock workers (New York), 87, 94–9, 100
  immigrants in UK, 112
  types of identity (UK), 88–9, 99, 117
  as 'white' in US, 35, 43
Irish famine, 90
Irvine, Alexander, 14
Italian Americans
  as New York longshoremen, 94, 96, 97, 98–9
  reaction to Italian invasion of Ethiopia, 19
Italy, invasion of Ethiopia, 18–19

Jackson, Tom, 142
Jamaica, 9, 11–12
Japan, migrants from, 3
Jewish immigration, and labour organization, 107, 112–13
Jews

in Leeds, 109
as telephone operators, 61
Johns, Ted, 93, 94
Johnson, George M., FEPC, 71
Jones, Jack, 140
Jones, Sir Alfred, 153
Joshi and Carter, 131

Kadalie, Clements, 198, 204
Kautsky, Karl, 4–5
Kay, Diana, 111, 117
Kazal, Russell A., 88
Kelley, Robin, 13
Kelly, J., 129–30
King, Martin Luther, visit to Britain, 134
Kraditor, Aileen, 12
Kru people
  ethnic identity, 156–61
  industrial action by, 162–4
  origins, 150–1, 156–7
  refusal to join union, 160
  as seamen, 151, 156, 164
  as stevedores, 151–6, 164
  tribal custom, 155, 163
Kushner, Tony, 113

labour
  racialized hierarchy of, 115–16, 172
  *see also* strikes; work
labour force
  homogenization of, 15–16, 22, 218
  variety within, 226–7
labour history, and ethnic history, 106–9, 118
labour market, control of, 227, 229–30
labour movement (UK), 104, 116–18

and Jewish immigrants, 107,
112–13
. racial exclusion practices,
123–4, 143–4
support for Grunwick strikers,
142, 144
labour organization, 217–18
East London casual dock
workers, 196, 197–8,
204–5, 207
Mexican, 55–6n
Nigerian miners, 176, 177–81,
182
*see also* trade unions
Labour Party (UK), 6, 20, 128–9,
131
and London dockers, 92
labour shortages
British post-war, 122–3
influenza pandemic, 171
for telephone operators, 67, 69
labour supply, 123
East London, 193, 199, 207–9
East London 'homeboy gangs',
194–5
Nigerian miners' work teams,
171, 177
transition to stability, 201–5,
207, 209
West Africa, 152, 154–6
*see also* casual labour
Labour Supply Company (South
Africa), 207–8
land, 9–10, 227
Lawless, Richard, 108
Leck, William, 172, 183
Lees, Lynn Hollen, 88–9, 92
Lewis, Earl, 13
Liberal Party (UK), 6–7
Lillie, N.W., 60
Lithuanian immigrants, 109

Liverpool
dockers, 150
racism among seamen, 161–2
Liverpool Negro Association, 108
locality, 1–2
and formation of identity,
93–4, 95, 99–100
importance of local meaning,
15
and roots of resistance, 228,
230
Logan, David, MP, 114–15
London
Irish dockers (Wapping), 87–8,
90–4, 99–100
mixed dockers' work gangs, 92
London Transport Executive, 123
Lourenço Marques, 193, 204,
206–7

McClure, D., 69, 70
McGreevy, John, 17
McIntosh, Eugene, 67
MacKenzie, John, 110
Malan, Daniel, 21
Malcolm X, 134
Mandlin, Father Constant, 32,
50n
Manley, Michael, 23
manliness *see* masculinity
Mann, Mae, 75
Manning, Cardinal, 90–1
Mansfield Hosiery Mills, strike
(1972), 136–7
Marks, Shula, 6
Martin, Carlotta Silvas, 43
Marxism, and class formation,
220, 226–7, 234n
masculinity
among Nigerian peoples, 175,
176–7

*masculinity continued*
  and ethos of mining, 177, 188
  and racism, 203
Melville, Herman, *Redburn*, 3–4
Mende people, as shipping
    labour, 152, 154, 157–60,
    166n
Mexicans
  class definitions of, 36–7, 46–8
  'ethnic', 34, 52n, 55–6n
  excluded from goldfields,
      39–40, 41–2, 53–4nn
  racial definitions of, 33, 45
Mexico, conquest of, 2
migration, 2–3
Miles, Robert, 105, 111, 114,
    117, 125
Mills, Charles, US copper worker,
    36–7, 49
Milner, Sir Alfred, 6–8
miners, work identity, 169,
    172–3, 176–7
mining
  Africa, 10, 170–3
  American gold, 40–3, 53–4nn
  Arizona copper, 32, 36–7, 44–9
  and employment practices,
      10–11, 173–4
  *see also* Nigeria
miscegenation, 38
Mombasa, 193, 198, 202, 204,
    205–6
Montejano, David, 3

National Committee for Trade
    Unions Against Racialism
    (NCTUAR), 137
National Front, 140, 148n
national identity
  American, 38, 43–4, 50–1n,
      55n, 88

British, 115–18
Irish, 88–9, 99, 117
role of culture in, 12–13
*see also* ethnic identity
National Maritime Board, 115
National Sailors' and Firemen's
    Union, 161–2
National Transport Workers
    Federation, 92
National Union of Hosiery and
    Knitwear Workers (NUKW),
    136
National Union of Seamen, 108,
    114, 115
nationalism, and race, 11–12
Native Americans, 33
*Negro Worker* journal, 20
Nelson, Bruce, 14
Netherlands, colonialism, 51n
networks
  community, 108
  and groups, 222
  *see also* labour organization
New Deal (US), 16, 18
New England Telephone &
    Telegraph Company, 61, 63
New York City
  Irish longshoremen, 87, 94–9,
      100
  mixed dockers' work gangs, 96
New York Foundling Hospital,
    32–3, 34–5
New York State, anti-
    discrimination legislation,
    68–9
New York Telephone Company,
    67–9
Newman, Watson and Newman
    (East London), 194
Nigeria
  colliery reforms, 179–80

Enugu mines, 168–9, 170–1, 181–6
  labour legislative reforms, 169–70, 178, 182
  miners' labour organization, 176, 177–81, 182
  mines Representative Councils, 179–80
  nationalist movement, 169, 184, 187
  trade unions, 182–8
Nigerian Defence Regulations (1941), 185
Nigerian labour, used to undermine Kru monopoly, 162–3
Nutt, Emma M., 60
*Nzuko* (meetings), 177–8, 179

O'Dwyer, Paul, 95
Ojiyi, Okwudili Isaiah, CWU leader, 183–7
Onselen, Charles van, 13
Ormsby-Gore, W.G.A., 178
Ottley, Roi, 19

Pacifico, Angelo, 96, 98, 99
packinghouse industry, in US, 17–18
Padmore, George, 20
Panayi, Panikos, 104
Paul, Kathleen, 116
peasant proprietorship, 9–10, 150–1, 176
Pelling, Henry, 6
Phizacklea, Annie, 125
Polanyi, Karl, 5–6
politics
  of difference, 231
  effect of multidimensionality, 230

  of identity, 219–20, 230
  in West African ethnicity, 161
postmodernist analysis, 12
Powell, Enoch, MP, 136
Przeworsky, Adam, 220
'psychological wage', 58–9, 73, 76, 78n

race
  and blackness, 114
  and class relations, 202, 207
  and ethnicity, 43
  and gender, 216
  internal differences, 12
  and nationalism, 11–12
  and religion, 32, 50n
  role of state in shaping meaning of, 2
  stereotypes of, 26n, 61, 62–3, 111–12, 203, 226
race relations
  as dynamic process, 107, 221–2
  factors in shaping, 33
  US regional variations, 33, 35–6, 49–50
Race Relations Advisory Committee (TUC), 141
Race Relations and Immigration, Select Committee on, 141
Race Today Collective, 123
Racial Action Adjustment Society (RAAS), 134
racial exclusion, 217
  in Bell System, 67–9
  black radical analysis of, 123–6
  in New York docks, 95–6
  organized resistance to, 134, 140–3, 144
  and quota system, 132–3
  South Africa, 202–3

*racial exclusion continued*
in US gold mines, 39–43,
53–4nn
racism
among seamen (Liverpool),
161–2
changing nature of, 22–3,
231–2
and class consciousness,
14–15, 132
development of, 5, 33–4
as legacy of empire, 109–10,
111
political will to combat, 131
resurgence in US. 220
scientific, 161
white resistance to, 148n
working-class solidarity
against, 140–3
*see also* South Africa, apartheid
Railway and Harbour Staff
Association (East London),
198
Ranger, Terence, 89
Regional Hospitals Board, 123
religion
influence in Liverpool, 91
and race, 32, 50n
*see also* Catholic Church
repatriation, Home Office
proposal (1920s), 162
resistance, 134, 140–3, 144
ideological sources of, 228–9
respectability
as class concept, 221
*see also* class, aspirations
restrictive practices, 127, 129
racial exclusions, 132, 133,
143–4
Roberts, Richard, 10
Rock Against Racism, 148n

Roediger, David, 88
Rosengarten, Theodore, *All God's
Dangers*, 9
Rozzelle, Frank, 60–1
Russian Revolution, 20
Rwanda, origins of conflict,
223–4
Ryan, Joe, 95, 97–8

Sampson, Gene, 98
Sanders, Lessie, 75
Saville, Julie, 13
Schmitt, Katherine M., 60, 62
Schuyler, George S., 68
seamen
American, 3
historiography of ethnic,
105–6, 108, 116
international role of, 20
Kru men as, 151, 156, 164
and racialized hierarchy of
labour, 115–16
racism among (Liverpool),
161–2
Seamen's Minority Movement,
15
Seamen's Union, 162
Second International, 4–5
Second World War, 20
and Enugu mines (Nigeria),
181–6
segregation, 24n, 231
settler consciousness, 3
Sewell, William, 213, 216
Shenton, Robert, 10
shipping companies
East London, 194
West Africa, 153–5, 159–60
shipping workers *see* dock
workers; seamen
shop stewards

power of, 138
role of, 129
Sierra Leone
colonial government, 159–60
ethnic conflict in, 158–60
Tribal Administration Rules,
163
Sierra Leone Native Seamen's
Benevolent Society, 159
Simpson, T.J., US copper worker,
36–7, 49
Sivanandan, A., 123, 124
skin colour, to define race, 35,
88, 111
slavery, 3, 224–5
abolition of, 10, 231
anti-slavery ideology, 225, 228
and ex-slave societies, 225–6,
228–9
Smith, D.J., 123
social status, compensatory, 71,
78n
South Africa, 6–8, 230
apartheid, 21, 202–3, 204, 209,
230–1
Natives Land Act (1913), 9
Rand Revolt (1922), 8
Urban Areas Act, 201–2
white racism, 14
*see also* East London
South African Railways and
Harbours (SAR&H), 194, 195,
197, 201
South African war (Boer War), 6
Spain, colonialism, 51–2n
state
intervention, 5–6, 127
role of, 2, 182, 218
Stedman Jones, Gareth, 90–1
Stephens, Scott, 75
Stevedores Union, 90

strikes
in 1950s, 129–30
in 1970s, 138
African general, 170
against discrimination, 135–7
'docker's tanner' (1889), 90–1
East London dockers, 195–6,
197–8
East London general (1930),
197, 199–200
Grunwick (1976-8), 141–3, 144
Imperial Typewriters (1973),
139–40
by Kru stevedores, 151–2,
163–4
Nigerian general, 186
Nigerian mines, 178, 187–8
telephone operators, 63
to support racist practices,
132
as trade union strategy, 127
transport, 132–3
US hate, 71, 84n
wildcat, 129, 138
*see also* trade unions
Sugrue, Thomas, 15, 17
Sullivan, Larry, 87, 95, 97–8
Sunny, B.E., 60
Swift, Roger, 92
Sylvan, T.P., 68

Tabili, Laura, 15, 89
*'We Ask for British Justice'*,
105–6
Tannahill, John, 113
Telephone Employees
Association, 70
telephone operators *see* African
American women; Bell
System; trade unions;
women

Telephone Traffic Union, 75
Temne people, West Africa,
    158–9, 160, 166n
TGWU, 133, 140
    refusal to support strikes, 135,
        139–40
    support for Grunwick strike,
        142
Thurmond, Strom, 21–2
Tillett, Ben, 90
Tooney, James, 90
trade unions, 217–18
    in colonies, 11, 182
    dockers', 92, 95, 96, 97–8
    exclusion of Mexicans, 47–8
    government attempts to curb,
        137–40, 144
    and ideology of working-class
        solidarity, 140–3
    internationalism of, 218, 229
    lack of support for strikes by
        black workers, 135–7,
        139–40
    Nigerian miners', 182, 183–7,
        188
    racism in, 14, 22, 71, 74–5,
        132–3, 162
    seamen's, 162
    and sectional class interests,
        126–8, 143
    strategies, 127, 128–30
    telephone companies, 70–1,
        74–6, 83n
    in US, 15–18, 20–1
    *see also* strikes; TUC
Trades and Labour Council
    (South Africa), 198
Traffic Employees Association,
    70
Trapido, Stanley, 6
TUC (Trades Union Congress)

and Nigerian CWU, 186–7
    reaction to Jewish
        immigration, 113
    recognition of need to combat
        racism, 125, 140–1, 142,
        143
    support for racist union
        policies, 133

unemployment, fear of, 113,
    132, 143
Union Castle Shipping
    Company, 194
Union of Post Office Workers,
    142
United Africa Company, 159
United States
    effects of Great Depression,
        15–18
    Fair Employment Practices
        Committee (FEPC), 69, 70,
        71
    former slaves in, 8–9
    and Mexico, 37–9, 49–50
    nature of colonialism, 2
    regional variations in race
        relations, 33, 35–6, 49–50
    restrictive mining legislation,
        53–4nn
    rise of corporate capitalism,
        44–5, 46, 48–50
    settler colonialism, 34, 51–2n
    trade unions, 15–18, 20–1
    use of convict labour, 10
    white supremacism, 14, 18,
        21–2
    *see also* African Americans;
        Arizona
urban areas
    rural social unrest in, 208–9
    and segregation, 24n

urbanization, of African
  Americans, 22

Vandervelde, Emile, 4–5
Virdee, Satnam, 22

wage labour, 8–11, 172
  expansion of, 225
  and separation from land, 9–10
wages
  differentiated, 8, 73, 115
  dual wage system, 48–9, 52n
  East London dockers, 195
  Kru shipping workers, 153,
    155, 160, 166n
  Nigerian mines, 179–80, 185
Wagner Act (1935) (US), 70
wakes, Irish, 91–2
Wallace, George, 22
Walter, Bronwen, 109–10
Webb, Sidney, 7
'Welfare Compromise', 128–9
welfare state, 6, 8
West Africa
  cotton production, 10
  *see also* Freetown
West Bromwich Corporation
  Transport, 132
West Indies, 178
  former slaves in, 8–9
  immigrants from, 122–3
Western Federation of Miners
  (US), 48
'white lady' idealization, 57–8,
  60, 76, 77n, 79n
White Man's Towns (Arizona
  and US), 33, 45, 48
white workers
  skilled, 124
  *see also* 'white lady'
whiteness, 3, 78n

and American identity, 38,
  43–4, 50–1n, 55n, 88
and British identity, 116–18
gendered in working class, 79n
'psychological wage' of, 58–9,
  76
US regional variations of, 33,
  35–6, 37, 42–3
Williams, Bill, 107
Williams, Walter D., 68–9
Winslow, Cal, 94
women
  black stereotypes, 61, 62–3
  as domestic labour in South
    Africa, 14
  income-earning labour, 9–10
  moral conditions for
    employment, 72–3
  wages (Mexican), 52n
  'white lady' idealization, 57–8,
    60, 76, 77n, 79n
  *see also* African American
    women; Bell System
work
  race and class aligned with,
    151, 217
  *see also* labour
work practices, and formation of
  identity, 156, 169, 170–4,
  176–7, 206
workers, and creation of
  whiteness, 66–7, 76, 77
working class
  and concept of family, 182
  and creation of racial ideology,
    58, 77–8n, 131
  and dual wage system, 49
  effect of Second World War
    on, 20–1
  ideology of solidarity, 139,
    140–3, 144

*working class continued*
racial distinctions within, 46–8,
    77, 111
  racial recomposition of, 22
  role of state in shaping
      meaning of, 2

and role of trade unions,
    126–7
  sectional interests, 126–8
  in South Africa, 8
World Federation of Trade
    Unions, 229

*St Antony's Series*

General Editor: **Eugene Rogan** (1997– ), Fellow of St Antony's College, Oxford

*Recent titles include*:

Craig Brandist and Galin Tihanov (*editors*)
MATERIALIZING BAKHTIN

Mark Brzezinski
THE STRUGGLE FOR CONSTITUTIONALISM IN POLAND

Reinhard Drifte
JAPAN'S QUEST FOR A PERMANENT SECURITY COUNCIL SEAT
A Matter of Pride or Justice?

Simon Duke
THE ELUSIVE QUEST FOR EUROPEAN SECURITY

Marta Dyczok
THE GRAND ALLIANCE AND UKRAINIAN REFUGEES

Ken Endo
THE PRESIDENCY OF THE EUROPEAN COMMISSION UNDER
JACQUES DELORS

M. K. Flynn
IDEOLOGY, MOBILIZATION AND THE NATION
The Rise of Irish, Basque and Carlist Nationalist Movements in the
Nineteenth and Early Twentieth Centuries

Anthony Forster
BRITAIN AND THE MAASTRICHT NEGOTIATIONS

Ricardo Ffrench-Davis
REFORMING THE REFORMS IN LATIN AMERICA
Macroeconomics, Trade, Finance

Azar Gat
BRITISH ARMOUR THEORY AND THE RISE OF THE PANZER ARM
Revising the Revisionists

Fernando Guirao
SPAIN AND THE RECONSTRUCTION OF WESTERN EUROPE, 1945–57

Anthony Kirk-Greene
BRITAIN'S IMPERIAL ADMINISTRATORS, 1858–1966

Bernardo Kosacoff
CORPORATE STRATEGIES UNDER STRUCTURAL ADJUSTMENT IN ARGENTINA
Responses by Industrial Firms to a New Set of Uncertainties

Huck-ju Kwon
THE WELFARE STATE IN KOREA

Cécile Laborde
PLURALIST THOUGHT AND THE STATE IN BRITAIN AND FRANCE, 1900–25

Eiichi Motono
CONFLICT AND COOPERATION IN SINO–BRITISH BUSINESS, 1860–1911
The Impact of the Pro-British Commercial Network in Shanghai

C. S. Nicholls
THE HISTORY OF ST ANTONY'S COLLEGE, OXFORD, 1950–2000

Laila Parsons
THE DRUZE BETWEEN PALESTINE AND ISRAEL, 1947–49

Shane O'Rourke
WARRIORS AND PEASANTS
The Don Cossacks in Late Imperial Russia

Karina Sonnenberg-Stern
EMANCIPATION AND POVERTY
The Ashkenazi Jews of Amsterdam, 1796–1850

Miguel Székely
THE ECONOMICS OF POVERTY AND WEALTH ACCUMULATION IN MEXICO

Ray Takeyh
THE ORIGINS OF THE EISENHOWER DOCTRINE
The US, Britain and Nasser's Egypt, 1953–57

Suke Wolton
LORD HAILEY, THE COLONIAL OFFICE AND THE POLITICS OF RACE IN THE SECOND WORLD WAR
The Loss of White Prestige

**St Antony's Series**
**Series Standing Order ISBN 0–333–71109–2**
(*outside North America only*)

You can receive future titles in this series as they are published by placing a standing order. Please contact your bookseller or, in case of difficulty, write to us at the address below with your name and address, the title of the series and the ISBN quoted above.

Customer Services Department, Macmillan Distribution Ltd, Houndmills, Basingstoke, Hampshire RG21 6XS, England